ROYAL HISTORICAL SOCIETY

STUDIES IN HISTORY

New Series

THE LABOUR PARTY AND THE POLITICS OF WAR AND PEACE, 1900–1924

THE LABOUR PARTY AND THE POLITICS OF WAR AND PEACE, 1900–1924

Paul Bridgen

THE ROYAL HISTORICAL SOCIETY
THE BOYDELL PRESS

First published 2009

A Royal Historical Society publication
Published by The Boydell Press
an imprint of Boydell & Brewer Ltd
PO Box 9, Woodbridge, Suffolk IP12 3DF, UK
and of Boydell & Brewer Inc.
668 Mt Hope Avenue, Rochester, NY 14620, USA
website: www.boydellandbrewer.com

ISBN 978–0–86193–303–7

ISSN 0269–2244

A CIP catalogue record for this book is available
from the British Library

The publisher has no responsibility for the continued existence or accuracy of
URLs for external or third-party internet websites referred to in this book,
and does not guarantee that any content on such websites is,
or will remain, accurate or appropriate.

This publication is printed on acid-free paper

Printed in Great Britain by
CPI Antony Rowe, Chippenham and Eastbourne

IN LOVING MEMORY OF MY PARENTS

BETTY BRIDGEN (1935–89)

JOHN BRIDGEN (1933–91)

Contents

Acknowledgements

I owe a great debt to a number of people for their assistance with this book. Academically, I am first extremely grateful to Patrick Renshaw and the late Ben Pimlott for their advice and ideas on this work as it developed. I am also very grateful to Jane Lewis and Rodney Lowe, from whom, while undertaking separate projects, I learned an enormous amount that has proved useful in the completion of this book. I received extremely valuable comments on the typescript from Kathy Burk, Chris Wrigley, Jon Lawrence and an anonymous reader. Finally, in terms of academic debts, I must also thank all my colleagues (past and present) in the Department of Sociology and Social Policy at the University of Southampton for their patient understanding.

This book has involved many long hours in archive reading rooms, during which time I encountered nothing but helpfulness and interest. I would particularly like to thank all the staff at the Museum of Labour History, Manchester, the LSE library archive section and the Bodleian Library, Oxford. I would also like to thank Christine Linehan for her patient and calm help in preparing the text for publication.

Finally, without the support of family and friends this book would never have neared completion. The unstinting, loyal support of my sister, Kay, has been very greatly appreciated. My partner, Astrid Davies, has my eternal love and gratitude for never wavering in her support even when I was close to giving up.

Paul Bridgen
August 2009

List of Abbreviations

ACIQ	Advisory Committee on International Questions
ASLE	Associated Society of Locomotive Engineers
BSIMF	British Section of the International Metalworkers Federation
BSP	British Socialist party
CID	Committee of Imperial Defence
DTMA	Draft Treaty of Mutual Assistance
ILP	Independent Labour party
JIC	Joint International Committee
LNS	League of Nations Society
LNU	League of Nations Union
LRC	Labour Representation Committee
MOWA	Memorandum on War Aims
NAC	National Administrative Council (ILP)
NCF	No Conscription Fellowship
NEC	National Executive Committee
PCTUC	Parliamentary Committee of the Trades Union Congress
PLP	Parliamentary Labour party
SDF	Social Democratic Federation
SFIO	*Section française de l'Internationale ouvrière*
SPD	*Sozialdemokratische Partei Deutschlands*
TUC	Trades Union Congress
UDC	Union of Democratic Control
USC	United Socialist Council
USPD	*Unabhängige Sozialdemokratische Partei Deutschlands*
WEWNC	War Emergency Workers' National Committee

BJL	Brynmor Jones Library, University of Hull
BLPES	British Library of Political and Economic Science, London School of Economics
Bodl. Lib.	Bodleian Library, Oxford
LPA	Labour party archive, National Museum of Labour History, Manchester
MRC	Modern Records Centre, University of Warwick
NLS	National Library of Scotland, Edinburgh
TNA	The National Archive, London

1

Re-Thinking The Labour Party's Approach To Foreign Policy, 1900–1924

The British Labour party has been the focus of considerable attention from historians and political scientists, but until recently[1] little of that attention has been directed towards the party's approach to foreign affairs.[2] This is particularly true with respect to the early decades of the twentieth century. Scholars of this period of Labour's history have focused on providing explanations for the emergence and nature of the Labour party, and its replacing the Liberal party on the left of British politics.[3] Labour's approach to foreign affairs has not generally been regarded as particularly important in explaining these developments and, mainly for this reason, the subject has been neglected.

This reflects a more general neglect of ideological and policy developments in the early Labour party, particularly by labour and social historians. The adoption of a socially deterministic approach to explain the party's electoral rise is one reason for this. It has encouraged the view that Labour only needed to establish itself organisationally to benefit from the economic and social changes that occurred in Britain in the later part of the nineteenth century and early twentieth century. Policy development played little part in this process. Labour's policy merely reflected the fact that the party was the beneficiary, and product, of the creation of an industrial working class, as a side-effect of modernisation.[4] Labour remained, up to 1931 at least, little more than a pressure group for organised labour, with no coherent set of policies or firm set of principles.[5] If the party was ideological at all, its ideology was 'labourism'.[6]

---

[1]   See, for example, R. Vickers, *The Labour party and the world: the evolution of Labour's foreign policy, 1900–1951*, Manchester 2004.
[2]   See J. W. Young, 'Idealism and realism in the history of Labour's foreign policy', *Bulletin of the Society for the Study of Labour History* i (1985), 14–19.
[3]   There is a massive literature on these debates which is usefully summarised by K. Laybourn, *The rise of Labour*, London 1998.
[4]   R. McKibbin, *The evolution of the Labour party, 1910–1924*, Oxford 1974, 243.
[5]   D. Howell, *British workers and the Independent Labour party, 1888–1906*, Manchester 1983.
[6]   See J. Saville, 'The ideology of Labourism', in R. Benewick, R. N. Berki and B. C. Parekh, *Knowledge and belief in politics*, London, 1973, 213–26, and G. Foote, *The Labour party's political thought: a history*, 3rd edn, London 1997. In his most recent book Howell

The dominance of this view has meant that, while the party's continued attachment to ideas associated with liberalism and radicalism has sometimes been noted, the ideas themselves, the party's use of them and their influence on policy development have rarely been investigated in any detail.[7] Only the nature of the party's commitment to socialism has received much attention, mainly with the intention of explaining either Labour's delayed and partial adherence to this creed, or the influence of Fabian thought.[8]

Concentration on Labour's socialism reflects in part the domination of the labour and social history of this period by Marxist (or Marxian) theory, which generally assigns a very limited and specific task to working-class politics and ideology. The role of working-class parties, on this reading, is to emphasise the essential unity of the working class and its fundamental clash of interest with the bourgeoisie, the inevitability of its oppression under capitalism and revolution as the only means of emancipation. Any other ideological approach distorts the 'real' interest of the working class and distracts it from its revolutionary task.[9] Thus, Labour's continued association with the 'outdated' ideologies of liberalism and radicalism has been regarded as evidence of its lack of ideological sophistication, especially in relation to its sister socialist parties in Europe.[10] Classical Marxists have generally blamed this historic 'failing' on Labour's leadership and intellectuals, who, it is argued, were either representatives of a privileged group of workers (i.e. the labour aristocracy), with interests closer to the bourgeoisie than the proletariat,[11] or intellectual lightweights unable to think themselves beyond the ideological *status quo*.[12]

makes clear the richness of this labourist culture, but does not depart in essence from this general approach: *MacDonald's party: Labour identities and crisis, 1922–1931*, Oxford 2002.

[7] S. Pierson, *Marxism and the origins of British socialism*, London 1973.

[8] See, for example, McKibbin, *Evolution of the Labour party*, and 'Why was there no Marxism in Britain?', in his *The ideologies of class: social relations in Britain, 1889–1950*, Oxford 1990, 1–41, and Saville, 'Ideology of Labourism'. On the influence of Fabian thought see A. M. McBriar (ed.), *Fabian socialism and English politics, 1884–1918*, Cambridge 1962.

[9] Even social historians less convinced of the revolutionary potential of the British working class have concentrated on Labour's non-adherence to Marxism: McKibbin, 'Why was there no Marxism in Britain?'.

[10] On Labour's association with radicalism see Howell, *British workers*, and D. Martin, 'Ideology and composition', in K. D. Brown (ed.), *The first Labour party, 1906–1914*, London 1985, 17–37. It has become increasingly clear that the commitment of European socialist parties to Marxism was not as great as has previously been thought. On Labour's relationship with European socialism see S. Berger, *The British Labour party and the German Social Democrats, 1900–1931*, Oxford 1994, 11–16, and D. M. Tanner, 'Socialist parties and policies', in M. Pugh (ed.), *A companion to modern European history, 1871–1945*, Oxford 1997, 138.

[11] E. J. Hobsbawm, 'The labour aristocracy in nineteenth century Britain', in his *Labouring men: studies in the history of labour*, London 1964, 272–315.

[12] Saville, 'Ideology of labourism', 224–6.

Dismissal of Labour's socialism, and its more general ideological and policy development, has had a strong influence on assessments of the party's early experiences of government. Labour's lack of ideological and policy sophistication, it is argued, became all too obvious once the party was in power, both in 1924 and 1929–31. Faced with the realities of office, Labour's lack of preparedness meant that it was a hostage to events and over-reliant on its officials. The 1931 crisis was the almost inevitable result.

Some labour and social historians, however, have increasingly questioned this dismissal of Labour's ideological and political development. Even some Marxists have queried the focus on the failings of the party leadership and intellectuals, and shown that they were not operating in the type of economic, social and political context that Marx had predicted.[13] This type of approach has been taken further by non-Marxists, who have shown that a considerable degree of sectionalism and diversity continued to exist within the 'working classes', both with respect to their working conditions and their cultural life.[14] Labour was not faced with a unified potentially revolutionary working class, but a considerably more varied latent constituency, whose material situation was often steady or improving. Politically, this constituency had reason to believe, in an increasingly democratic system, that social reform – to the extent that it was supported – was feasible. Together, these factors explained the continued commitment of many workers to moderate trade unionism and Liberal politics.

These insights, combined with more general doubts about socially deterministic explanations for Labour's rise, have led some commentators to suggest that a reformist strategy, compatible with the varied interests of the trade unions and appealing to the party's diverse potential constituency, was the only option for Labour if it wanted to bring about social and economic change, socialist or otherwise.[15] Such an approach was bound to involve the party in debates with existing reformist strategies associated with Victorian and Edwardian liberalism and the popular radical tradition. The real issue with respect to Labour's ideological and policy sophistication, therefore, becomes not the extent of its socialism, but its success in combining insights from a number of ideological approaches in a coherent policy programme capable of maximising its electoral support.

---

[13] P. Anderson, and T. Nairn, 'Origins of the present crisis', *New Left Review* xxiii (1964), 26–54.

[14] See, for example, E. F. Biagini and A. F. Reid, 'Currents of radicalism, 1850–1914', in their *Currents of radicalism: popular radicalism, organised labour and party politics in Britain, 1850–1914*, Cambridge 1991, 14–15.

[15] On growing doubts about the class thesis of Labour's rise see D. M. Tanner, *Political change and the Labour party, 1900–1918*, Cambridge 1990, 11. For an analysis of the interpretative basis for this 'new political history' see L. Black, '"What kind of people are you?" Labour, the people and the "new political history"', in J. Callaghan, S. Fielding and S. Ludlum, *Interpreting the Labour party: approaches to labour politics and history*, Manchester 2003.

With regard to domestic ideology and policy, some attempts have been made to reassess the Labour party on this basis. These have generally shown that the party used and developed liberal and radical ideas creatively, in combination with socialist insights, to construct policy positions that were far more sophisticated than has generally been suggested.[16] However, the construction of a credible reformist strategy had also to include the development of a coherent policy on foreign affairs. This subject was of great importance to Labour during this period. It remained at, or close to, the top of the political agenda throughout the period of Labour's rise, and particularly after 1914. As a party, from 1918, with ambitions to govern, Labour had to show how it would deal with international issues. It had to neutralise its opponents' claims that the emerging party could not be trusted on foreign affairs and was, thus, not fit to govern.[17] More positively, as Catherine Cline has shown, a firm stand on foreign affairs was a way of attracting the support of disillusioned former Liberals.[18] Moreover, foreign affairs also had a direct effect on the interests of the trade unions. The First World War had a profound impact on the social and economic conditions of the working classes, but even after the conflict was over, the perceived consequences of the post-war settlement for international trade meant that foreign affairs was at the heart of debates on the post-war depression.[19] Foreign affairs also impinged directly on Labour's relationship with its international sister parties, an important aspect of the party's history which has also received less attention than it deserves.[20]

Yet inadequate attention has been given in the reassessment of Labour's ideological and political development to international affairs. While there are important studies of Labour's approach to specific international areas (for example, the empire[21]), there is a lack of broader archive-based studies of the

---

[16] See, for example, D. M. Tanner, 'Ideological debate in Edwardian labour politics: radicalism, revisionism and socialism', in Biagini and Reid, *Currents of radicalism*, 271–93, and 'The development of British socialism, 1900–1918', *Parliamentary History* xvi (1997), 48–66. See also M. Worley, *Labour inside the gate: a history of the British Labour party between the wars*, London 2005. This reassessment will be considered in more detail in the conclusion below.

[17] See M. Cowling, *The impact of Labour*, London 1971.

[18] C. Cline, *Recruits to Labour*, New York 1963. See also R. Dowse, 'The entry of the Liberals into the Labour party, 1910–1920', *Yorkshire Bulletin of Economic and Social Research* xiiii (1961), 78–88.

[19] For the impact of the war on the economic and social conditions of the working classes see K. Burgess, *The challenge of labour: shaping British society, 1850–1930*, London 1980; K. Burk, *War and the state*, London 1982; and B. Waites, *A class society at war*, Leamington Spa 1987.

[20] Berger, *British Labour party*; C. Collette, *The international faith: Labour's attitude to European socialism, 1918–39*, Aldershot 1998.

[21] See S. Howell, *Anticolonialism in British politics: the left and the end of empire, 1918–1964*, Oxford 1992, and P. S. Gupta, *Imperialism and the British Labour movement, 1914–1964*, London 1975. Another important study looks at some of the issues raised by international

party's 'thinking about peace and war', to use Martin Ceadel's phrase, and in particular its attitude towards Europe.[22] As a result, until recently, reliance has had to be placed on studies mainly undertaken by diplomatic historians, American political scientists and historians interested in liberal or radical ideas, individuals and organisations. Most of these try to establish the ideological bases of Labour's policy and tend to assume that Labour's approach can be understood on the basis of a unifying ideology, with political and institutional factors discounted as an influence on policy development. Generally, they conclude that up to 1924 Labour adopted a relatively unsophisticated 'idealistic' approach to foreign affairs, strongly influenced by nineteenth-century liberal and/or radical ideas, which had to be reined back, in the face of international realities and official opposition, when the party entered office in 1924.[23] However, most of these accounts are extremely impressionistic, none being based on systematic research of the party's records, or those of the leading figures of the period.

These accounts have recently been supplemented by Rhiannon Vickers's welcome attempt to update understanding of Labour's early foreign policy as part of a broad-ranging study of international policy developments up to the Blair government.[24] However, while this work emphasises to a greater extent than previous studies the degree of ideological division in the early Labour party, it is over-reliant on previous work for the period up to 1924 and does not explain why some ideas were influential in the party while others were not. Partly for this reason, it concludes, like many earlier studies, that Labour's 'rhetoric in opposition' was 'significantly to the left of actions taken once in power'.[25]

The main aim of this book is to trace the development of Labour's policy on 'peace and war' between its formation as the Labour Representation Committee (LRC) in 1900 and the end of its first period of government in 1924. Its central concerns are thus to untangle the main ideological and interest influences on the party's approach to foreign affairs, show which of these assumed a dominant position and investigate how and why this process occurred. It will place particular emphasis on the interaction of old ideas and new intellectual influences in the development of Labour's approach, situate these in their political context and analyse how political factors affected the

affairs, but from the perspective of their effect on the level and nature of patriotism in the Labour party: P. Ward, *Red flag and the Union Jack: Englishness, patriotism and the British left, 1881–1924*, Woodbridge 1998.

[22] M. Ceadel, *Thinking about peace and war*, Oxford 1987. For an important exception dealing with the foreign policy of the second Labour government see D. Carlton, *MacDonald versus Henderson: the foreign policy of the second Labour government*, London 1970.

[23] See n. 56 below.

[24] Vickers, *Labour party and the world*

[25] Ibid. 28. Vickers regards this as a tendency evident throughout the twentieth century, but clearly includes the 1924 government in reaching this conclusion.

evolution of Labour policy. In so doing, it hopes to contribute to the broader current debate about the early Labour party's ideology and policy. The study makes no claim to be an exhaustive account of Labour's foreign policy during this period, rather it concentrates on the party's attitude towards Europe, and particularly the issues raised with respect to security and reconstruction by the First World War.

The main argument of the study is that the development of Labour's foreign policy during this period has been fundamentally misinterpreted. Existing accounts exaggerate the level of agreement on foreign affairs within the party,[26] overstate the influence of certain high-profile individuals and groups, such as E. D. Morel and the Union of Democratic Control (UDC), underestimate the sophistication and practicality of Labour's approach to this issue in the early post-war period and, as a result, substantially misjudge the foreign policy record of the first Labour government. As a result, while few existing accounts relate their findings to the more general history of Labour's ideological and policy development, they nevertheless tend to support the prevailing view.

One reason for these misinterpretations is the narrow range of sources upon which previous commentaries have been based. However, they also stem from the adoption, either explicitly or implicitly, of a doctrinal interpretative framework.

Interpretations of the Labour party

A number of different approaches have been taken to the interpretation of the history of the Labour party. Of these the doctrinal, pluralist and labourist approaches are the most common, although insights gained from elitist and rational choice theories have also been utilised. These frameworks are important because they provide different explanations of how party policy came to be made and the forces that influenced the process.[27]

The doctrinal approach to Labour's history is most commonly associated with the work of Samuel Beer. He argued that it was possible to establish a socialist ideological framework within which the large majority of the party's actions could be understood.[28] Labour's adoption of a socialist constitution in 1918, he argued, signified a major shift in the nature of the party: before this Labour was little more than a 'coalition' of interest and ideological groupings. After the acceptance of the new constitution 'a new orthodoxy, a

---

[26] Vickers's study is an exception in this regard.

[27] The importance of combining the theoretical insights of political scientists with the empirical work of historians in the study of the Labour party has recently been emphasised in Callaghan, Fielding and Ludlum, *Interpreting the Labour party*.

[28] S. H. Beer, *Modern British politics: a study of parties and pressure groups in the collectivist age*, 3rd edn, London 1982.

unified doctrine, even a system of thought' knitted together the pluralism of views within the party.[29] Thus, while Labour always remained to some extent a coalition, its approach to issues was henceforward framed by a commitment to socialism: 'all groups had the same object, the Socialist Commonwealth'.[30] Labour became a doctrinal party.

Beer's argument has always been controversial. It was constructed as an alternative to – and repudiation of – Labour Revisionists, who argued in the late 1950s and early 1960s that socialism was only one of a number of ideological influences on the party in its early years. Thus, Bernard Crick had insisted in 1960 that the party was 'a coalition of diverse class, union, regional, ideological and even ethnic interests … And Socialism itself, except in a very broad sense, is only one element in this coalition.'[31] Despite Beer's efforts, this pluralist view remains influential. The extent to which the 'socialist' constitution represented a major change in the nature of the Labour party has repeatedly been challenged. Ross McKibbin, in his influential study of Labour's organisational development up to 1924, argued that clause IV (ie the socialist commitment) merely had an 'umbrella function', acting as an 'acceptable formula in a party where there was otherwise little doctrinal agreement'.[32] Brian Harrison made a similar argument. For him, clause IV 'did not indicate … the presence of a coherent ideology. It is better understood as a rallying point around which the adherents of different ideologies and the representatives of different interests assembled'.[33] In short, Labour remained, after 1918, the same coalition of interest and ideological groupings that it had been before 1918. Moreover, this situation was reinforced by the federal nature of the party's organisational structure which, although it became more centralised in the period after the First World War, continued to allow the socialist societies to exist as separate entities within the party.

This type of approach to the study of the Labour party finds considerable support in the wider political science literature on political parties. For example, in a classic 1964 study of British politics Richard Rose argued that the differences within parties were at least as important in explaining the development of public policy as those between them.[34] The Labour party

---

[29] Ibid. 126.

[30] Ibid. 127.

[31] Quoted ibid. 107.

[32] McKibbin, *Evolution of the Labour party*, 97.

[33] R. Harrison, 'The War Emergency National Workers' Committee, 1914–1920', in A. Briggs and J. Saville, *Essays in labour history, 1886–1923*, London 1971, 211–59. See also Tanner, *Political change*, 13.

[34] R. Rose, 'Parties, factions and tendencies in Britain', *Political Studies* xii (1964), 33–46. See also R. Zariski, 'Party factions and comparative politics: some preliminary observations', *Midwest Journal of Political Science* iv (1960), 27–51, and F. P. Belloni and D. C. Beller (eds), *Faction politics: political parties and factionalism in comparative perspective*, Santa Barbara 1978.

since its foundation, he suggested, has always been a prime example of a factional party.[35] In recent years, increasing attention has been focused on the internal politics of parties rather than their wider role in political systems.[36] Parties have come to be viewed as complex organisations or 'miniature political systems' in which policy comes to be made on the basis of bargaining and negotiation as facilitated by the party leadership.

However, a purely pluralist view of the Labour party is not accepted by all commentators. Labourists, while accepting that Labour is made up of a diverse group of ideological and interest groups, have stressed the overwhelming influence of one particular interest group: the trade unions. They have retained a dominant position, according to this view, in the various party institutions (the Executive Committee, the Conference etc.) throughout its history. McKibbin's analysis of the 1918 constitution was based on this type of approach. He argued that the most important part of the document was not clause IV, but the organisational changes it also proposed. The constitution 'embodied not an ideology but a system by which power in the Labour Party was distributed', and in this regard it was the trade unions rather than the socialist societies whose position was strengthened. Clause IV was an 'adornment' which was included in response to fears of a leftward shift in working-class politics after the Bolshevik revolution and which the unions accepted in return for their improved position within the party's organisation.[37] This labourist view argues that debates in the party have always been carried on 'within specific ideological limits' set by the trade union character of the party.[38] Thus, Labour's overwhelming concern has been with improving the immediate material condition of the working classes within the existing capitalist system of production. It has been hostile to capitalists but not to capitalism *per se*.[39]

All the interpretative frameworks outlined so far tend to downplay the role of the Labour party leadership. For pluralists, the role of the party leadership is restricted to facilitation, both of agreement between the competing party factions and of increased support from other societal and political groups. In

---

[35] Rose, 'Parties, factions and tendencies', 323. He defines factions as 'a group of individuals … who seek to further a broad range of policies through consciously organised political activity'. A 'tendency', in contrast, did not consist of individuals, but referred to the existence of 'a stable set of attitudes' within a party.

[36] See, for example, A. Panebianco, *Political parties: organization and power*, Cambridge 1988; R. Mule, 'Explaining the party-policy link: established approaches and theoretical developments', *Party Politics* iii (1997), 493–512; and R. Harmel and K. Janda, 'An integrated theory of party goals and party change', *Journal of Theoretical Politics* vi (1994), 259–87.

[37] McKibbin, *Evolution of the Labour party*, 259. See also, for example, L. Minkin, *The contentious alliance: trade unions and the Labour party*, Edinburgh 1992, and Foote, *The Labour party's political thought*.

[38] Foote, *The Labour party's political thought*, 6.

[39] Ibid. 12.

the labourist view, the leadership, like the rest of the party, is constrained by the need to reflect the concerns of the trade unions. However, this neutral view of the role of the party leadership separates these perspectives from elite theories. Since Robert Michels's classic study of the oligarchic tendencies of parties, the power and influence of the party leadership has repeatedly been stressed.[40] What this literature emphasises is the degree to which the interests of party leaders may diverge from those of the rank-and-file. Michels argued that as parties develop, the primary goal of leaders becomes to maintain their own positions and ensure the survival of the organisation. Their commitment to the original goals of the party diminishes. The existence of a divergence of goals has also been accepted by rational choice theorists. However, their view of leadership motivation is that party leaders mainly desire power, and approach policy-making on this basis. Leaders thus seek to encourage the party to accept policies that will maximise its electoral support.[41] In contrast to their more ideologically-driven party members and groups, they are amoral, non-ideological vote-seekers. Empirical testing of this theory confirms the vote-seeking motivation of leaders, but also indicates that they are more policy-oriented than rational choice theory would suggest. Leaders also retain a strong desire to implement the party's programmes.[42]

Varying interpretative frameworks for analysing Labour's history are important because they provide different explanations of the party's policy-making process. Understanding policy formation on the basis of the doctrinal interpretation of the Labour party is relatively straightforward: it merely involves the translation of the party's doctrine into measures and proposals in each policy area. However, if it is accepted that no one doctrine unified the whole party, and that many of its members were not interested in ideology but in the material interests of the groups they represented, explaining policy development becomes more complex. Pluralists argue that, in these circumstances, policy is made as the result of a bargaining process between the different groups involved in the party. Thus, party policy is a composite of the goals of the various groups.[43] It is deliberately vague in order to ensure the adherence of all the main party factions, and is designed to rally the party in its contest with opposing parties. It may also have the aim of increasing the party's support amongst other groups in society. The labourist view accepts that policy develops on the basis of competition and bargaining between the

---

[40] R. Michels, *Political parties: a sociological study of the oligarchical tendencies of modern democracy*, London 1915.
[41] A. Downs, *An economic theory of democracy*, New York 1957.
[42] See K. Strom, 'A behavioural theory of competitive political parties', *American Journal of Political Science* xxxiv (1990), 565–98, and H. Klingemann, R. I. Hoffbert and I. Budge, *Parties, policies and democracy*, San Francisco 1994.
[43] A summary of the pluralist approach and Labour is in Beer, *Modern British politics*, 105–9.

different groups in the party, but argues that ultimately the trade unions can veto any policy with which they disagree. Elitist and rational choice theories stress the distinct role of the leadership in these processes, with the latter emphasising, in particular, the importance of electoral and political calculations in the leadership's approach to policy-making.

What the empirical and theoretical literature on party policy-making suggests, therefore, is that a doctrinal approach may not provide the best framework for analysing policy developments in the Labour party. What may also need to be considered are the ideological and interest group differences in the party, the organisational structures within which policy is made, particularly the role of the trade unions, the leadership's role in the policy process and the importance of political, as well as ideological, considerations in their approach to policy development. This book will argue that it is only by considering such factors that Labour's approach to foreign policy between 1900 and 1924 can be properly understood.

The historiography of the Labour party's foreign policy development, 1900–24

Of the possible interpretative frameworks, the doctrinal approach has, either explicitly or implicitly, dominated accounts of Labour's foreign policy development between 1900 and 1924. Commentators have sometimes differed in their view of which doctrine influenced Labour's approach in this area, but they have generally agreed that a single ideological approach dominated the party's policy development.[44] On the basis of this approach a prevailing explanation of the party's international policy during this period has developed.

One group of commentators, influenced by Beer, has argued that Labour's approach to foreign affairs can best be understood within a socialist ideological framework. For example, M. R. Gordon, an American political scientist, referred directly to the Beerian model in his 1969 study and claimed that 'what was true of socialist orthodoxy at home was equally true of socialist orthodoxy in matters of foreign policy, the latter being regarded ... as merely the application of the former to the international scene'.[45] On this basis, Gordon sought to define the characteristics of Labour's 'socialist' approach. Thus he identified four broadly-drawn 'essential principles', which he suggested lay at the root of Labour's policy and together constituted an 'ideal' 'socialist' foreign policy. These were an emphasis on internationalism, rather than nationalism, a belief in international working-class solidarity,

---

[44] For the purposes of this book a 'patriotic', nationalistic approach to foreign affairs is not treated as a foreign policy ideology.

[45] M. R. Gordon, *Conflict and consensus in Labour's foreign policy, 1914–65*, Stanford 1969, 8.

opposition to capitalism and opposition to 'power politics'. These principles, he suggested, went largely unchallenged during the period up to 1945: they represented the party's unifying 'doctrine' and 'orthodoxy' in foreign affairs. Differences that arose were over tactics rather than strategy.

In outlining the development of these principles, Gordon concentrated upon the views of Labour politicians and thinkers of the early twentieth century. He said little about the influence of liberal and radical thought on Labour's thinking. His aim was to emphasise the degree of unity rather than any differences of approach. In this regard, he accepted, his four principles were 'ideal typical abstraction … [which] purposely emphasise, even exaggerate, in an effort to distil the inner logic of a complex reality'.[46] The justification for such simplification, he argued, rested on the success of such a framework in accounting for the most important facts of Labour's history with respect to foreign policy. It is highly questionable whether this is the case.

Kenneth Miller's 1967 study adopted a different methodology, but nevertheless characterised Labour's approach as 'socialist'.[47] Unlike Gordon, he sought to trace the development of Labour's 'socialist theories' by examining the interaction of liberal and radical ideas of the nineteenth century with the various types of socialist thinking that developed at the beginning of the twentieth century. With regard to the former, he argued that the thinking of Jeremy Bentham, Richard Cobden, John Stuart Mill and William Gladstone was influential. With regard to socialist thinking, Miller outlined the Marxist ideas of the Social Democratic Federation (SDF), together with the thinking of the Socialist League, the Fabians and the Independent Labour Party (ILP). However, having marked out the development of these various ideas and indicated the differences between them, Miller made little attempt to explain how they were incorporated into Labour's thinking on foreign policy. He did not explain which ideas were most influential, how the differences between them were resolved or the extent to which Labour's approach could be described as 'socialist', given the influence of liberalism and radicalism.

These Beerian-based approaches have not been unique in stressing the degree of ideological coherence in the Labour party's foreign policy development. In a separate literature, historians, mainly from a diplomatic history background, have also approached the subject from this perspective. However, rather than attempting to explain Labour's policy on the basis of a socialist framework, they have emphasised the continuity of Labour's approach, particularly after 1917, with that of their liberal and radical predecessors.[48]

---

[46] Ibid.10.

[47] K. E. Miller, *Socialism and foreign policy: theory and practice in Britain to 1932*, The Hague 1967.

[48] Miller's approach differs from this literature because he stresses the extent to which Labour's policy transcended its radical and liberal origins and could thus be regarded as

11

This type of interpretation is reflected most in A. J. P. Taylor's 1957 classic and extremely influential book *The troublemakers*, which traced the development of the radical tradition of foreign policy dissent from the end of the eighteenth century to 1939.[49] For Taylor the essential characteristic of this tradition was its utter repudiation of the 'aims, methods and principles' of traditional British diplomacy.[50] The 'dissenters' did not just disagree with a particular line of British diplomacy, they rejected the general assumptions upon which it was based (for example the maintenance of the balance of power in Europe).[51] Such an approach, Taylor argued, could be traced through the nineteenth century in the thinking of Charles James Fox, Richard Cobden, John Bright and William Gladstone. It was on the basis of this tradition that radicals of the Edwardian period, such as Arthur Ponsonby and E. D. Morel, opposed the Liberal government's foreign policy and, when war came in August 1914, formed the UDC to maintain their critical stance. When Labour constructed a foreign policy in 1917, it was to this tradition that it turned.[52] Henceforward up to 1939, Labour became 'the nearest thing there has ever been to a party of Dissent'.[53]

In terms of policy ideas, Taylor based this assertion on Labour's repudiation, in its 1917 Memorandum on War Aims (MOWA), of 'the old diplomacy', its refusal to discriminate between enemies and allies, and its emphasis on reconciliation with Germany. Labour's attachment, as the war neared its close, to Woodrow Wilson's approach to peacemaking, as laid down in his fourteen points, also signified for Taylor its closeness to the approach of the UDC. On this basis Taylor went on to make a number of empirical claims about Labour's policy development in the early post-war period. The most important of these were that Labour absolutely condemned the Versailles peace treaty, and rejected completely its economic clauses; that the party's approach, simply put, was 'pro-German' and 'anti-French'; that Labour was ambivalent about a League of Nations and rejected the concept of collective security; and, finally, that the influence of the international socialist movement on Labour's policy development was marginal.[54] Taylor was characteristically open about the limitations of his study. He accepted that within

'socialist'. Vickers's recent study combines both approaches, but is closer to that of Taylor in that she explicitly repudiates the notion that Labour's approach can be characterised as 'socialist', although she is more broad-ranging than Taylor in her assessment of the ideological influences on the early Labour party: *Labour party and the world*, 4–9, 32–53.

[49] A. J. P. Taylor, *The troublemakers: dissent over foreign policy, 1792–1939*, London 1957. On the writing on the book and its reception see K. Burk, *Troublemaker: the life and history of A. J. P. Taylor*, New Haven–London, 2000, 296–300.

[50] Taylor, *Troublemakers*, 13.

[51] The nature of the radical critique will be outlined in more detail in chapter 2 below.

[52] Taylor, *Troublemakers*, 154.

[53] Ibid. 20.

[54] Ibid. 151–81. Strangely, Vickers in her recent study of early Labour party foreign policy makes no mention of the Memorandum on War Aims: *Labour party and the world*.

the radical tradition there were important differences of approach which he had downplayed in his narrative. He also conceded that he had understated the influence of less 'idealistic' sections of the Labour party in the inter-war period.[55] Nevertheless, like Gordon, Taylor regarded the simplifications involved in establishing his framework as justified, on the basis that it provided a generally valid guide to the behaviour and actions of the Labour party and other dissenters.

Despite Taylor's acknowledgement of the limitations of his approach, his book has been a major influence on most subsequent studies of Labour's foreign policy up to 1924. His view of the influence of radical dissent on the party, especially as represented by the UDC, quickly became the consensus. The empirical claims he made about Labour's policy development up to 1924 have remained largely unchallenged. Thus, Catherine Cline, in her 1963 study of the politicians and intellectuals who joined the Labour party after 1914, claimed that '[t]he Labour Party adopted [in 1917] the foreign policy of the anti-war group'.[56] She cites as evidence for this assertion the fact that Labour party conferences up to 1924 'called annually for the revision of the Treaty of Versailles' and 'enthusiastically received ... proposals for disarmament'. Similarly, Marvin Swartz argued in 1971 that 'In seeking an independent course ... British Labour turned to the Union of Democratic Control for an articulation of its views on foreign policy.'[57] Despite the passage of forty-three years since Taylor's essay, this interpretation of the events of 1917 remains dominant. In the most recent study of Labour's foreign policy development during this period and in both centenary histories of the Labour party, for example, the Taylorian line has been left largely unrevised.[58]

Although the Taylorian and Beerian interpretations have developed separately, there are nevertheless important similarities between them. They differ with respect to the nature of the ideology that they regard as influen-

[55] Taylor, *Troublemakers*, 20.

[56] Cline, *Recruits*, 21.

[57] M. Swartz, *The Union of Democratic Control in British politics during the First World War*, Oxford 1971, 147. See also, for example, F. L. Carsten, *War against war: British and German radical movements in the First World War*, London 1982; Cline, *Recruits*; H. Hanak, 'The Union of Democratic Control during the First World War', *BIHR* xxxvi (1963), 168–80; D. Marquand, *Ramsay MacDonald*, London 1977; A. J. Mayer, *The political origins of the new diplomacy*; New Haven 1959; S. Spear, 'Pacifist radicals in the post-war British Labour party: the case of E. D. Morel, 1919–1924', *IRSH* xxiii (1978), 193–223; and H. Winkler, 'The emergence of a Labour party foreign policy in Great Britain, 1918–29', *JMH* xxviii (1956), 247–58, and *Paths not taken: British Labour and international policy in the 1920s*, Chapel Hill–London 1994.

[58] Vickers, *The Labour party and the world*, 10, 33, 61, 74; D. Keohane, 'Labour's international policy: a story of conflict and contention', in B. Brivati and R. Heffernan (eds), *The Labour party: a centenary history*, Basingstoke 2000, 366. See also S. Howe, 'Labour and international affairs', in D. M. Tanner, P. Thane and N. Tiratsoo (eds), *Labour's first century*, Cambridge 2000, 128.

tial, but nevertheless they share the view that Labour's policy was based on an 'idealistic' or 'utopian' rejection of mainstream diplomatic opinion, either from a socialist or liberal internationalist perspective.[59] In this respect, both further argue that the ideological aspect of Labour's policy only changed as it moved closer to government. The party was then forced to reconstruct its foreign policy in the light of the realities of the international situation. This was because Labour would otherwise have left itself open to accusations from its opponents that it could not be trusted in government to defend the nation's interests; and because any form of diplomatic progress was only likely if 'international realities' were accepted. Thus, both the Beerian and Taylorian approaches argue that the development of Labour's foreign policy can be understood during this period, and up to 1945, on the basis of an 'idealistic'/'realistic' continuum, with the party gradually moving away from the former and towards the latter.[60]

It is on the basis of these arguments that both types of approach analyse Labour's period in office in 1924. Both argue that in important respects the foreign policy of the MacDonald government involved a 'compromise with the party's principles'.[61] What they are generally referring to is the government's acceptance of the Dawes Plan on reparations and its sympathetic attitude towards the Geneva Protocol on the security apparatus provided by the League of Nations. The Dawes Plan, it is suggested, constituted a major break with previous Labour commitments on reparations because Germany's payments were only reduced and not abolished. The Geneva Protocol would, if implemented, have introduced an unambiguous measure of collective military security to the League of Nations. This, it is suggested, was also inconsistent with the party's largely pacifist-inspired rejection, when in opposition, of any military involvement in international affairs.

Rethinking Labour's approach to foreign policy, 1900–24

Most existing accounts substantially misinterpret Labour's approach to foreign affairs up to 1924, and for this reason considerably exaggerate the first Labour government's 'betrayal' of previous commitments. Labour's approach to international policy in the years before it entered government cannot simply be dismissed as 'idealistic'; the party was not primarily influenced by a 'dissenting' approach to foreign affairs, either of a socialist or

---

[59] See, for example, Winkler, 'Emergence', 251, and *Paths*, 4, 14.
[60] For an elucidation of 'idealism' and 'realism' with respect to international affairs see E. H. Carr, *The twenty year' crisis, 1919–1939*, 2nd edn, Basingstoke 1946.
[61] See Cline, *Recruits*, 83–5, and Gordon, *Conflict and consensus*, 55. See also Marquand, *Ramsay MacDonald*, 333, and R. W. Lyman, *The first Labour government, 1924*, London 1957, 167–70, 180.

radical variant; and Labour's policy remained generally consistent with the mainstream thinking of leading Liberal individuals and groups.[62]

This book will show that while Labour was, like most progressive commentators at this time, strongly critical of the Treaty of Versailles, its criticism was different both in tone and content from that of more absolutist voices, such as Morel. The party always focused its criticisms on certain aspects of the treaty (i.e. the extent to which it deviated from the 1918 armistice) and, after 1922, developed its approach into a coherent and practical policy for the incremental revision of the post-war settlement. This took place largely on the basis of Keynesian thought and in association with moderate European socialists. On the League of Nations, Labour was always more pragmatic and constructive in its approach than is usually suggested.[63] The concept of collective security was largely accepted by most leading Labour party figures by 1918. It was only MacDonald's reticence towards the League that prevented this support being made more explicit. Labour did briefly show interest in a more economic interventionist League in 1918/19, but this quickly died away once it became clear that wartime inter-allied economic bodies were not to be continued into the post-war period.[64]

Labour did not, therefore, enter office in 1924 with an uncompromisingly idealistic approach to foreign affairs, which was diluted in the face of international realities and official opposition. Rather, it had developed during the previous few years a generally moderate, constructive and, with respect to reparations and reconstruction in particular, a relatively sophisticated approach to international policy. Seen in this context, Labour's decision in 1924 to accept the Dawes Plan can be judged less as a betrayal of past commitments, than as an almost inevitable consequence of developments in its policy since the war. Similarly, the government's decision to contemplate acceptance of the Geneva Protocol represented no more than the continuation of a policy debate that had been taking place in the party since 1917/18.

To understand why misinterpretations of Labour foreign policy have occurred it is necessary to move away from the doctrinal interpretative framework adopted, either explicitly or implicitly, by previous commentators. In fact, Labour was not a party with a single ideologically-coherent

---

[62] In this regard, the main problem with Vickers's recent study, which similarly emphasises the influence of liberal ideas, is that she does not sufficiently distinguish between the two traditions within liberal internationalism (radical and Gladstonian): *Labour and the world*, 40–2, 70–5. These, as will be seen in chapter 4 below, led to markedly different conclusions about the causes of the war and policy prescriptions for the post-war world.
[63] For a contrasting view see H. Winkler, *The League of Nations movement in Great Britain*, Metuchen 1967. Vickers is right to emphasise more than in previous studies the importance of the League of Nations and collective security to Labour's approach. However, she wrongly attributes the adoption of this attitude to the influence of the UDC: *Labour party and the world*, 70–5
[64] See A. Orde, *British policy and European reconstruction after World War One*, Cambridge 1990, 28–9.

approach to foreign affairs. It was, rather, a party in which a variety of foreign policy ideologies existed. Of these four were most important: Gladstonian liberalism, UDC radicalism, democratic socialism and ILP pacifism. Labour's policy cannot be properly understood by attempting to merge and combine these different ideological approaches. Rather, the exact nature of the differences between them has to be more clearly elucidated, so as to allow a proper assessment of which was the most influential.

Of these four groupings, two emerged out of the rich nineteenth-century liberal internationalist tradition. The importance of this source of ideas has been recognised by some commentators.[65] However, two important points about this tradition, and its existence within the Labour party, have not been given sufficient attention. The first is that within the liberal internationalist tradition there were important differences of approach, which developed further during this period. Liberal internationalism was not the static remnant of the previous century, but was continuing to develop in the face of new international problems. As chapter 2 will demonstrate, the fundamental belief upon which the tradition was founded was that there existed a harmony of interests between nations based on free trade: international peace and stability which would be maintained so long as the free international exchange of goods and capital was not obstructed by national governments. However, important differences had begun to emerge within this overall framework by the early part of the twentieth century, the most important of which concerned the question of non-intervention.[66] Firm adherents to the Cobdenite view, that British intervention abroad should be resisted in all circumstances, were challenged by those who argued, often on the basis of William Gladstone's approach to international affairs, that intervention had to be accepted both to manage the international system and to support liberal movements abroad.

It was on the basis of this cleavage that liberal radical thought split during the war. The Cobdenites, such as Morel, Trevelyan and Ponsonby, who were instrumental in the formation of the UDC, continued to argue unwaveringly that free trade and a more democratic approach to domestic diplomacy were sufficient for the avoidance of future wars. In contrast, Gladstonian liberals, such as Gilbert Murray, Lord Bryce and Willoughby Dickinson, whose belief in a harmony of interests between nations had even prior to the war been more sceptical and contingent than that of the Cobdenites, responded to the war by arguing that future conflicts could only be avoided if embryonic ideas on the management of the international system were developed much further. It was on this basis that the idea of a League of Nations was to

---

[65] Most recently by Vickers, *Labour party and the world*.
[66] See, for example, A. J. A. Morris, *Radicalism against war*, Harlow 1972; A. J. A. Morris (ed.), *Edwardian radicalism, 1910–14: some aspects of British radicalism*, London 1974; and W. Hinde, *Richard Cobden: a Victorian outsider*, New Haven 1987.

emerge.[67] For the most part, this idea developed outside the UDC. It was not one that the Cobdenites, who dominated that organisation, played much of a role in developing, or supporting thereafter, although democratic socialists in the organisation adopted a much more positive attitude. The UDC radicals paid lip service to the League concept, but always regarded free trade and democratic control as more important.[68] Rather, it was the Gladstonian liberals who cultivated the idea separately, first in the secret meetings and then, after May 1915, in the League of Nations Society (LNS). In this task, significantly, they received explicit support at an early stage from leading trade unionists, such as J. H. Thomas, J. R. Clynes and Tom Shaw. By the end of the war, therefore, the cleavage in the liberal tradition on foreign affairs had hardened, with the existence of two distinct ideological groupings – the UDC radicals and the Gladstonian liberals – both of which, with the entrance of Morel, Ponsonby and Trevelyan into the ILP, were represented in the Labour party.

The second important point in respect of the liberal tradition concerns its relationship with socialist thinking. Some existing accounts have simply included liberal ideas, together with ideas from other sources, in a list of principles which are then said to constitute a 'socialist' approach.[69] However, much socialist thought on international affairs involved a rejection of the basic tenets of liberalism. The two traditions did not merge in the Labour party, but remained distinct and in competition. As will be shown in chapters 2 and 4, two main strands of socialist thought were evident during this period: the democratic socialist and the ILP pacifist. Given the broad definitions of the term 'socialist' often given, it is important to be clear about how this term is being used in this book. In this regard the two strands identified have been categorised as 'socialist' because, unlike the two liberal strands, both were grounded on a fundamental critique of the international capitalist system.

Of the socialist strands of thought on foreign affairs, the democratic socialist strand was the most important. It came out of the work of J. A. Hobson on imperialism, which was developed further before, during and after the war by H. N. Brailsford.[70] Hobson argued in his classic *Imperialism: a study* (1902), that there were deep-seated problems with the international structure of capitalism, caused by the domination of foreign policy by international financiers.[71] Brailsford took this argument forward and argued that

[67] See Ceadel, *Thinking about peace and war*, 111.

[68] See Taylor, *Troublemakers*, 141–2. Ponsonby played a small role in the early development of the League idea but quickly lost interest once it became clear that the organisation would rely on force: K. Robbins, *The abolition of war: the peace movement in Britain, 1914–1919*, Cardiff 1976, 135.

[69] See Miller, *Socialism and foreign policy*.

[70] J. A. Hobson, *Imperialism: a study*, 3rd rev. edn, London 1938.

[71] Ibid. See also P. J. Cain and A. G. Hopkins, 'Variations on a famous theme: Hobson, international trade and imperialism, 1902–38', in M. Freeden (ed.), *Reappraising J. A.*

British foreign policy operated in the direct interests of the capitalist class.[72] It sought to protect its imperial investments from foreign competition. Thus, in a competitive economic system there would always be a temptation for disadvantaged nations to use force to bring about a change in their favour, by gaining guaranteed access to scarce resources and privileged opportunities for capital investment. Absolute reliance could not, therefore be placed, as Cobdenite radicals argued, on the shared benefits of free trade as a guarantor of peace. Nor were the limited schemes for the extension of arbitration and establishment of collective security likely to be as effective as the Gladstonians liberals supposed. Rather, what was required was greater supranational control of the international economy.[73] This was an idea in which Fabians, such as Sidney Webb and Leonard Woolf, who had initially co-operated with Gladstonian liberals in the development of ideas for a limited League, grew increasingly interested during the war.

The second socialist ideological strand also differed in important respects from liberalism. It developed out of connections on the left with pacifist thought.[74] As will be seen in chapter 4, some in the ILP and British Socialist party (BSP), argued for an absolute rejection of all 'capitalist wars', either from a Christian socialist standpoint or as the result of variants of Marxist thought. This strand was an important feature of the ILP's reaction to the war: the avowedly pacifist No Conscription Fellowship (NCF), which was formed in 1914, was dominated by young ILP figures such as Clifford Allen, Fenner Brockway and J. H. Hudson.[75] However, for most of this period pacifism was to have only a marginal effect on the development of Labour policy.

The politics of Labour party foreign policy-making

The failure of past accounts to separate out the different ideological strands, combined with their neglect of the role of political and institutional elements in policy development are the root causes of their misinterpretation of Labour's approach to foreign policy during this period. Politically,

---

Hobson, London 1990; and P. J. Cain and A. G. Hopkins, *British imperialism: innovation and expansion, 1688–1914*, London 1993.

[72] H. N. Brailsford, *The war of steel and gold: a study of the armed peace*, 3rd rev. edn, London 1915.

[73] Idem, *A League of Nations*, 2nd edn, London 1917.

[74] The term 'pacifist' is used in this book in accordance with Ceadel's categorisation of thinking on peace and war. In this regard, it refers to an absolute opposition to the use of force to resolve disputes and is contrasted with 'pacificism'. The latter holds that war can be prevented and, in the long term, abolished by reforms to the international system and the domestic diplomatic process. Pacificists argue that war is only generally justified in defence of these reforms: Ceadel, *Thinking about peace and war*, 5–6, and *Pacifism in Britain, 1915–45*, Oxford 1980.

[75] Robbins, *Abolition*, 77.

what requires more explicit recognition is the fact that, despite ideological differences, individuals and groups often had an interest in building coalitions in order to increase their political power or maximise their influence on policy development. When Labour's foreign policy development is analysed on this basis the prevailing view of the role of the UDC, in particular, is thrown into question.

Existing work assigns a strong influence to the UDC in the development of Labour's foreign policy during this period, on the basis that Labour's 1917 MOWA was strongly reminiscent of the UDC's policy on the war and its proposals for peace; that once the peace settlement was agreed Labour rejected it using similar language to that used by the UDC; and, finally, that after the peace was signed both organisations called for a revision of the treaty.

Three main points can be made about these arguments. First, that existing accounts misunderstand the ideological nature of the UDC because they fail to put the organisation into its political context. Second, that the UDC's ideas did not dominate the MOWA, but that ideologically the document was an extremely eclectic mix of approaches, a fact that can again be explained if it is put into its political context. Third, that if greater attention is given to the actual meaning assigned by individuals and groups to terms such as 'a Wilsonian peace' and 'revision of the treaty' clear differences are apparent between leading UDC figures and Labour leaders.

So, if the UDC was not the dominant influence on Labour's foreign policy development, what was? Is, indeed, a Labour party foreign policy identifiable during this period, or was policy, as the pluralists would suggest, always merely an incoherent amalgam of recommendations proposed by the different ideological groupings in the party? To answer these questions greater attention needs to be given to the institutions within which Labour party policy was made, the organisation of the party's policy-making process and the distribution of power within it.

Existing accounts have not entirely ignored this issue. They have suggested that members of the UDC exercised influence through their membership of the Advisory Committee on International Questions (ACIQ), which was set up, along with other such committees, as part of Labour's re-launch in 1918.[76] However, there are a number of problems with this view, the most important of which is that the committee was only 'advisory': it had no executive power and the party as a whole was not bound by its decisions.[77] In contrast, on those bodies that did exercise executive power – the party lead-

---

[76] See, for example, Miller, *Socialism and foreign policy*, 83; Taylor, *Troublemakers*, 154; and Vickers *Labour party and the world*, 74.

[77] The question of where executive power lies within the Labour party has long been debated by historians and political scientists. See, for example, L. Minkin, *The Labour party conference: a study in the politics of intra-party democracy*, London 1978; R. McKenzie, *British political parties*, 2nd edn, London 1963; and Worley, *Labour inside the gate*, 9.

ership, the Parliamentary Labour party (PLP) and the executive committee – the representation of the leading figures of any of the ideological groupings was often extremely small.[78] Trade unionists dominated the executive committee, a domination that was reinforced in 1918 with the adoption of the new constitution and establishment of joint committees with the parliamentary committee of the TUC (PCTUC) on many issues including foreign affairs. Other sections of the party were only allowed a minority representation.[79] Trade unionists also dominated the PLP for most of the period, although the number of ILP representatives did rise at the 1922 election.

The situation with respect to the party leadership was not so clear-cut. Here, MacDonald, an ILP member and founding member of the UDC, remained an important figure, even after his resignation from the leadership in August 1914. After 1922, with his return to the party leadership, he undoubtedly had a significant impact upon policy development.[80] However, the figures who surrounded MacDonald were all from a trade union background. In this regard Henderson,[81] the leading figure in the party after MacDonald's resignation, and Thomas, Clynes[82] and Shaw, who all exercised a strong influence on the way in which the party was run and the decisions that were made made, were the most important. Moreover, ideologically, MacDonald's approach to foreign affairs was always idiosyncratic. His views on the war were complex, if not confused, and his continued attachment to the international socialist movement led him to adopt a much more tolerant view of France in the post-war period than many of his UDC colleagues.[83]

Overall, then, representatives of the trade union wing of the party dominated its foreign policy-making apparatus. Existing accounts have either side-stepped or ignored this situation. Some commentators, such as Cline, Winkler and Swartz have suggested that the trade unions themselves were converted by the views of the UDC in 1917.[84] As chapter 5 will show, however, this view is simply wrong. In fact, even those trade unionists who favoured a less passive approach to the war than the one taken by Labour in 1914, made strenuous efforts to ensure that the party kept its distance from the peace-by-negotiation groups. Rhiannon Vickers, on the other hand, accepts that the trade unions had 'a massive influence on the Labour Party's foreign policy in the first half of the [twentieth] century', but does not explain how this interpretation is consistent with the 'resounding impact'

[78] On the developing relationship during this period between the NEC, the PLP and the leadership see Howell, *MacDonald's party*, 55–6
[79] From 1917 onwards a joint trade union and executive committee body was given responsibility for conducting Labour's approach to international policy: see chapter 5 below, and Howell, *MacDonald's party*, 56–7
[80] See ibid. 58.
[81] On the 'centrality' of Henderson see ibid. 65.
[82] Clynes was also a member of the ILP.
[83] See chapters 8 and 9 below.
[84] See, for example, Cline, *Recruits*, 17–18, and Winkler, *Paths*, 19.

she also assigns to the UDC, given that the views on foreign policy associated with the latter and of the TUC were different.[85]

An alternative view is that the trade unions were only interested in foreign affairs at times of national crisis and, at all other times, left party intellectuals to debate the issue amongst themselves.[86] Such an argument is based on the labourist notion that ultimately the trade unions were only interested in the material interests of their members. However, while there is a certain amount of truth in this view it should not be overstated. What it ignores is the fact that, despite their trade union origins, individuals such as Henderson, Thomas, Clynes and Shaw were more than just representatives of the trade union interest. They became, as they climbed the party leadership ladder, politicians in their own right, with political ambitions and views of their own.[87] This was particularly the case in areas where the trade unions did not always have a clearly-defined interest. As spokesmen for the party in parliament and elsewhere, they had to develop an interest in all aspects of public affairs and, given the centrality of foreign affairs during this period, this was not an area that they could neglect. Moreover, as Labour increasingly presented itself as a competitor for power, these leaders had to fight off accusations that the party was deficient in this area, or dominated by extremists. On a personal level, any claim that they might have had to be considered as future leaders of the party, rested on their ability to credibly represent it in each policy area. And, in this regard, Thomas and Clynes, in particular, saw themselves as potential future leaders of the Labour party.

Moreover, Labour's moderate leaders, like a number of trade union leaders, were not blank canvases upon which party intellectuals could construct their own approach to foreign affairs.[88] Rather, while none was in any sense an intellectual, each had strong and firmly grounded views of his own on international policy. These stemmed in part from their close past associations with the Gladstonian Liberal party, which explains the close attachment of Thomas and Clynes to the League of Nations movement during the war and thereafter.[89] However, they were also a product of the international links of the Labour party and the trade union movement. As a result leading Labour figures were used to meeting foreign nationals and exchanging views; and, as will be seen in chapters 8 and 9, repeatedly showed themselves prepared to listen, and occasionally take on board, views critical of Britain's position. As a result, all these figures had strong but moderate internationalist incli-

---

[85] See Vickers, *Labour party and the world*, 33–4. It is possible that Vickers's argument is that the trades unions' influence was mainly felt in the 1930s, but this is not explicitly stated.

[86] See Foote, *The Labour party's political thought*.

[87] For a recent acceptance of this view see Howell, *MacDonald's party*, 57

[88] Howell makes clear the dangers of adopting a one-dimensional approach to the views and opinions of trade unionists: ibid. 95

[89] On Henderson's early contacts with the Liberal party and association with Gladstonian radicalism see C. Wrigley, *Arthur Henderson*, Cardiff 1990, 32, 36, 72.

nations, strongly reminiscent of the Gladstonian liberal ideological strand. Indeed, there is good evidence that, in this respect, their views were typical and representative of a significant body of opinion in the broader Labour movement.[90] Thus, all supported the war as a just fight against German militarism, and all believed that while Germany should be treated fairly during the peacemaking process, she should nevertheless pay for the damage that she had caused. All supported a limited form of League of Nations, based on the notion of collective security.

Given their position in the policy-making apparatus of the Labour party, Henderson, Thomas, Clynes and Shaw were strongly placed to ensure that their approach to foreign affairs dominated. And they could often rely on the backing of the significant strain of moderate internationalism running throughout the party. When the statements and resolutions emanating from the main institutions of the party are closely and systematically analysed, it is clear that this, for the most part, is what they did. After recovering from the shock of the war in 1914, Labour gradually developed between 1917 and 1924 a moderate approach to international policy, which was consistent with its increasingly critical support for the war, and which was little different from the Liberal mainstream views of Keynes and the LNU.

This approach certainly came under pressure from UDC radicals and democratic socialists in the party, and, as will be seen in chapter 6, some small successes were achieved during the early post-war period, when most of the Labour party and its moderate leadership were distracted by other events. Overall, however, the Labour moderates prevailed, especially after 1921.

It was therefore with this moderate and practical policy, rather than one influenced by the UDC radicals, democratic socialist or ILP pacifists in the party, that Labour entered office in 1924. Moreover, as chapters 8 and 9 will show, Labour remained largely true to this policy in government. Compromises were, of course, made in the face of external constraints, but there was certainly no general betrayal of previous commitments. Indeed, judged on the basis of the party's actual policy aims, rather than those proposed by dissident factions, and given the international situation that the government inherited, Labour's first effort at international diplomacy was remarkably successful.

---

[90] See chapters 2–4 below.

2

Labour and International Affairs before the First World War

The formation in 1900 of the Labour party (initially as the Labour Representation Committee) took place at a time when debate about foreign affairs and Britain's role in the world was becoming increasingly heated. The most immediate reason for this was the Boer War, which had been in progress since 1899. Britain, the greatest imperial power of the age, was experiencing severe difficulties in overcoming a small guerrilla army of Boers. Her resources were stretched and the tactics employed to quash the rebellion were becoming increasingly desperate. Among domestic 'pro-Boer' critics of British imperialism, the 'immoral' war was outspokenly condemned. British foreign policy, it seemed, had been hijacked by protectionist imperialists.

To a large extent, however, the South African controversy was part of – and seemed to make more urgent – a larger debate about Britain's future in the face of broader economic and political changes in the industrialised (or industrialising) world. The rise of Germany and the USA, as potential rivals to Britain's global position, was the major concern. How should Britain respond to this new, more competitive environment? Should she maintain her longstanding commitment to free trade, or should the state take a more active role in safeguarding Britain's competitive position, through greater domestic intervention and tariff reform? Was British intervention abroad ever justifiable?

These debates, most historians agree, were largely ignored by the Labour party. It is generally accepted that before the First World War 'working class interest in foreign affairs was sporadic and slight'.[1] This reflected the dominant position of the trade unions in the party. They had agreed to the formation of the new party in the belief that it was the best way to advance the economic and social interests of their members. International affairs were not seen as exercising much influence on this question; therefore, they were largely ignored.[2]

Interest in foreign affairs, it is argued, was largely confined to the ILP, with even the Fabians showing little concern. The ILP had a long tradition

---

[1] Winkler, *Paths*, 12. See also Howe, 'Labour and international affairs', 127, and D. J. Newton, *British labour, European socialism and the struggle for peace, 1889–1914*, Oxford 1985.
[2] This view fits closely with Labourist interpretations of the Labour party. See, for example, Foote, *The Labour party's political thought*.

of internationalism and managed, through its members' central role in the leadership of the Labour party, to ensure that Labour's limited interventions on foreign policy reflected this stance. However, even the ILP's internationalism was influenced more by the nineteenth-century liberal internationalist campaigns of Cobden and Gladstone than by the anti-national internationalism of socialism.[3] Labour thus associated itself in the pre-war period with Liberal Radical demands for 'national self-determination, disarmament, compulsory arbitration and the abolition of secret diplomacy', and not with the international socialist campaign for a general strike against war.[4]

The extent to which even these liberal internationalist values were supported, rather than just tolerated, by the wider Labour movement has also been questioned.[5] Labourist historians, such as Geoffrey Foote, for example, have suggested that the Labour movement always 'rallies to the national flag' in a national emergency.[6] This knee-jerk nationalism in the Edwardian period, Gareth Stedman Jones has suggested, reflected a working-class culture that if it did not 'actively promote jingoism … passively acquiesced to it'.[7]

There is much in this traditional view of Labour's response to pre-war debates on international affairs that is correct. Nevertheless, it contains a number of important simplifications and gaps, which need to be addressed if a better understanding is to be gained of the party's subsequent approach to foreign affairs, and particularly its reaction to the coming of war in 1914. These concern the relationship between foreign affairs and Labour's political strategy, the party's foreign policy ideology and the level of support within the broader labour movement for the leadership's approach. These issues must also be considered in relation to the changing international context within which British elites were grappling with foreign policy issues during this period, the nature of the policy reappraisal that followed and the resulting debate among liberal internationalists.

British foreign policy and its critics, c.1854–1903

For much of the nineteenth century, there was a general consensus among Britain's political elite that the country's basic interests were served by the pursuit of a foreign policy that in many respects was consistent with the

---

[3] See Ward, Red flag, 103–4, and Vickers, Labour party and the world.
[4] See J. N. Horne, Labour at war: France and Britain, 1914–18, Oxford 1991, 30.
[5] Ibid.
[6] Foote, The Labour party's political thought, 13. See also Marquand, Ramsay MacDonald, 169. For a slightly different interpretation see Keohane, 'Labour's international policy', 364.
[7] G. Stedman-Jones, Languages of class: studies in English working class history, 1832–1982, Cambridge 181.

liberal principles of free trade, peace and low military expenditure.[8] As a trading nation which, unlike most of her competitors, undertook as much trade with the rest of the world as she did with continental Europe, the maintenance of free trade and peace was a vital national requirement.[9] Indeed, given her geographical position, free trade was regarded as Britain's only real security concern. The English Channel provided security against invasion and Britain had no territorial interests on the continent. It was the navy, therefore, not the army, that was regarded as the ultimate guarantor of Britain's position.[10] Britain's relationship with Europe was largely determined by the global nature of her interests. Her only real concern was that a balance of power be maintained between the great European states; that one power, or a combination of powers, did not become too dominant. If this occurred, it was feared that Britain's wider imperial interests might be threatened.[11]

What, however, should Britain do to prevent this from happening? It was on this issue that the link between the national interest and liberal principles was most strained. A small army and limited military expenditure was vital to the maintenance of Britain's liberal values, but it greatly constrained her ability to intervene effectively to ensure the maintenance of the balance of power. For most of the nineteenth century this was not a pressing problem: no European country was as industrialised as Britain, none posed a major threat to her world role and no one power – or group of powers – seemed determined to gain a dominant position on the continent. It was only when this situation began to change at the beginning of the twentieth century that the unresolved tension at the heart of British policy became more problematic.

For mid nineteenth-century ideological liberals, even the consideration of intervention in Europe was anathema. Of this group, the most important and influential individual was Cobden. He was an ardent proponent of free trade who, on the basis of the work of the great *laissez-faire* thinkers, Adam Smith and Jeremy Bentham, believed firmly that the necessary and sufficient requirement for the maintenance of international peace and stability was the free international exchange of goods and capital: there existed a harmony of interests between nations based on free trade. The use of military force in international relations or the protection of exclusive markets by one power was thus economically irrational.[12] Britain's best policy in defence of liberty

---

[8] See B. Porter, *Britain, Europe and the world, 1850–1986: delusions of grandeur*, 2nd edn, London 1987.

[9] See Cain and Hopkins, *British imperialism*, 202–25, 449–73.

[10] A large army was also regarded unfavourably because it would be too costly, imply higher taxes and thus disrupt economic stability.

[11] See, for example, Cain and Hopkins, *British imperialism*, 450.

[12] On Cobden see Hinde, *Richard Cobden*; D. Read, *Cobden and Bright: a Victorian political partnership*, London 1967; Taylor, *Troublemakers*, 40–66; and F. R. Flournoy, 'British liberal theories of international relations', *JHI* vii (1946), 195–217.

was to stand aside in all military disputes. She would thus set a positive example of the prosperity to be gained from non-intervention.

Despite the British Foreign Office's apparent commitment to liberal principles, Cobden was deeply suspicious of its motives. Britain's liberalism was half-hearted: she remained too interventionist, too imperialistic and too much reliant, with respect to the navy, on the use of (or threat of) force. Cobden dismissed as a 'chimera', the policy of maintaining the balance of power in Europe:[13] it was costly, distorted the natural harmony of interests and created the type of suspicions and distrust which led to war. Imperialism, he argued, presupposed the maintenance of a large and expensive navy to defend it from predators, and a standing army to hold down the native population. It was maintained, he argued, mainly to provide careers for the aristocracy.[14] Indeed, Cobden, as a confirmed radical, believed that many of the problems of British foreign policy could be traced to its domination by aristocratic influences and permanent bureaucrats.[15] They were incapable of representing the real interests of the British populace. Thus, domestic political reform was a prerequisite for the achievement of a rational foreign policy.[16] Without it, the state would continue to pursue a militarist and imperialist policy on behalf of an unrepresentative minority.

When disputes did arise between nations or access to markets was blocked the solution proposed by Cobden was mediation or conciliation. If there was a harmony of interests between nations, all disputes were ultimately capable of solution by rational negotiation. This should be organised in the form of bilateral agreements between nations, not on a collective basis.[17] As Wendy Hinde suggests, Cobden's 'profound distrust of government' led him to 'emphatically disclaim any wish to establish a permanent court or congress for the settlement of disputes'.[18] He was thus firmly opposed to the idea that conciliation should be backed by the threat of military force.

Most liberals accepted the basic tenets of Cobdenism: free trade, retrenchment, disarmament and non-intervention. However, some were unwilling to accept the almost isolationist 'no foreign politics' creed that radically-inspired Cobdenism seemed to imply. This reflected a gradually developing division between liberals and radicals.[19] Some sympathetic liberal critics of Cobden

---

13 Quoted in Miller, *Socialism and foreign policy*, 7
14 See Hinde, *Richard Cobden*, 207.
15 On the radical tradition with respect to foreign affairs see Ceadel, *Thinking about peace and war*, 114–21.
16 However, Cobden was cautious in his support for universal suffrage: Hinde, *Richard Cobden*, 192. The importance of some form of public control over diplomacy had first been stressed by Bentham: Miller, *Socialism and foreign policy*, 6.
17 See Hinde, *Richard Cobden*, 200. It was not entirely clear, however, whether the nations involved would be compelled to comply with the award of the arbitration.
18 Ibid.
19 For an excellent summary of the nature of this division see Ceadel, *Thinking about peace and war*, 109–19.

were more prepared than he was to consider systematic and structured forms of international conciliation and mediation. These, they argued, were necessary to manage the international system and give nations more confidence in the idea of free trade.[20] International, as well as domestic, reform was necessary to preserve peace. Others were critical of Cobden's passivity in support of liberal or national liberation movements abroad and argued, especially in the later part of the century, that Britain had a moral responsibility to promote and protect freedom abroad, as well as at home. Gladstone's ideas on foreign policy were the main inspiration for these arguments.[21] He seemed more prepared to accept that Britain, as the home of liberty, had a duty to support and protect movements for freedom abroad.[22] Whereas Cobden balked at the idea of any systematic means of regulating the international system, Gladstone accepted the need for regular conferences to help maintain order. In 1880 he wrote that 'It is the working of the European Concert for the purposes of justice, peace and liberty, with efficiency and success, which is the great matter at issue. This has always been the ideal of my life in Foreign Policy.'[23] If mediation and arbitration failed, Gladstone even seemed prepared to use force, particularly in the case of Belgium. However, generally he had no intention of presiding over an ever-increasing armament budget, nor a general policy of intervention. Thus, while Gladstonians were often prepared to engage in greater rhetorical condemnation of oppressive regimes (particularly Tsarist Russia) than their more Cobdenite colleagues, few were prepared to propose a policy of widespread British intervention. In what circumstances (if any), and in what form, Britain should intervene abroad remained the classic liberal dilemma.

The foreign policy of Edward Grey

Despite Cobden's complaints, the tensions between liberal principles and the national interest remained relatively slight while Britain remained the only truly industrialised nation with global trading interests. After 1880, however, the stresses gradually became more profound. Intense imperial rivalry in Africa, and the rise of German *Weltpolitik* after 1900, seemed to put Britain's world position at risk.[24] The clearest and most poignant manifestation of this threat for Britain was the seemingly inexorable growth of the

---

[20] In so doing, they were reflecting a strand in liberal thinking begun by Bentham: Miller, *Socialism and foreign policy*, 5.
[21] These ideas were, in turn, strongly influenced by those of John Stuart Mill: ibid. 11.
[22] Flournoy, 'British liberal theories', 196; Hinde, *Richard Cobden*, 222.
[23] Quoted in H. Temperley and L. M. Penson (eds), *Foundations of British foreign policy from Pitt (1792) to Salisbury (1902)*, Cambridge 1938, 410.
[24] On the background to Germany's change of policy see P. Kennedy, *The rise of the Anglo-German antagonism, 1860–1914*, London 1980, 157–288.

German navy. Everywhere it seemed that the economic interests of Britain were threatened. Could the government really stand aside and let her ever-powerful rivals, particularly Germany, gain the spoils, in the belief that ultimately they would have to pay a greater price to defend their gains?

Few policy-makers believed that such a stance was sensible. As a result, the aim of foreign policy from 1900 became increasingly to protect Britain's world role in the face of the German threat and the growing realisation that she lacked by herself the means to do so. As a result, in the early 1900s, agreements or treaties were signed with the USA (1901), Japan (1902), France (1904) and Russia (1907), all of which made concessions in the hope that specific imperial threats would be neutralised.[25]

These developments began under the Conservative premiership of Lord Salisbury. Nevertheless, despite the election in 1906 of the apparently radical prime minister, Henry Campbell-Bannerman, foreign policy was continuous.[26] Under the tutelage of Sir Edward Grey, there was little obvious change in Britain's European diplomacy, and defence spending, after initial reductions, increased steadily. To Liberal radicals it seemed that the government's foreign policy had been captured by the imperialist 'Liberal League' wing of the party.[27]

As a result, an eight-year campaign of criticism and opposition was mounted by the radicals, which focused upon the refusal by a hard-core group to vote in favour of increases in military expenditure.[28] These pre-war radicals were the remnants of a pro-Boer movement, which had united older Liberals who subscribed to the views of Cobden and Gladstone, with new Liberals, such as Hobhouse, Hammond and Hobson, who up until this time had concentrated on domestic affairs.[29]

[25] See, for example, Temperley and Penson, *Foundations*, 456.
[26] This was despite Campbell-Bannerman's explicit support for 'a League of Peace' in 1906: *Concord* (Jan. 1906).
[27] Somewhat confusingly, Liberal opponents of Grey's foreign policy were generally referred to as 'Radicals'. However, as the coming of the war was to show, not all of them were ideological radicals; some were Gladstonian liberals (see chapter 4 below). Formed by a new generation of Liberal politicians in 1903, the Liberal League aimed to modernise the party's approach by moving it away from its reliance on the principles and policies of its past statesmen. In particular the 'Limps' wanted the party to accept and embrace the renewed international imperial expansion, which had built up at the end of the nineteenth century.
[28] For the Radical's campaign on foreign policy and defence spending see Morris, *Radicalism*.
[29] As Howe suggests, the nature and content of Cobdenism had changed since the mid-1800s to reflect the concerns of the New Liberals: 'Towards the "hungry forties": free trade in Britain, *c.* 1880–1906', in E. F. Biagini (ed.), *Citizenship and community: Liberals, radicals and collective identities in the British Isles, 1865–1931*, Cambridge 1996, 193–218. This was part of a broader debate taking place within new Liberal circles about free trade, which was largely instigated by Hobson's work on imperialism. For Hobson's ideas see chapter 4 below. See also P. F. Clarke, *Liberals and social democrats*, Cambridge 1978, and

The main areas of concern for the radicals were the agreements made in the 1900s with the other great powers in Europe. Increasingly, from 1906, the suspicion grew that the main aim of British policy was to 'pen in' Germany as a threat to the balance of power in Europe. However, this was the most pessimistic view of Grey's foreign policy. There were important differences of emphasis within radical circles about the extent of the government's deviation from the liberal path.[30] While some Cobdenite radicals concentrated merely on the level of defence expenditure, others were more prepared to take a wider view of the overall aims of Grey's policy. Older politicians, such as Lord Loreburn and Lord Courtney, believed that as long as peace was maintained, the means by which it was achieved were largely irrelevant. They were prepared to accept Grey's assertion of pacific intentions in the Gladstonian belief that *entente* with France was the first step towards a Concert of Europe, rather than an entangling alliance.

However, on the primary question of pre-war British diplomacy, the relationship with Germany, there was consensus among radicals: there was no reason why an agreement could not be reached, a belief that was boosted immeasurably by the work of the journalist and publicist Norman Angell on the interdependence of the European economy.[31] Most accepted that Germany was an expansionist power, but there was genuine incomprehension that, given the 'proven' irrationality of war between the European powers, Britain and Germany could still not come to some agreement. Arthur Ponsonby summed up the radicals' bemusement in 1912, writing that 'We do not understand what obstacles lie in the way.'[32]

After the Agadir Crisis of 1912 – caused by a dispute between Germany and France over trading rights in Morocco – there was a concerted radical campaign urging Grey to re-establish links with Germany.[33] With the government's failure to recognise the possibility of encouraging a harmonious international system, many radicals, in true radical Cobdenite fashion, looked to the workings of the governmental process for an explanation. The formation of the Liberal Foreign Affairs Committee in 1912 was primarily motivated by this contention.[34] Its main aim was to exert a greater democratic control on foreign policy. As Arthur Ponsonby told the House of Commons, this

F. Trentmann, 'The strange death of free trade: the erosion of "liberal consensus" in Great Britain, *c.* 1903–1932', in Biagini, *Citizenship and community*, 219–50.

[30] See Ceadel, *Thinking about peace and war*, 109–19, and Clarke, *Liberals and social democrats*, 78–9.

[31] See, for example, N. Angell, *The great illusion: a study of the relation of military power to national advantage*, London 1913, 32.

[32] A. Ponsonby, *Democracy and the control of foreign affairs*, London 1912, 15. See also HC, Debates, xli.1411 (25 July 1912).

[33] See Morris, *Radicalism*, 269.

[34] On the Liberal Foreign Affairs Committee see T. P. Conwell-Evans, *Foreign policy from the back-bench, 1904–18: a study based on the papers of Lord Noel-Buxton*, London 1932.

was necessary because foreign policy was being dictated by 'a certain section of the press, specialist and experts, a small body of jingoes and last but not least, those who are interested in the manufacture of war'.[35]

However, there was a paradox in the radicals' position. While many were critical of the immorality of the new imperialism and the treatment of native races, they defended Britain's world role.[36] As Ponsonby told the House of Commons on 25 July 1912, 'As to patriotism, I have an almost superstitious belief in the British race, in British characteristics, and in the position of domination which we hold in the world.'[37] It was clear that the harmony of interests between nations that they envisaged would be based on the *status quo*.[38] Only the real mavericks envisaged a cut in British naval strength relative to other world powers. [39]

Thus, the radicals tended not to move beyond the British perspective when looking at foreign affairs. Seen from abroad, however, Britain retained a hegemonic international position in the early part of the twentieth century, albeit a weakening one.[40] The aim of Grey's foreign policy was to safeguard this situation, while remaining as true as was possible to liberal principles. The radicals, while implicitly accepting the aims of this policy, consistently rejected its methods.[41]

Despite such inconsistencies and ambiguities in the radicals' campaign, the Labour party leadership closely associated the party with the anti-Grey crusade. To understand why it did this, and to examine the extent to which this approach accurately reflected the views of the wider labour movement, it is necessary to examine the nature of the Labour party in the pre-war period: its structure, ideology, policy-making process and political strategy.

Policy-making and political strategy in the pre-war Labour party

In the years before the First World War the Labour party was a political body unsure and divided about its aims, purpose and tactics. Although the formation of the LRC in 1900 had signalled a general recognition among socialists and the majority of the trade unions that their interests could be most adequately served by mutual co-operation, behind this pragmatic agree-

---

[35] HC, Debates, xli.1407–8 (25 July 1912).

[36] See Howe, *Anticolonialism in British politics*, 31–3.

[37] HC, Debates, xli.1412 (25 July 1912). See also M. Swartz, 'A study in futility: the British radicals at the outbreak of the First World War', in Morris, *Edwardian radicalism*, 246–61.

[38] Carr, *The twenty years' crisis*, 69.

[39] See Morris, *Radicalism*, 110

[40] The nature of this hegemony is explained in Cain and Hopkins, *British imperialism*, 161–80.

[41] On Grey's foreign policy see K. Robbins, *Sir Edward Grey: a biography of Lord Grey of Fallodon*, London 1971, 129–36.

ment there remained a host of fundamental differences over its ideological function and its relationship with other parties. Labour remained little more than a loose coalition of interests, many of them deeply suspicious of the others' intentions.[42] At the head of this disparate body was a leadership structure which had only recently been recognised as necessary, had still to gain the acceptance of many and which could still not count on internal party discipline.

With respect to policy-making, party policy in the pre-war period was determined, according to the Labour party's constitution, by the annual conference. On many issues this did occur. The subjects raised by the PLP in the House of Commons often mirrored very closely resolutions passed by the conference,[43] which generally dealt with issues of concern to the trade unions affiliated to the Labour party.[44]

In policy areas that were less obviously of interest to the unions, the aims and purpose of policy, and the process by which it was agreed, were more confused. While the labourist view of the Labour party can be exaggerated, there is little doubt that many within the pre-war party had little interest in policies on subjects outside their own narrow concerns. Nevertheless there was no general attempt to inhibit policy-making on non-union subjects.[45] The result was that the party leadership in particular, but also the party's ideological factions, had much greater room for manoeuvre on policy development in these areas. Motions could be passed at conference and party leaders could make speeches in parliament, the content of which was largely ignored by much of the party's membership.

For most of the first thirty years of the twentieth century the political leadership of the Labour party was dominated by two men: James Ramsay MacDonald and Arthur Henderson. MacDonald, a member of the Independent Labour Party (ILP) from its earliest days, was a clear-minded political strategist with an absolute commitment to the parliamentary process as the forum within which to press for social reform.[46] Arthur Henderson was a union man.[47] He had started his political career as an organiser in the Iron Founders' union. His first political experience had been in the Liberal party and he remained close to many of those politicians associated with its radical wing.

The political position facing these two leaders in the pre-war period was precarious. This had a profound effect on the political strategy that

---

[42] As Henry Pelling suggested it was more reminiscent of a pressure group than a political party: A short history of the Labour party, 9th edn, Basingstoke 1991, 18.

[43] Beer, Modern British politics, 116–20.

[44] See McKibbin, Evolution, 90

[45] Ibid.

[46] The best biography of MacDonald remains Marquand, Ramsay MacDonald.

[47] On Henderson see Wrigley, Arthur Henderson; F. M. Leventhal, Arthur Henderson, Manchester 1989; M. A. Hamilton, Arthur Henderson, London 1938; and Howell, MacDonald's party.

they pursued and, therefore, the development of policy. Labour was still a relatively new third party operating in a political system biased strongly in favour of two large parties. The primary electoral concern, therefore, was not how to compete for power, but how to safeguard the party's separate existence and maximise its influence. For this reason the Labour leadership adopted an extremely cautious approach, regarding the prospect of a Labour government as very much a long-term goal. The immediate need was to consolidate and gradually improve the party's electoral performance, further develop its organisation and attempt within these constraints to make Labour more distinctive. In practice this strategy involved an informal, but strictly enforced, electoral agreement with the Liberals up to 1914, co-oper-ation with the Liberal government on the bulk of its programme in parlia-ment, strong representation in parliament of the interests of the unions and a campaign to increase the number of unions affiliated to the party. This strategy safeguarded those seats already held by Labour, ensured against a Unionist government, identified the party as the defenders of the organised working class and bolstered the foundations of the party's support.[48]

The strategy was also consistent with MacDonald's conception of socialism and the methods by which it would be achieved. Recent reassessments of MacDonald's political thought reveal him as a more serious and innovative socialist thinker than had previously been suggested and, with respect to his ideas on domestic affairs, it is no longer possible simply to categorise him as a liberal.[49] His contribution to debates on the development of modern capitalism and the role of the state show him to have moved well beyond the *laissez-faire* dogmas that continued to influence some centrist Liberals.[50] Nevertheless, in showing interest in these and other ideas, MacDonald's thought did not separate him entirely from the Liberal party. Many of the ideas and policies with which he was associated were consistent with advanced liberal thinking, particularly as represented by early Edwardian liberal thinkers such as J. A. Hobson, L. T. Hobhouse and J. L. Hammond.[51] They had been instrumental in laying the foundations for a new liberalism which focused on the social consequences of traditional economic *laissez-faire*. In common with the Fabians they looked to the state to sponsor social

[48] See Marquand, *Ramsay MacDonald*, 137–63; R. McKibbin, 'James Ramsay MacDonald and the problem of the independence of the Labour party, 1910–1914', *JMH* xlii (1970), 216–35; and Tanner, *Political change*, 19–44, 317–50.

[49] See P. Thane, 'Labour and local politics: radicalism, democracy and social reform, 1880–1914', in Biagini and Reid, *Currents of radicalism*, 244–70, and Tanner, 'Ideological debate in Edwardian Labour politics', and 'The development of British socialism'.

[50] See J. R. MacDonald, *The zollverein and British industry*, London 1903; Tanner, 'The development of British socialism', 55–7; and F. Trentmann, 'Wealth versus welfare: the British left between free trade and national political economy before the First World War', *Historical Research* lxx (1997), 70–98.

[51] See Thane, 'Labour and local politics', 261–70, and Clarke, *Liberals and social demo-crats*.

reform in the collective interest. They regarded socialism as the inevitable out-growth of liberalism.[52] MacDonald shared this belief. He had strong links with reform-minded Liberals, which he maintained throughout the period.[53] He was thus sympathetic to the social legislation introduced by the Liberal government in the early part of the century. His ultimate aim was for Labour to become the organisational expression of the movement for social reform. In the short run, however, efforts to present Labour as the only party committed totally to social reform were constrained by its continuing electoral weakness.[54]

Henderson had been closer to the Liberal party than MacDonald and was strongly influenced by Gladstonian liberalism. However, he was always firmly on the left of the Liberal party.[55] After joining Labour, his commitment to the party's independence and its gradual development into a competitor for power grew steadily the more he became involved in its administration.[56] He came to share most of MacDonald's ideological and strategic assumptions. His strong links with the unions made him well aware that gaining the full trust and support of organised labour would be a slow process. Nevertheless, he regarded this as the essential prerequisite for the eventual electoral independence of the party.

For those sections of the party, such as the ILP and British Socialist party (BSP), which were committed firmly to a socialist transformation of society, the cautious strategy pursued by MacDonald and Henderson was deeply frustrating.[57] In terms of actual policy, this discontent was not expressed in an alternative programme of action. The nature of the ideological debate taking place within the ILP was richer than has sometimes been suggested, but it had yet to result in a coherent body of policies.[58] However, many within the ILP had determined that Labour could not be socialist unless it was truly independent.

---

[52] There were, however, important differences between the 'new' Liberals and the Fabians: Clarke, *Liberals and social democrats*, 28–61.

[53] See, for example, *Minutes of the Rainbow Circle, 1894–1914*, ed. M. Freeden, London 1989.

[54] On the relationship between MacDonald's political ideas and his political strategy see *Ramsay MacDonald's political writings*, ed. B. Barker, London 1972, and R. Barker, 'Socialism and progressivism in the political thought of Ramsay MacDonald', in Morris, *Edwardian radicalism*, 114–30.

[55] See Wrigley, *Arthur Henderson*, 12–13, 17.

[56] Ibid. 21–39.

[57] See McKibbin, 'James Ramsay MacDonald'; A. F. Brockway, *Inside the left: thirty years of platform, press, prison and parliament*, London 1942; and Marquand, *Ramsay MacDonald*, 150–63. The Fabians, while often showing impatience at the reticence of union leaders to move beyond the most narrow definition of their role, accepted that the permeation of socialist ideas would be a gradual process: McBriar, *Fabian socialism*.

[58] For recent reassessments of the ILP's thinking see Tanner, 'Ideological debate', and 'The development of British socialism', and Trentmann, 'Wealth versus welfare'.

Despite the vociferous nature of the ILP's challenge to its strategy, the Labour leadership successfully resisted demands to adopt a more adventurous approach. The dominant force in the party remained the unions and they were generally content with the leadership's cautious measures and suspicious of the ILP.[59] Indeed, up to 1914, MacDonald and Henderson were able to keep the dissonance within the party to manageable proportions. It was only when the party found itself having to respond to a world crisis that the leadership found it impossible to mask and overcome the fundamental divisions that had existed within the movement since its formation.

Labour's 'principled opportunism' on foreign policy

Labour's pre-war approach to foreign policy was strongly affected by the party's structure and the political strategy pursued by its leaders. Foreign affairs was a good example of a policy area in which most trade unionists took only a passing interest, with debates at Labour's annual conference normally short and uncontroversial.[60] The party's approach was largely determined by the leadership on the basis of their own ideological predilections and the political strategy that they had adopted.[61]

Yet, while this general conclusion accords with the traditional view of Labour's foreign policy up to the First World War, if the party's response to the war in 1914, and the development of the party's policy thereafter, is to be properly interpreted a fuller understanding of three issues is important: first, the relationship between Labour's approach to foreign affairs and its political strategy; second, the level of support for the party leadership's policy within the broader Labour movement; and third, the nature of Labour's ideological approach and its relationship with socialist ideas on international affairs.

With regard to the first of these areas, Labour's independence was constrained by the electoral necessity of its pact with the Liberals. However, within the constraints, the Labour leadership was determined that the party should maximise its influence and, where possible, establish distinctive policies, which set it apart from mainstream Liberalism. Foreign policy was an area in which Labour was able to do this. The government's pursuit of a largely traditional foreign policy meant that there was a natural majority for Grey in the House of Commons. This lessened the political imperative

---

[59] Howard is wrong to say that Labour had decided on a strategy of independence during 1914: Tanner, *Political change*, 317–48.

[60] See, for example, *Report of the annual conference of the Labour party*, London 1912, 98. During the debate on foreign affairs, Hardie complained about the short time allowed for the issue.

[61] According to Newton 'The TUC Parliamentary Committee … remained silent at all the great moments of international tension in the period 1899 to 1914': *British Labour*, 70–1.

on the Labour leadership to support it on this issue. Given the chance to present an independent line, MacDonald and Henderson grasped the opportunity.[62]

However, Labour did not attempt to formulate an entirely new policy, based on a wholly distinctive analysis of the international system. Ideologically, there is little doubt that the party's approach to foreign affairs in the pre-war period owed a lot to liberalism.[63] What Labour attempted to do was present itself as the most effective advocate of liberal ideas.[64] This approach was consistent with the ideological background of the Labour leadership. MacDonald's personal attitude to foreign affairs, in the pre-war period, was fundamentally that of a liberal. In this regard, his thinking on international affairs was less advanced than his thinking on domestic policy.[65] He had opposed the Boer War on grounds of morality, and had split from the Fabians in the process.[66] On occasions during the next decade MacDonald explicitly stated that it was the principles of a 'Liberal foreign policy' that he was seeking to defend.[67] Thus, he rarely mentioned capitalism in his comments on foreign affairs and never used any analysis of its international structure to help formulate his ideas. Free trade and *laissez-faire*, while increasingly regarded as a problem at home, were unassailable in international affairs. He thus ignored the work of advanced liberal and socialist thinkers who regarded the dynamics for war as resting inherently within the capitalist system. The views he expressed on the empire, for example, were barely distinguishable from those of the radicals.[68]

Henderson's pre-war comments on foreign affairs reflected similar concerns.[69] His Liberal origins imbued him with a strong interest in international matters, which led him, in his early political career, actively to campaign for free trade and against British links with the Russian regime.[70] However, in one significant respect Henderson's approach to international affairs was different from that of MacDonald. Unlike the Labour leader, he was closely associated, through his membership of the International Arbitration and Peace Association, with Gladstonian liberal calls for a more

---

[62] Marquand has described this approach as a policy of 'principled opportunism': *Ramsay MacDonald*, 93

[63] The resolution on disarmament and international affairs at the party's conference in 1911, for example, protested against increased armaments and called on all disputes to be solved by 'reason and arbitration': *Report* (1911), 111–20.

[64] See, for example, ibid; Morris, *Radicalism*, 206; and Wrigley, *Arthur Henderson*, 73.

[65] See Trentmann, 'Wealth versus welfare', 91–2.

[66] See Howe, *Anticolonialism*, 35–6. For the debate between MacDonald and the Fabians on the Boer War see James Ramsay MacDonald papers, TNA, PRO 30/69/1143, 1144.

[67] See, for example, HC, Debates, xxvii.78 (27 Nov. 1911).

[68] See J. R. MacDonald, *Labour and the empire*, London 1907.

[69] See, for example, *The Times*, 20 Mar. 1909, 11 Jan. 1912; HC, Debates, clxxxix.1118 (27 May 1908); ii.1133–8 (7 Mar. 1909).

[70] See Wrigley, *Arthur Henderson*, 32, 36, 72.

systematic form of international conciliation and mediation.[71] In the pre-war period, this difference did not appear to be particularly significant. It was to become increasingly important after 1914, when the split between liberalism and radicalism on foreign affairs became more pronounced.

Nevertheless, there was one aspect of Labour's approach to foreign affairs that did represent a new departure: its relationship with the international socialist movement. Since the late nineteenth century the Second International had included representatives of all the leading socialist parties in Europe. Considerable effort had to be expended in the years after Labour's formation to negotiate a special dispensation allowing the party to affiliate with the organisation, despite its ideological idiosyncrasies.[72] MacDonald and Henderson played a full part in these negotiations and remained committed to the International throughout the pre-war period.

Even so, this attachment had more to do with differences in the practice rather than the ideological foundations of Labour's internationalism compared with liberalism.[73] MacDonald certainly had a strong ideological commitment to working- class internationalism. He was 'an instinctive internationalist' and had particularly close contacts with Eduard Bernstein and the revisionist wing of the *Sozialdemokratische Partei Deutschlands* (SPD).[74] He saw the international socialist movement as an increasingly important force for peace which, once the working class was fully enfranchised in all states, would make it extremely difficult for governments to commit their people to war.[75] However, this argument owed more to Cobden than to Marx: it was a re-working of the idea that if diplomacy acted in the general interest – in this case democracy – a more peaceful world would result. Thus, MacDonald sought to incorporate working-class internationalism within a radical-inspired approach to foreign affairs. It was on this basis that he criticised Grey's policy towards Germany. By treating her as a monolithic militarist state, the Labour leader argued, the Foreign Secretary made no attempt to encourage the growing ranks of the SPD in Germany, who opposed their government's policy.[76]

71 See ibid. 74; *Concord* (June/July 1907); *The Times*, 20 Mar. 1909.
72 For details see Newton, *British Labour*, 48–9, 196–202. See also E. McNeilly, 'Labour and Internationalism, 1906–14', *Twentieth Century British History* xx (2009), forthcoming.
73 There were also political reasons for this attachment. Labour's active support for working-class internationalism was important for the maintenance of the labour alliance given the ILP's commitment to this concept. See also C. Wrigley, 'Widening horizons? British Labour and the Second International, 1893–1905', *Labour History Review* lviii (1993), 8–13.
74 As Fletcher shows, however, even Bernstein's approach to foreign affairs was strongly influenced by British radicalism: 'British radicalism and German revisionism: the case of Eduard Bernstein', *IHR* iv (1982), 339–70. For MacDonald's contacts with Bernstein see MacDonald papers, PRO 30/69/1152, 1153, 1155.
75 See, for example, HC, Debates, xxvii.1830–1 (27 July 1911).
76 See Marquand, *Ramsay MacDonald*, 165.

Thus, both because it was consistent with their ideological assumptions and their political strategy, the Labour party leadership firmly aligned the party with liberal internationalism. Was this an approach, however, that had much support within the wider Labour movement?

The Labour movement and international affairs before 1914

Traditionally it has been argued that the bulk of the pre-war Labour movement were not interested in international affairs. It has also been suggested that among trade unionists and Labour's broader working-class constituency nationalistic and patriotic opinions were common, if not predominant, by the early part of the twentieth century.[77] It is certainly the case that there was a strong current of nationalist patriotism in the pre-war Labour movement.[78]

However, there are good grounds for treating the claims that these views were predominant with caution. While most trade unionists may not have been fervently internationalist, or even have had a strong interest in international affairs, the evidence suggests that a significant minority nevertheless held moderate internationalist opinions similar to those expressed in Labour's pre-war policy. Connections between popular politics and internationalism, both working-class and liberal, were after all of long standing. Throughout the nineteenth century, working-class organisations, including trade unions, had taken an active interest in international events, particularly as they were perceived to affect the conditions of the working classes abroad. The Workmen's Peace Association, for example, was the 'largest political organization supported by working men in the 1870s'.[79] While there is little doubt that in the later part of the century working-class internationalism began to ebb, this decline should not be exaggerated. As H. Cunningham suggests, while patriotism became a cross-class phenomenon after 1870 'it was by no means unopposed by either the lower middle class or the working class'.[80]

---

[77] See Newton, *British Labour*, 73–80, 118–23. Vickers has recently indicated that the international affiliations of the trade unions might suggest that there are problems with this general view but she does not fully develop this point: *Labour party and the world*, 34, 44–5.

[78] See Newton, *British Labour*. As Ward shows, patriotism can take a number of forms: *Red flag*, 3–7. The type being referred to here, and the sense in which the term is used throughout this book, was characterised by xenophobia and jingoism. See also n. 80 below.

[79] H. Cunningham, 'The language of patriotism, 1750–1914', *History Workshop Journal* xii (1981), 8–33.

[80] Ibid. 25. Moreover, as Ward has suggested, even some of those who embraced patriotism adopted a 'radical patriotic stance'. This was tolerant of other nations' patriotism but emphasised the particular perceived strengths of the British people, particularly their liberalism: *Red flag*, 7.

Working-class organisations responded to the Boer War, for example, with little enthusiasm and some opposition.[81]

One reason for the continued rejection of natonalistic patriotism among some working-class organisations and individuals was the connections they developed or maintained with Liberal politics and causes. As Anthony Howe has shown, for example, free trade had been 'adopted as a working-class cause' by the late 1800s, despite the undoubted tensions that had existed between free trade campaigners and the Chartists in the middle part of the century.[82] Free trade pressure groups (for example the Cobden Club) could rely on significant support from mainstream working-class organisations such as the growing trade union movement in the period up to the tariff reform controversy of 1903.[83] This connection was reinforced by the shared interest of many working-class leaders and midde-class radicals in religious non-conformism and temperance. It was through these connections that many leading trade unionists became involved in politics, gaining their political education in the Gladstonian Liberal party.[84] As John Shepherd has shown, the practice of Lib-Lab politics in the late 1800s, through which the first trade unionists entered parliament 'was the formal expression ... amongst working men and their leaders ... of a genuine attachment to Gladstonian Liberalism'.[85]

On the basis of these long-standing connections between working-class politics, radical free trade and Gladstonian liberalism, a number of Lib-Lab trade unionists became imbued with moderate internationalist attitudes.[86] Of these, the most obvious example is Arthur Henderson. However, Tom Shaw (Textile Trades Federation), J. R. Clynes (National Union of General Workers) and G. H. Wardle (Railwaymen's Union) were also active in support of a moderate internationalist stance during this period.[87] Moreover,

---

[81] Cunningham, 'Language of patriotism', 27. See also Ward, *Red flag*, 59.

[82] Howe, 'Towards the "hungry forties"', 194. See also Wrigley, *Arthur Henderson*, 32, 36–7.

[83] Howe, 'Towards the "hungry forties"', 215–16.

[84] See Martin, 'Ideology and composition', 17–37, and J. Shepherd, 'Labour and parliament: the Lib-Labs as the first working-class MPs, 1885–1906', in Biagini and Reid, *Currents of radicalism*, 187–213.

[85] Shepherd, 'Labour and parliament', 198.

[86] As Alastair Reid has shown it is possible to exaggerate the conservatism and caution of leading trade unionists during this period: 'Old unionism reconsidered: the radicalism of Robert Knight, 1870–1900', in Biagini and Reid, *Currents of radicalism*, 214–43.

[87] See *The Times*, 8 June 1909, and 25 May 1910. Clynes, also unusually a member of the ILP, spoke regularly on foreign affairs in the pre-war period. See, for example, HC, Debates clxxxv.430–4 (2 Mar. 1908), and *The Times*, 1 Feb. 1911 and 29 Jan. 1914. After the war, Shaw was to become a leading spokesperson for a moderate internationalist policy (see chapter 5 below), an interest that appears to have been developing in the pre-war period: *The Times*, 27 Jan. 1910. George Wardle's views became more patriotic after 1914. For further evidence of support for a moderate internationalist stance within the broader labour movement see *Report* (1911), 111–20; *Report* (1912), 10–11; *Concord* (Aug./Sept. 1908); and Collette, *International faith.*, 12–14.

'a number of Labour members' were involved with the International Arbitration League, the aims of which were endorsed by PCTUC in 1905 and 1906.[88]

The second reason for questioning the traditional view of the trade unions' approach to foreign affairs in the pre-war period concerns the extent to which the practice of working-class internationalism, through the various international labour, socialist and trade union organisations, was a normal and accepted activity within the Labour party at this time. Some commentators have questioned the importance of Labour's pre-war internationalism and doubted the extent to which it amounted to 'the coming of a real internationalist consciousness'.[89] However, while there is no doubt that for some trade unionists international activities were a tolerated, rather than a welcomed, part of their duties, this was not the case for everyone. The sheer scale of party members' involvement in these activities would suggest otherwise. The Labour movement's record in terms of affiliation was, as even the more sceptical voices accept, 'quite respectable', and international trade unionism 'progressed handsomely' in the last years of the 1800s.[90] By 1914 there were fifteen labour organisations that were affiliated to international working-class organisations, including the Miners Federation of Great Britain, the Transport Workers Federation, the National Union of Railwaymen and the Iron and Steel Trades Confederation.[91] Of these, no organisation could compare in terms of effectiveness, the PCTUC was later to suggest, with the International Metalworkers Federation.[92] This was formed in 1891 on the basis of the involvement of representatives from France, Switzerland, Germany, Austria/Hungry, America and Belgium, in addition to the British. By 1913 it represented more that a million trade unionists from thirteen nationalities. Like the other international trade union organisations, it was 'distinctly industrial': it exchanged information, collected statistics, offered support to national bodies involved in industrial disputes. It did not generally engage with matters of international affairs.[93] However, while there is no doubt that these international relationships developed largely for instrumental reasons, they nevertheless helped to engender a developing internationalist consciousness among a significant minority of trade unionists. The existence pre-1914 of this spirit was commented upon regretfully by the editor of *Railway Review* on the outbreak of the war:

---

[88] See *The Times*, 20 Mar. 1909; Newton, *British Labour*, 81–2; and *Concord* (Sept./Oct. 1906).

[89] Newton, *British Labour*, 89

[90] Ibid. 87–8.

[91] BSIMF, advisory committee minutes, 9 July 1918, MRC, MS 036/IMF/7/1. See also International Union of Woodworkers, ibid. MS 78/ASC&J/3/1/17

[92] BSIMF, advisory committee minutes, 9 July 1918, MRC, MS 036/IMF/7/1MS036/IMF/7/1.

[93] Ibid. 6 Sept. 1918.

During recent years there has been a very real rapprochement between the trade union movement of the various continental countries and other in which the great German trade union movement had taken the lead. There was a genuine international trade union movement ... brotherhoods and municipalities have all been exchanging visits and workers representative have been fraternising in various ways.[94]

Moreover, in this regard, the problem many trade unionists had with the international socialist movement was not its internationalism, but its domination by Marxists. As Chris Wrigley suggests, in an assessment of Labour's pre-war connections with the Second International, for example, 'Peace was an issue which could unite Lib-Lab working men, admirers of William Gladstone and John Morley, with the socialists, even if they differed on what action was desirable.'[95] At the very least, then, these international connections challenged the influence of 'knee-jerk' nationalism among trade unionists; for some they inculcated a genuine concern for the views and perspectives of other nations, particularly those emanating from the working-class organisations of these nations. This was to become evident, for example, in the wartime actions of the British Section of the International Metalworkers Federation (BSIMF).[96]

In raising these queries about the traditional view of trade unionists' attitudes towards international affairs in the pre-war period, this is not to deny that many were uninterested and that some held strongly patriotic views. However, this was not true of everyone. For a significant minority the connections that they maintained with the various international working-class and labour organisations were the practical expression of, and reinforced, the liberal-inspired internationalism with which they had come into contact in the Gladstonian Liberal party. The existence of such attitudes among some trade unionists in the pre-war period helps to explain the Labour party's attitude towards the war in 1914 and the development of its ideas on foreign policy thereafter.

The emergence of a socialist challenge

While the Labour party leadership was content merely to present the party's foreign policy as a more fervently oppositional, effective and working-class-inspired variant of liberalism, others on the left adopted a more distinctly socialist perspective. In a significant move away from the analytical constraints of liberalism, they were prepared to consider the risks of war inherent within

---

[94] *Railway Review*, 21 Aug. 1914, ibid. MS 127/NU/4/1/2.
[95] See Wrigley, 'Widening horizons?', 9.
[96] See chapter 5 below

the capitalist system. In the pre-war Labour party this alternative approach remained embryonic and undeveloped, but it was to play an important part in debates after 1914 about the development of the party's foreign policy.

Among Marxists, democratic socialists and even some left-wing radicals there was considerable scepticism about many liberal assumptions. They questioned whether a pacific international system based on free trade was the most likely development of capitalism. There may be a general interest in a freely competitive world system, but large and significant sections of the capitalist economy had vested interests in avoiding competition and securing exclusive world markets. This criticism of capitalism as a major cause of war was not new in the British socialist tradition.[97] However, from the mid-1890s onwards, Marxist-inspired analyses of the international political economy of capitalism became increasingly influential. The Marxist philosopher, and some-time editor of the Social Democratic Federation's *Justice*, Balfort Bax, had been airing such views since 1896. Imperialism, he explained in that year, was the latest stage of capitalism desperate to maintain profits by seeking new markets. Without this expansion, capitalism would collapse.[98]

With the outbreak of the Boer War, the links between capitalism, imperialism and war became an issue for debate within mainstream political circles. Keir Hardie, for example, wrote in the *Labour Leader* in January 1900, that the war was 'a Capitalist war, begotten by Capitalists' money'.[99] This view was subsequently given greater intellectual credibility by the most influential study on the British left during this period of capitalism, imperialism and war, J. A. Hobson's *Imperialism* (1902).

Hobson based his book on the first-hand experience of the Boer War that he had gained by covering the conflict as a journalist. As a materialist and economist, he was not prepared to accept that the war was caused merely by immorality. Instead he explained the war and imperialism as a whole in terms of his controversial 'underconsumptionist' theory of the British economy. British imperialism resulted from the maldistribution of wealth in the domestic economy: wealth was concentrated in the hands of a small minority of the population, thus home demand was inhibited. In order gainfully to employ this excess wealth investors were forced to export capital and Hobson concluded that this 'growing pressure for foreign investments must be regarded as the most potent and direct influence in our foreign policy'.[100] When this small, but powerful, band of financiers felt their interests to be at risk they enlisted the support of the state in their defence.

[97]   See Miller, *Socialism and foreign policy*, 15–24.
[98]   See B. Porter, *Critics of empire*, London 1968, 99, 103.
[99]   Ibid. 128. As Trentmann suggests, however, on other occasions Hardie's views seemed much closer to those of the Radicals: 'Wealth versus welfare', 92.
[100]   Quoted in Clarke, *Liberals and social democrats*, 91.

Despite this conclusion, as some historians have noted, Hobson remained to some extent wedded to Cobdenite ideas.[101] Unlike some Marxist theorists of imperialism, he did not believe that either imperialism or war were inevitable under capitalism.[102] Cobden had merely failed to take into account 'two counteracting influences' which could subvert the pacific tendencies of free trade: the maldistribution of wealth and the control of foreign policy by special interests. These influences could be countered by traditional radical means: social and governmental reforms in the domestic sphere, particularly the democratic control of foreign policy.[103]

Some on the ILP left went further. They were more prepared than Hobson to use his analysis, mixed with a more overtly Marxist view of the state, to take a firm step away from the Cobdenite thesis.[104] The journalist and ILP member, Henry Noel Brailsford, was the most noteworthy in this regard. He argued in 1913 that the function of the state was being systematically perverted in the interests of adventuring and emigrating capital: 'The hunting of concessions abroad and the exploitation of the potential riches of the weak states and dying empires [was] fast becoming an official enterprise, a national business.' Britain, he said, was engaged in 'Imperial trading, with the flag as its dispensable asset but the profits go exclusively into private pockets.'[105] Like Hobson, however, Brailsford looked mainly to domestic reform for the solution. Socialists must 'win at home the power to control [the] export of capital [and] ... use it as a potent servant of a humane diplomacy'.[106] If this failed international control of 'exported capital' might be necessary.[107] These ideas were to be further developed by Brailsford after the outbreak of war.

On the basis of these arguments, Brailsford and other leading figures on the ILP left refuted directly and unambiguously the Cobdenite thesis.

---

[101] Ibid. See also P. J. Cain, 'Variations on a famous theme: Hobson, international trade and imperialism, 1902–38', and B. Porter, 'Hobson and internationalism', in Freeden, *Reappraising J. A. Hobson*, 167–81.

[102] See D. H. Kruger, 'Hobson, Lenin and Schumpter on imperialism', *JHI* xvi (1955), 252–9. There is some debate among historians about whether Hobson believed that imperialism could be explained entirely in terms of structural maladjustments of the British economy or whether it was primarily the result of a financial conspiracy. For a summary of this debate see Freeden, *Reappraising J. A. Hobson*. A good summary and defence of Marxist theories can be found in E. Stokes, 'Late nineteenth century colonial expansion and the attack on the theory of economic imperialism: a case of mistaken identity', *HJ* xxii (1969), 285–301.

[103] Clarke, *Liberals and social democrats*, 91.

[104] Those historians, such as Cain, who argue that Hobson envisaged 'fundamental economic, social and political reform' to prevent imperialism would draw less of a distinction between his views and those of the ILP left: 'Hobson's developing theory of imperialism', *Economic History Review* xxxiv (1981), 315.

[105] Brailsford, *War of steel and gold*, 61.

[106] Ibid. 263.

[107] Ibid. 171.

Bruce Glasier, for example, argued that to dismiss territorial conquest as against the national interest, as Angell and his admirers tended to do, was to miss the point. He wrote in September 1912 that 'The interests in which wars are waged are never national. They are sectional – the interests of a piratical class of financiers.'[108] There was little point, suggested Brailsford, in campaigning for a reduction in armaments while the reasons for their exist- ence remained.[109]

The conclusions that some European Marxists reached on the basis of these types of argument were that conflict between states was inevitable under capitalism and that the working class had no interest in whether their country won or lost a war. The latter view had some support in the ILP but, while anti-capitalism was the dominant ethos of the party, few accepted that it would lead inevitably to war.[110] Despite the influence of Marxist theorists, most in the party had not yet given up on the potential power of democracy.[111] If socialism could be brought about by democratic and peaceful means, as most in the ILP believed, war could be prevented using similar methods. Thus, while the establishment of socialism was the only way of making war impossible, there were other methods by which it could be prevented in the meantime. It was on this basis that the ILP, in its statements on foreign affairs, declared its support for many of the liberal- inspired proposals to decrease international tensions made by the Labour leadership.[112] In addition, the party launched regular campaigns of its own against conscription and militarism.

However, there was one tactic supported by the ILP which was rejected by Labour: an international general strike against war should such a conflict break out.[113] For much of its existence, the International had debated the efficacy of such a ploy if their governments seemed determined on war. In Britain, Hardie and Glasier were its leading proponents. Unlike most issues of foreign affairs, however, the proposal impinged directly on the interests of the unions: not only would they be asked to organise the strike, but by doing so they would appear to be adopting an overtly and potentially subversive position. This was considerably further than most in the Labour party were prepared to go. Henderson, in particular played a leading part in resisting the party's commitment to the idea.[114] He successfully argued that it was a

---

[108] See Robbins, *Abolition* , 65.

[109] Brailsford, *War of steel and gold*, 313.

[110] Some, indeed, remained wedded to the Radicals' position that war would not happen in Europe because it was economically irrational. See, for example, J. T. Walton-Newbold, *The war trust exposed*, Manchester 1913, and W. C. Anderson's editorial in the *Labour Leader*, 30 July 1914. Most also believed in national defence: Ward, *Red flag*, 103.

[111] See *Labour Leader*, 9 Apr. 1914.

[112] See, for example, ibid. 9 Jan., 7 June 1912, and 8 Jan. 1914.

[113] For the campaign on an international general strike see Newton, *British Labour*, 251–93. See also G. Haupt, *Socialism and the Great War*, Oxford 1972, 161–80.

[114] See Wrigley, *Arthur Henderson*, 75.

distraction from parliamentary action. While he would support international working-class demonstrations against war he would not support concerted industrial action.[115]

The general strike against war, then, like the rest of the ILP socialists' analysis of the international situation was rejected by the pre-war Labour party. It was only when the war, and the political changes it wrought, encouraged Labour to think more seriously about foreign affairs, that the policies advocated by Brailsford received greater attention, along with other ideas developed during the war and based on more orthodox liberal foundations.

Thus, on the eve of the First World War, Labour's approach to foreign affairs was opportunistic, ill-thought-out and commanded the committed support of only a minority in the party. These characteristics were of little significance while peace was maintained. However, with the coming of war, Labour was forced to construct an intellectually coherent international policy that commanded the support, and not just the acquiescence, of the majority in the party.

[115] Ibid. MacDonald was more positive about the idea but did nothing to promote it as party policy: *Socialist Review* (Sept. 1910, Nov. 1911); *Labour Leader*, 15 Aug. 1912.

3

Labour and the Outbreak of War,
August–October 1914

There had been intermittent crises in international relations since 1900, the most serious of which had been the 1912 Agadir dispute, but none had led to war. Many commentators believed that a major conflict between the European powers was unlikely ever to occur. It was in this context that the increased tension that followed the assassination of the Austrian Archduke Franz Ferdinand, by Serb and Croat nationalist rebels at the end of June 1914, was initially viewed. Few thought that the event would lead in less than a month to a general European war, let alone a conflict which would last for four years and transform the social, economic, political and international landscape in its wake. In its early days, the crisis was thus treated with relative complacency. It was only from the weekend of 1 August 1914 that the seriousness of the situation, and Britain's likely involvement, came to be realised. It took much longer for many politicians and commentators to accept that the conflict could drag on for years, rather than months. It was in an atmosphere of shock, horror and apprehension, as the full implications of the European situation slowly became apparent, that political and policy decisions were made. Politicians were forced to respond to events that they only partially understood, and which were, for the first three months of the war, extremely volatile. They tended to be led by events rather than taking the lead themselves, and their views on the situation shifted as more information became available or circumstances changed. No politicians, and particularly not the Labour leaders, were masters of the situation.

On the face of it Labour's reaction to the worsening international situation should have been relatively straightforward. Labour had espoused during the pre-war period a foreign policy based on strong anti-militarist and internationalist principles. Leading party members had openly and frequently declared their unity with the working class of foreign nations and accused the British government of being inspired by militarism and jingoism. The party leadership, while sometimes speaking in more moderate language, did little to distance itself from this approach. Indeed, with respect to foreign affairs, MacDonald had sanctioned a largely independent line, under which Labour emphasised the advanced nature of its policy in comparison to the more cautious and traditional approach of the Liberals. On this basis the July/August crisis seemed initially like another opportunity for Labour to put itself at the head of the opposition to the Liberals' diplomatic policy.

Thus, at a meeting on 31 July of the British representatives of the Inter-national, which was attended by Henderson, Glasier, Henry Hyndman and MacDonald, and chaired by Hardie, it was agreed that Labour's opposition to any British involvement in a European war should be made explicit.[1] A resolution was passed blaming 'secret alliances and understandings' for the crisis. Any alliance by Britain with Russia in the war, it was argued, would be 'offensive to the traditions of this country and dangerous to Europe'. Labour would demonstrate against war. A Trafalgar Square rally, organised for the following Sunday by George Lansbury's Herald League, would be supported and local branches of the ILP and the Labour party were encouraged to show their opposition to Britain's involvement in the war.[2]

Within three months, however, Labour's position had fundamentally altered. The party had unequivocally accepted the conflict, supporting largely uncritically the government's reasons for entering it, it had agreed to allow its organisational apparatus to be used in the recruiting campaign, and it had accepted a political truce with its opponents. MacDonald had resigned from the leadership of the party and the labour alliance seemed at risk due to the ILP's strong criticism of Labour's stance. During the next three years, despite the slaughter on the Western Front, the introduction of conscription and the formation of a Conservative-dominated coalition government at the end of 1916, Labour displayed little willingness to question the decision made in 1914.

This dramatic change of direction has been explained in a variety of ways. The traditional, largely labourist, interpretation emphasises the extent to which the party's pre-war policy was at variance with the views of Labour's rank-and-file. When war came the party leadership sought to maintain its pre-war stance but was 'easily overwhelmed' by a 'deep vein of old-fashioned patriotism' that was entrenched within the party.[3] MacDonald, whom some commentators have regarded as maintaining a position of outright opposi-tion to the conflict, was brushed aside, while Henderson bowed to the new consensus, despite his own reservations.[4]

Christopher Howard takes this labourist perspective to its extreme and in the process downplays the importance of ideology on the decisions made by Labour politicians at this time. He suggests that self-interested motivations 'rather than a concern for the fate of the nation determined the decisions taken by MacDonald and Henderson, the parliamentary Labour party, and

---

[1] See Newton, *British Labour*, 325–8.
[2] For details and reports of the anti-war demonstrations see *Labour Leader*, 6 Aug. 1914.
[3] Marquand, *Ramsay MacDonald*, 169. See also Foote, *The Labour party's political thought*, 13.
[4] See, for example, Keohane, 'Labour's international policy', 365–6.

the wider labour movement in the first months of the war'.[5] MacDonald saw the war as an opportunity to construct 'a new party', which combined the Labour party with the left of the Liberal party in opposition to the war. The trade unions, in contrast, insisted on a policy of support for the conflict, mainly because they were concerned that without government support they would be bankrupted by the unemployment that was expected to accompany the conflict.[6] Henderson, who was first and foremost a trade unionist, backed this line, hence his split from MacDonald.

In contrast John Horne insists that an important ideological principle underpinned Labour's support for the conflict. The party's stance was Gladstonian in that it was based on a belief that the war represented 'a conflict between opposed political systems' in which the democratic values of Britain and France were being challenged by an authoritarian Germany.[7] If there was an element of self-interest in this support it was, he suggests, the 'quite explicit ... connection', made in Labour's October 1914 manifesto on the war, 'between the self-preservation of democracy and the nation, and the conditions for the continued growth of the labour and socialist movements'.[8]

In fact, however, Labour's response to the war was far less straightforward than existing accounts suggest. This was because the pre-war Labour party was a complex body with respect to foreign affairs: the ideological influences on the party's foreign policy were more diverse than is often supposed, and the wider labour movement was not one-dimensional in its attitude to foreign affairs. Thus, there were some members of the Labour party who wanted to support the war for reasons of simple patriotism. There were others who could justify such a policy ideologically. Some in the party, particularly in the trade unions, were more interested in the domestic implications of the crisis. Others, particularly in the ILP, argued strongly for a policy of total opposition. As a result of this diversity, the party was initially thrown into a state of utter confusion, a situation from which it did not really emerge for three months.

What occurred during this period was an attempt by the Labour leadership to construct a compromise, 'centrist' policy on the war, sufficiently supportive of the conflict to secure the support of the party's newly assertive patriotic wing, while retaining a sufficiently critical distance to reassure internationalists.[9] This attempt was unsuccessful. Events in France strengthened the patriots' case and ended any chance that the bulk of the party

---

[5] C. Howard, 'MacDonald, Henderson and the outbreak of war, 1914', *HJ* xx (1977), 871.
[6] The unions were concerned that their unemployment funds would be run dry by wartime unemployment: ibid. 876–7.
[7] Horne does not describe this view as 'Gladstonian' but it was consistent with this type of approach: see chapter 4 below.
[8] Horne, *Labour at war*, 45–6.
[9] The term 'centrist' was used in 1918 to describe an approach similar to that which Henderson and MacDonald tried to construct in 1914: *Labour Leader*, 12 Sept. 1918.

would accept any policy overtly critical of the government. Moreover, for some in the labour movement this policy was, in any case, made attractive by concerns about the effect of the war on the material interests of the trade unions and the preservation of a Liberal government, which was trusted to uphold the interests of labour. Thus, while, at the instigation of moderate internationalists in the Labour party a Gladstonian gloss was put on some of Labour's statements in support of the conflict, no attempt was made to place limits on the party's backing of the government. By the spring of 1915 Labour had set aside any pretence of independence and was a fully signed-up supporter of a 'fight-to-the-finish' policy.

The Labour party and the coming of war

Labour's initial reaction to the 1914 European crisis at the end of July had been framed while there was still a chance that a general war might be avoided. As the weekend of 1 August progressed, however, it became increasingly apparent that the circumstances were different from similar crises during the previous two decades. The situation was running out of control, with Germany likely to attack France by passing through neutral Belgium, and Britain almost certain to support France. The nature of the decisions that political leaders faced was transformed: from being an issue which required a tactical response, the crisis was gradually developing into one which could affect many of the assumptions upon which previous ideological and political decisions had been made.

For the Labour party this situation was complicated further by the fact that, for many in the party, the coming of war was the first time that they had contemplated, at any length, an issue of international affairs. Foreign affairs, from being an issue of peripheral interest for most within the movement, became the central political question, and it was unclear which way the bulk of the party would swing. Among those who had shown an interest in foreign affairs, the coming conflict accentuated the differences in their approach. For the patriotic wing, the issue was relatively simple. They were prepared to trust absolutely and uncritically the judgement of the political and military elite that Germany's action posed a threat to the British national interest, which had to be resisted. Labour should adopt a bipartisan approach and give its total support to the war effort. At the other end of the spectrum, socialist internationalists also had a relatively clear-cut view of the situation: the war was a capitalist war, the result of imperial rivalries, which was of no interest to – and should be resisted by – the international working class.[10]

---

[10] This view was reflected on the front page of the *Labour Leader* on the 6 Aug. 1914, the banner headline of which was 'Down with the War'. It was not a view that was endorsed by the national administrative committee of the ILP: Brockway, *Inside the left*, 47.

However the patriots and the international socialists were at the two extremes of Labour's approach to foreign affairs. In the middle was a significant group of moderate internationalists. For them, the coming of the war posed considerable problems. Indeed, the way in which the conflict developed in its initial stages seemed almost designed to expose the contradictions and ambiguities at the heart of the liberal internationalist approach. Germany's invasion of neutral Belgium raised the classic dilemma for liberals: when, if ever, was British military intervention overseas justifiable? Should Britain support an anti-militaristic government abroad in the face of aggression by an anti-democratic militaristic foe? Or would such intervention inevitably prove counter-productive, both in terms of escalating the conflict and because of the damage it would do to the international economy? Those located towards the Cobdenite end of the liberal internationalist spectrum tended to answer 'no' to the first two questions and 'yes' to the third. Gladstonians, on the other hand, tended to adopt the opposite attitude.

The issues raised by the war, however, were not just ideological; they were also political. In this regard there were three important likely consequences of the coming of war. First, Britain's involvement in a European conflict made the chances of a split in the Liberal party much greater. The most sustained opposition to the government from within its own party in the pre-war period had been on foreign policy. There seemed little doubt that many radicals would feel compelled openly to oppose any British involvement in a European war. If this opposition was substantial, it was conceivable that the existing party system could fracture. Secondly, the war seemed likely to have serious effects on the social and economic conditions of the British working classes. A massive increase in unemployment and a general reduction in the living standards of Labour's natural constituency was widely expected. The interests of the unions and their members were at stake; the latitude that they had allowed the party in its approach to foreign affairs was unlikely to be continued. Thirdly, the war ensured that Labour's internationalist convictions, from previously appearing to be harmless principles, could suddenly be used by opponents to question the patriotism of the party and its members. With the great wave of jingoistic nationalism that accompanied the coming of war, the whole labour movement had to decide whether it was prepared to resist the prevailing mood in order to defend the party's pre-war internationalist stance.

The coming of the war thus accentuated ideological divisions on foreign affairs within the Labour party and threatened to disrupt the political strategy pursued by it in the pre-war period. It was this complex situation that MacDonald and Henderson, as leaders of the party, had to manage and make sense of. They were suddenly forced, in a period of great uncertainty, to construct a foreign policy which could unite the whole party. The decisions that needed to be taken in this rapid re-evaluation of policy went to the heart of the continuing debates on the party's ideology and political strategy.

A policy of 'wait and see'

In attempting to construct a policy, the Labour leadership's attitude was far more flexible than is often supposed. With the future development of events so uncertain, it was difficult to establish a firm position on either ideological or political grounds, and for this reason MacDonald and Henderson sought to keep their options open.[11] In this regard it is particularly important to appreciate that the policy initially outlined by the party leadership was not one of unequivocal opposition to Britain's intervention in the war regardless of events. There were circumstances under which the party would support Britain's involvement. Labour would not, however, be rushed into supporting the conflict on the basis of a patriotic impulse or because the Liberal government told them that they ought to.

MacDonald's position on the war, in particular, has been widely misunderstood.[12] As David Marquand has shown he 'was not a pacifist. For him, the possibility of a British defeat could not be left out of the reckoning.'[13] However, given his consistent criticism of Grey's diplomacy in the pre-war years and his closeness to, and admiration for, the SPD, he could not unequivocally support a war which he believed, initially at least, to have been caused by major errors in British diplomacy. In fact, there is evidence that MacDonald could see justifications for British intervention beyond mere national defence even before the war had started. He conceded to Liberal Cabinet ministers on 2 August, for example, that Britain would be justified in declaring war on Germany if Belgium's neutrality were infringed.[14] In the *Manchester Guardian*, the previous day, he had been recorded as saying that 'If we are to fight surely we can arrange that our intervention will be for some righteous cause and for some worthy government.'[15] Thus, while MacDonald later argued that the government had used the Belgian invasion to maximise support for the conflict, he was undoubtedly sympathetic to Belgium's plight. He was stuck in the liberal dilemma of having profound sympathy for the victim of aggression, but balking at the costs of British intervention. As events stood on 3 August, MacDonald argued, in his reply to Grey's House of Commons speech announcing Britain's support for France, that Britain

[11] Marquand, *Ramsay MacDonald*, 167–79.
[12] The most reliable and least self-conscious statement by MacDonald of his views on the war, and the tactics that he believed socialists should adopt, can be found in Ramsay MacDonald to 'Lander', 2 Nov. 1914, MacDonald papers, PRO 30/69/1158.
[13] Marquand, *Ramsay MacDonald*, 174.
[14] Marquand dismisses this report as 'so contrary to the position MacDonald took up publicly, and to that expressed in his diary, that it seems highly unlikely that he ever expressed it'. However, there can be little doubt that MacDonald felt enormous sympathy for the plight of Belgium. He probably indicated this to Riddell. There seems little reason for Riddell deliberately to misrepresent MacDonald's views: Marquand, *Ramsay MacDonald*, 164 n. 2.
[15] See *Manchester Guardian*, 1 Aug. 1914.

should have remained neutral. However, he was very careful to indicate that events in Europe might change matters.[16] Britain, he intimated, should be prepared to intervene if the country was in danger and '[i]f France [was] really in danger, if as a result of [the war] ... the power, civilisation and genius of France [was] removed from European history'.[17] He was later to tell Henderson that he sympathised with the view that Britain should intervene on France's behalf 'in any quarrel into which she might be drawn in her own interest'.[18]

In fact, as the following weeks were to show, there was no more than a razor's edge between MacDonald and many Gladstonian liberals, like Gilbert Murray, who were convinced by Grey's speech that Britain had a moral duty to intervene in the conflict.[19] MacDonald did not call for outright opposition to the war on 3 August, he merely asked his party to reserve its final position and wait upon events.

MacDonald's decision not immediately to follow the lead of other Gladstonians was also influenced by political considerations. MacDonald believed that even if Labour was forced by circumstances to adopt a more positive view on the war, it was important for the political future of the party that its support was of a limited and critical nature. In proposing this stance, MacDonald was not, as Howard suggests, veering off dramatically from the strategy that had been agreed upon during the pre-war period. He was not looking to reconstruct the party system. He merely believed that Labour should not jump back into the arms of the Liberals on foreign affairs at the first sign of trouble. Initially this view was shared by Henderson.[20] It was only once it became clear that any equivocation about support for the government was unacceptable to many in the Labour movement that his view diverged from that of MacDonald. [21]

Opposition within the Labour party to MacDonald's line was evident to some even as the 3 August speech was delivered. Despite agreeing to the content of MacDonald's reply, the PLP was 'about equally divided'.[22] MacDonald and Henderson still believed, however, that they could hold the line that had been agreed. On 4 August Henderson called a conference of a wide cross-section of labour and socialist leaders, with the intention of forming a National Peace Emergency Committee. The main aims of this

[16] See HC, Debates, lxv.1800–31 (3 Aug. 1914).
[17] Ibid.
[18] MacDonald suggested that his main objection to the *entente* with France was that it committed Britain to support her in 'quarrels' that came about 'in consequence of her alliance with Russia': Marquand, *Ramsay MacDonald*, 171.
[19] See Clarke, *Liberals*, 166.
[20] Wrigley, *Arthur Henderson*, 70, 75–6.
[21] For alternative interpretations see Howard, 'MacDonald, Henderson and the outbreak of war', and Marquand, *Ramsay MacDonald*, 167–85.
[22] Quoted in Howard, 'MacDonald, Henderson and the outbreak of war', 880. See also MacDonald to Arthur Henderson, 21 Aug. 1914, MacDonald papers, PRO 30/69/1232.

new body, Henderson suggested in his introductory circular, were 'to urge the strictest neutrality possible' and 'to take all steps to secure a permanent peace'.[23] At the same time he called a special meeting of the NEC to consider the party's response to events in Europe.[24]

However, by the time that meeting took place, Britain was irrevocably involved in the European conflict. The Cabinet had become aware around noon on the 4 August that German troops were moving into Belgium. An ultimatum, calling on Germany to withdraw, had passed at 11 p.m. and from that moment Britain was at war. A jingoistic bandwagon was already gaining momentum and the opinions of those in the Labour movement opposed to the leadership's equivocal stance were hardening.

Even so, the position that the Labour leadership had taken was not immediately brushed aside. Despite considerable disquiet on the part of some of its members, the NEC refused to endorse the war.[25] A compromise resolution was agreed, which reiterated the party's opposition to the 'policy which has produced the war', and unreservedly criticised Grey for misleading the House of Commons over the extent of the commitment to France. It ended with a deeply ambiguous conclusion: it was now the Labour movement's duty 'to secure peace at the earliest possible moment on such conditions as will provide the best opportunities for the re-establishment of amicable feelings between the workers of Europe'.[26] For the time being, it was clear, a small majority of the committee was prepared to accept the leadership's policy. Labour was to retain a distinctive and sceptical position, albeit one based on an extremely fragile compromise of tortuous ambiguity.[27]

The Labour party's resolution of 5 August was critical of government policy leading up to the conflict and looked forward to a permanent peace in the future. What it failed to do, however, was to provide a policy for the immediate present. The central issue was avoided. Did Labour support its country in the war it was about to wage? Within twenty-four hours it was clear that answering this question could not be put off for long. The patriotic wing of the party began to flex its muscles. At the inaugural meeting of Henderson's proposed National Peace Emergency Committee, it was evident that the mood of the Labour movement was moving ever faster in a pro-war direction. Attempts by Glasier to discuss the merits, or otherwise, of the

---

[23] For details of the setting up of the War Emergency Committee see J. M. Winter, *Socialism and the challenge of war: ideas and politics in Britain, 1912–18*, London 188–9, and Harrison, 'The War Emergency National Workers' Committee'.

[24] Wrigley, *Arthur Henderson*, 76.

[25] NEC minutes, 5 Aug. 1914, LPA.

[26] Ibid.

[27] George Wardle told the Labour party conference of 1916 that the NEC resolutions of 5 and 6 Aug. 1914 were 'a compromise agreed upon with the object of attaining unity in the party': *Report* (1916), 103.

war were brushed aside.[28] This mood was carried over into the meeting that evening of the PLP.[29] It had been called to consider the party's response to the government's request for a war credit of £100m. MacDonald, in line with the general intentions of the NEC resolution agreed that afternoon, argued that the PLP should abstain on the vote. In the debate, MacDonald would merely read out the NEC resolution. However, to do this Labour would have to force a division. The reaction of the meeting to this proposal was bitter and explosive. As the party's assistant secretary, James Middleton, later admitted 'tempers were lost'.[30] John Hodge, soon-to-be president of the rabidly pro-war Socialist National Defence Committee, led the rebellion against MacDonald's suggestion. He later claimed that 'after (MacDonald) sat down it appeared as if no-one was anxious to move one way or another. [W]hen I spoke I stated that as far as I was concerned, if I stood alone, I would vote for the war credit; that I was not a believer in a policy of sitting on the fence – either we were for our country or we were against it'.[31] This was not an argument for supporting the war as 'a conflict between opposed political systems and values'. It was rather a knee-jerk patriotic response and, apparently to Hodge's surprise, was backed up by 'many others' in the PLP. MacDonald attempted to save the situation by suggesting that each member of the party could vote according to his conscience. But even this face-saving formula was rejected. A motion calling upon the party to support the government was passed with four dissenters. The pro-war elements in the PLP had succeeded in overturning the leadership's 'wait and see' policy.

MacDonald resigned, but this was not made public until the following day. The delay may have been the result of an attempt to encourage him to reconsider his position. This would explain a resolution (proposed by Sanders and seconded by MacDonald), passed by the Executive Committee the following day which seemed designed to re-establish a compromise position on the war. It stated that

> without in any way receding from the position that the Labour movement has taken in opposition to our engaging in a European war, the Executive of the party advises that, whilst watching for the earliest opportunity for taking effective action in the interests of peace and the re-establishment of good feeling between the workers of the European nations, all Labour and Socialist

---

[28] Quoted in L. Thompson, *The enthusiasts: a biography of John and Katherine Bruce Glasier*, London 1971, 205.

[29] On the PLP's meeting of 6 August see MacDonald to Henderson, 21 Aug. 1914, MacDonald papers, PRO 30/69/1232; Winter, *Socialism*, 189; and J. Hodge, *Workman's cottage to Windsor Castle*, London 1931, 166–7. Hodge's recollection of the date of the meeting is mistaken, but there is little doubt that he is referring to the same event.

[30] Quoted in Winter, *Socialism*, 189.

[31] Quoted in Hodge, *Workman's cottage*, 167.

organisations should concentrate their energies, meantime, on the task of carrying out the resolutions passed by the [WEWNC].[32]

If a reunification of the party behind MacDonald was the intention of this resolution, it failed. His resignation was reported in the *Manchester Guardian* the following day.[33] However, what it did succeed in doing was ensuring that Labour's position on the war remained deeply unclear throughout the next two months.

MacDonald and Henderson attempt to re-forge the Labour alliance

Despite MacDonald's resignation, he and Henderson continued to search for a formula on the war around which the majority of the party could unite and which would allow the former Labour leader to resume his position. These negotiations are important because they reveal an attempt by the two men to hammer out in more detail the policy of critical and limited support for the war that MacDonald had indicated was necessary in the first few days of August. There were certainly indications that support for such a policy still existed among some trade unionists. Thus, for example, the first edition of the *Railway Review* published after the outbreak of war adopted a thoroughly Gladstonian approach. It called for a redrawing of the map of Europe at the end of the war, and continued: 'If "never again" is to be a reality the workers must organise so as to inaugurate the reign of democracy to create a real concert of Europe to end "Kruppism" and private traffic in blood and also to establish a new era in diplomacy and government which shall not rely on the balance of power, but which shall make the enemy of one, the enemy of all.'[34] Henderson's main aim in his negotiations with MacDonald was to minimise the split in the party. MacDonald shared this aim. There is no doubt that he was angry and felt slighted by the PLP's action, but there is little evidence that he remained anything other than committed to the Labour party at this time.[35] Nevertheless, he also remained convinced that Labour's best interests would not be served by moving to an unquestioningly pro-war position. This would prevent it from taking advantage of the disillusionment with the conflict that MacDonald believed would inevitably occur once the initial enthusiasm had subsided.

Henderson began attempts to persuade MacDonald to resume his position

---

[32] NEC minutes, 6 Aug. 1914, LPA.
[33] See *Manchester Guardian*, 7 Aug. 1914.
[34] See *Railway Review* 21 Aug. 1914, MRC, MSS 127/NU/4/1/2.
[35] On MacDonald's views about the PLP see MacDonald diary, MacDonald papers, PRO 30/69/1753, entry for 23 Sept. 1914.

soon after his resignation.[36] In the negotiations that followed, MacDonald began by reiterating his view that the party's stance must retain a critical element. It was essential that the movement was prepared to express his views regarding

'1. The Cause of War;
2. Our duty to keep these causes before electors;
3. Our duty to prepare the public mind for a settlement which will be in accordance with the international policy of labour; and specifically;
4. Our duty to formulate our objections to the military and diplomatic policies which have been pursued just as much in this country as on the continent, and to prepare at once to advocate an alternative.'[37]

If Labour was not prepared to do this, MacDonald indicated that he felt compelled to cooperate with a 'movement' that did. There is no record of a reply, but, three days later, MacDonald wrote again. This time he enclosed (probably at Henderson's request) a circular letter 'for the party' outlining in detail the more positive aspects of his position on the war. He stated considerably more frankly than previously that now that the war had started he was not prepared to oppose it. He wrote: 'The war has broken out, we are in it. We must see it through. Every step to that necessary end must be taken. Let there be no mistake about that.' Labour's particular task was to prevent the peace, when it came, from being inspired by jingoism and imperialism. He ended the letter with an appeal for unity, arguing that 'If the Labour Party is broken by the war none of these things can happen.'[38]

In his accompanying letter to Henderson, MacDonald apologised for not striking a more conciliatory line. He remained sceptical about whether, after the bitterness of the last PLP meeting, even the less ambiguous statement that he had enclosed would allow a compromise to be agreed. He remained insistent, however, that Labour must retain an independent stance. He argued that 'The Party must make up its mind what it is to do for the next month or two. Is it to throw itself out of action altogether and allow each individual to drift whither it seems good to him? Or is it to attempt to take up a distinctive position which will be in due course the rallying centre for those who wish this war shall not have been fought in vain.'[39] This was not, however, MacDonald's final word. News of military retreats in Belgium and France in early September caused him temporarily to reassess his whole position. Suddenly, the spectre of the crushing defeat of France that MacDonald had mentioned in his 3 August speech actually appeared possible. Throughout

[36] A deputation had been despatched to the former chairman with this aim in mind: MacDonald to Henderson, 21 Aug. 1914, ibid. PRO 30/69/1232.
[37] Ibid.
[38] Ibid. See also MacDonald to Henderson, 24 Aug. 1914, ibid.
[39] MacDonald to Henderson, 21 Aug. 1914, ibid.

August his comments on the war had been based on the assumption that Germany would be defeated. The Germans' advance across a wide front on the continent ended once and for all any complacency about the difficulty of the task confronting the allies. MacDonald's reaction was immediate. On 4 September he wrote to Hardie that 'I have heard some rather alarming news about the military situation which, if it is true, ... will necessitate a meeting to discuss our position. Paris will be occupied without much doubt and a new move made against us. I am just dropping you this line to let you know what is passing in my mind.'[40] If the war became one to defend the independence of France or of national defence, MacDonald, as he had indicated in his speech of 3 August, believed that Labour would have no option but to support the government.

It was with these thoughts 'passing in [his] mind' that he agreed to attend a recruiting meeting to be held in Leicester on 12 September – only failing to attend at the last minute and sending instead a letter of support.[41] In this note MacDonald stated firmly that 'Victory must be ours. England is not played out. Her mission is not accomplished.' Directing his comments to the purpose of the meeting, he added: 'Should any opportunity arise to enable me to appeal to the pure love of country ... I shall gladly take that opportunity. I want serious men of the Trade Union, the brotherhood and similar movements to face their duty. To such men it is enough to say "England has need of you".'[42]

There was now little separating MacDonald from Henderson who was delighted by MacDonald's actions. 'Nothing has given me so much satisfaction for a long time', he told MacDonald in a letter on 14 September. 'It enables the movement to see that we are not apart as some imagine ... I am convinced that whatever our views we ought not to stand apart at the critical moment.'[43]

MacDonald, the European crisis and progressive politics

It thus appeared possible by mid-September that MacDonald and Henderson might be able to resolve their differences on the war. The exact nature of a compromise policy was not entirely clear, but, given the negotiations that had taken place, it seems likely that it would have involved Labour adopting a position of critical and limited support for the conflict. But was MacDonald genuine in his desire to reach such an agreement? Was the unity of the Labour party important to him by this stage, or did he have much grander plans?

[40] MacDonald to Keir Hardie, 4 Sept. 1914, Francis Johnson papers, BLPES, ILP4.
[41] See extract from the *Daily Citizen*, 12 Sept. 1914, MacDonald papers, PRO 30/69/1232
[42] Ibid.
[43] Henderson to MacDonald, 14 Sept. 1914, ibid.

Christopher Howard suggests the latter. He argues that MacDonald was primarily motivated throughout these events by political considerations and viewed the 1914 crisis almost entirely instrumentally. Motivated mainly by personal ambition, he determinedly and purposefully set out to exploit the situation to transform the existing party system. The crisis represented 'an issue of national magnitude and national importance' which MacDonald attempted to use to break 'the constraints of pre-war politics'. Taking advantage of emerging rifts on the Liberal left, he 'believed he could take the *majority* of the [Labour] party into a new combination' which he would lead and which would take the form of an 'anti-war alliance'.[44]

A major split in the Liberal party was certainly plausible. It had become by 1914 an increasingly unstable coalition of opinions, in which there were wide and fundamental differences on a variety of policies.[45] Despite its ineffectiveness, the radicals' campaign on foreign policy had been damaging for party unity. Previously it had always foundered due to Grey's skill in exploiting the radicals' differences and appeals to party loyalty. For many radicals, however, a Liberal government which committed the country to war would be barely worth the name.[46] As a result, splits quickly developed in the party in the early days of the war. The Liberal Foreign Affairs Group met twice at the end of July and Ponsonby communicated to Grey, on 29 July, the group's concern.[47] Outside parliament, J. A. Hobson and Graham Wallas were already well advanced in their organisation of a British Neutrality League: likely sympathisers had been contacted with the intention of sending a letter to the press (subsequently printed on Monday 3 August).[48] However, despite the existence of splits on the Liberal left there are a number of problems with Howard's argument. When taken together these suggest that, while MacDonald was undoubtedly interested in and sought to exploit these developments, his actions in so doing were considerably more cautious than Howard suggests.[49]

The first problem is that the premise upon which Howard's argument is based appears in the light of recent scholarship to be mistaken. Howard claims that just prior to the war MacDonald and Henderson had agreed that Labour should fight the coming election as a 'truly independent party of the left and of the trade union movement', that the progressive alliance had been abandoned.[50] As a result, MacDonald was looking for an issue around

---

[44] Howard, 'MacDonald, Henderson and the outbreak of war', 879 (my emphasis).
[45] See Tanner, *Political change*, 317–48.
[46] See Morris, *Radicalism*, 410; Clarke, *Liberals*, 167.
[47] See Morris, *Radicalism*, 408–11.
[48] See *Manchester Guardian*, 3 Aug. 1914; Clarke, *Liberals*, 164–74; and J. L. Hammond, *C. P. Scott of the Manchester Guardian*, London 1934, 178.
[49] Much of Howard's argument is based on Fenner Brockway's analysis of MacDonald's actions at this time. Brockway was neither a close personal nor political friend of MacDonald: *Inside the left*, 56.
[50] Howard, 'MacDonald, Henderson and the outbreak of war', 872.

which he could 'polarise public opinion'. The outbreak of war proved to be this issue. As Duncan Tanner has shown, however, 'The size and geographical distribution of [a 1914] parliamentary campaign would [have been] compatible with the idea of progressive alliance.'[51] There had not been in 1914 the definite abandonment of Labour's pre-war political strategy that Howard has suggested. This makes his overall argument less convincing. In this regard, MacDonald had been prepared to follow an intensely patient strategy of gradual growth and consolidation over the previous four years, despite the concerted opposition of many of his colleagues. It is unlikely, therefore, that he would have been prepared to risk the perceived benefits of this project on a political gamble in the midst of a national crisis. Rather, in the face of the fevered speculation about a major Liberal split, MacDonald reacted cautiously. When informed by Illingworth on 1 August that war was inevitable and that it was likely to be unpopular, he replied that 'no war was at first unpopular'.[52] The precedent he clearly had in mind was the Boer War. This had started as a patriotic crusade, but had gradually lost a large amount of public support as its aims and purpose became confused. Many of MacDonald's actions during the early days of August 1914 can best be understood in the context of his experience as an opponent of the Boer War and his interpretation of its political effects. MacDonald guessed, as did many others, that the conflict in 1914 would be relatively short, that it was likely to end in inconclusive stalemate and that this, when combined with the social and economic dislocation that the conflict would inevitably produce, was likely to lead to a widespread repudiation of the initial decision in favour of Britain's involvement. The political benefits of such disillusionment would accrue to the party that was prepared to adopt a critical stance at the outset of the war. Labour did not need to attempt the launch of a new combination to benefit politically from the war. It merely needed to maintain the sceptical approach to the Liberals' foreign policy of the pre-war years to inevitably benefit from the distaste with which the war would come to be regarded. Labour could remain true to its previous announcements by declaring that the party could not support unconditionally a war caused by a failure of British diplomacy. It was on this basis that MacDonald confided to Lord Riddell, during dinner with the newspaper proprietor and three Liberal Cabinet members on 2 August, that 'In three months there will be bread riots and we (the Labour Party) shall come in'.[53] This was more bravado than prediction but it does indicate the Labour leader's thinking at this time.

MacDonald's caution was also based on the fact that he was aware well before the outbreak of war that the split in the Liberal party was likely to be only partial. By the 2 August he knew that the majority of the Cabinet would remain in place. While John Simon was 'broken', according to MacDonald,

---

51 Tanner, *Political change*, 317, and also pp. 318–48.
52 MacDonald memorandum, 23 Sept. 1914, MacDonald papers, PRO 30/69/1232.
53 *Lord Riddell's war diary*, London 1933, entry for 2 Aug. 1914.

Charles Masterman was 'jingo' and Lloyd George was searching for excuses with which he could justify supporting Britain's involvement in the war.[54] If the leading radical in the Cabinet was to stay put, it was likely that the vast majority of the Liberal party would also stay loyal. There was not to be a climactic break-up of the Liberal party on the outbreak of the war to accelerate the coming together of the progressive forces that MacDonald regarded as inevitable in the longer term. Only this would have encouraged MacDonald to contemplate the launch of a new combination. After all, he had a lot to lose by attempting such a venture. It would, for example, almost certainly result in the breaking up of the labour alliance. Any permanent link-up with the radicals would be resisted firmly by the ILP, which remained MacDonald's sole power base within the Labour party.[55]

In addition, it also seems unlikely that MacDonald would have sought to spark a party realignment at a time when there was so much uncertainty about how matters would develop. Like the greater majority of the Commons and many within the Cabinet, he was confused and unsure about the full significance and implications of the crisis. In such circumstances, his main intention was to leave Labour with room for manoeuvre. This was reflected in MacDonald's Commons reply to Grey's speech on 3 August in which he committed the party to neutrality, but also outlined the scenarios in which this commitment might be relaxed. In adopting this line, MacDonald was simply urging his party to remain consistent with its previous criticisms of the government's foreign policy and on all other matters adopt a policy of 'wait and see'. He had no intention, while the situation remained so unpredictable, of launching off on some new and risky venture.

Nevertheless, while MacDonald's actions are not consistent with an attempt to launch a new political combination, he did recognise that by maintaining an independent stance on the war Labour was stretching the progressive alliance to breaking point. After ten years of electoral co-operation with the Liberals and tacit support for their legislative programme, a crisis had arisen in the one area of policy where Labour, with MacDonald's sanction, had adopted a position of sustained and overt criticism. If the party retreated now, any claim to distinctiveness would be discredited. Labour, MacDonald believed, had to remain the 'party of challenge' in foreign affairs, even if, in doing so, the umbilical cord linking it to the Liberal party was finally cut. It was on this basis that MacDonald speculated that 'a great break had come'.[56] This was not a strategy that MacDonald adopted with any degree of enthusiasm or confidence. He was responding to events rather than leading them. It was mainly in hope rather than with certainty that MacDonald summed

---

[54] MacDonald memorandum, 23 Sept. 1914, MacDonald papers, PRO 30/69/1232
[55] For the ILP's opposition to any connections with the Liberal Radicals see Robbins, *Abolition*, 45. See also Hardie to T. N. Benson, 29 Oct. 1914, Johnson papers, ILP4.
[56] MacDonald diary (supplement), MacDonald papers, PRO 30/69/1232, entry for 23 Sept. 1914.

up his Commons speech in reply to Grey on 3 August with an explicit allusion to what he had seen as the eventual political vindication of the pro-Boers: 'I not only know but I feel that the feeling of the House is against us. I have been through this before and 1906 came as part recompense. It will come again.'[57]

There is no doubt that after his resignation MacDonald felt at greater liberty to investigate developments on the left of the Liberal party. They also gave him valuable bargaining power in his negotiations with Henderson. However, it was dissident Liberals (for example Charles Trevelyan), rather than MacDonald, who took the initiative in raising the question of 'party reconstruction'.[58] While sympathetic to the general aim of cross-party co-operation in criticism of the government's war policy, MacDonald was working to a different political agenda. He remained wedded to the belief that if there was to be a change in the political system resulting from the war, it would consist of the creation of a more broadly-based Labour party. This approach caused concern and insecurity among dissident Liberals and distrust among the constituency that they were trying to attract.[59] MacDonald's unwillingness to rule out a return to the chairmanship of the Labour party created suspicions about his political motives.[60] Indeed, there is evidence that MacDonald's involvement seriously inhibited the growth of what was eventually to become the UDC.[61] Many radicals were cautious of links with Labour and socialism. They were not interested in becoming part of MacDonald's long-term plan for an expanded Labour party. A wariness of Labour remained a significant factor throughout the war in their unwillingness to join the UDC's campaign.[62]

Thus, by the end of August the political situation was in a state of flux. The Labour party's precise policy on the war remained ambiguous. MacDonald had resigned, but was still engaged with Henderson in negotiations about how Labour's differences could be patched up. At the same time, developments on the left of the Liberal party suggested that, although a major split in the older progressive party was unlikely, a partial fracture was still probable. During September and October, however, the situation began to resolve itself. Gradually, it became clear that the split between the ILP and the rest of the Labour party was too wide to be bridged by any compromise policy.

---

[57] HC, Debates lxv.1800–31 (3 Aug. 1914).

[58] Although reaction against the war within the governing party was more muted than many had expected, predictions of a changes in the party system remained common. The phrase 'party reconstruction' was regularly used at the time. See, for example, C. P. Scott to E. D. Morel, 24 Aug. 1914, E. D. Morel papers, BLPES, F6/1, and Emily Hobhouse to MacDonald, 2 Sept., 1914, MacDonald papers, PRO 30/69/1233.

[59] See chapter 4 below.

[60] See Marquand, Ramsay MacDonald, 172.

[61] See, for example, Arthur Ponsonby to Morel, n.d., c. Aug. 1914, Morel papers, F8/123.

[62] See Robbins, Abolition of war.

Labour divided

It was not, therefore, a lack of will that prevented a *rapprochement* between the two Labour leaders. The main problem that MacDonald and Henderson faced in trying to construct a compromise policy was that the ILP and the rest of the Labour party remained massively divided. If anything, opinions became more polarised during the first two months of the war. After MacDonald's resignation, pro-war majorities of various sizes and degrees of enthusiasm were established on all the Labour party's most important bodies: the NEC, the PLP and the PCTUC. Gradually, during August, they began to tighten their grip on party policy. The first manifestation of this was the agreement of the PLP on 27 August that all the Labour whips should join the Parliamentary Recruiting Committee. This was presented to the NEC on 29 August as a *fait accompli*. After 'considerable discussion', it was agreed by 7 votes to 4 that Labour should '[support] the campaign to strengthen the British Army [by placing] the central organisation at the disposal of the campaign'. At the same meeting an electoral truce between the main political parties was agreed. This ensured that a free run in by-elections would be given to the party that had previously held the seat.[63] Whatever MacDonald and Henderson's equivocations about the war might be, they were not shared by the majority of the movement. At a time of perceived national strife, it was becoming clear that many believed that Labour's place should be at the side of the government.

Meanwhile, as the pro-war majority imposed their will on the Labour party, the ILP began to move in the opposite direction. At the outbreak of the war, the party had been split between those, like MacDonald, W. C Anderson and F. W. Jowett, who favoured a centrist line and were anxious to prevent a break-up of the labour alliance, and pacifist elements, led by Glasier, Brockway and Allen, who insisted that the party should adopt a policy of outright opposition and resistance to the war, based on its socialist internationalist ideology.[64] Gradually, during the first two months of the war, the latter grouping began to make substantial progress. The ILP's National Administrative Council (NAC) vigorously rebuked MacDonald for his equivocation on the conflict.[65] Meanwhile, in the pages of the *Labour Leader*, pacifist elements pushed hard for an ILP campaign against conscription and for peace.[66]

Indications that the ILP was moving to a policy of outright pacifism, in combination with the worsening situation in France in early September, had

---

[63] NEC minutes, 29 Aug. 1914, LPA.

[64] When the NAC did make their views known, they consisted merely of a restatement of the ILP's internationalist principles: Brockway, *Inside the left*, 47.

[65] Ibid. 56.

[66] The pacifist elements came close to converting the party to this position at the beginning of 1915.

the effect of further hardening pro-war sentiment in the Labour party. At the instigation of the PCTUC and George Wardle (of the Railwaymen's union), a manifesto for the British Labour movement was drawn up. It was 'prepared with a view to removing the misapprehension which exists in regard to the Labour Party's attitude on the war and the confusion between the Labour members and the ILP'.[67] This was passed by the PCTUC on 7 October 1914, and sent individually to Labour members for them to sign.[68] Its content reflected its aim: blame for the war was apportioned directly to Germany's 'ambition to become the dominant military power of Europe'. MacDonald's criticisms of Grey's pre-war diplomacy were explicitly repudiated.[69] The manifesto stated that the Labour movement 'recognised that Great Britain, having exhausted the resources of peaceful diplomacy was bound in honour as well as by treaty, to resist by arms the aggression of Germany'. It concluded that '[u]ntil the power which has pillaged and outraged Belgium and the Belgians, and plunged nearly the whole of Europe into the awful misery, suffering and horror of war, is beaten, there can be no peace'.[70]

As John Horne suggests, the manifesto did seek in places to justify Labour's support for the war on the basis of principle.[71] The moderate internationalist body of opinion evident within the trade unions in the pre-war period retained an influence. Thus, the manifesto stated that 'the victory of Germany would mean the death of democracy in Europe'. However, while there undoubtedly were some moderate internationalist Labour members who continued to regard the war as a principled fight against German militarism, Horne's argument that the allied socialist and labour parties generally saw the war in these terms is stronger for France than it is for Britain.[72] For most of the British labour movement these considerations did not weigh particularly heavily by the end of 1914. They certainly placed no constraints on the party's support for the conflict, which after the release of the October manifesto was absolute and uncritical. Most of the Labour movement was prepared to fall into line behind the policy proposed by the patriotic wing. For some, this was probably due to the self-interested motivations suggested by Howard.[73] For others in the party the decision was made easier by the fact

---

67 PCTUC minutes, 7 Oct. 1914, LPA.

68 For details of how the manifesto was drafted and distributed see George Wardle to MacDonald, 14 Oct. 1914, MacDonald papers, PRO 30/69/1232, and Wardle to Hardie, 14 Oct. 1914, Johnson papers, ILP4.

69 In response, MacDonald denounced the document as 'imperfect in statement and ... absurdly inadequate in its conclusions': MacDonald to Henderson, 20 Oct. 1914, MacDonald papers, PRO 30/69/1232. For Hardie's view see Hardie to Arthur Peters (Labour's national agent), 12 Oct. 1914, Johnson papers, ILP4.

70 See G. D. H. Cole, *Labour in wartime*, London 1915, 55–6.

71 Horne, *Labour at war*, 45.

72 Among those refusing to sign the manifesto were a number of trade unionists: *Labour Leader*, 3 Dec. 1914.

73 See Howard, 'MacDonald, Henderson and the outbreak of war', 875–7.

that it was a Liberal government that was asking for support: the continued ties between the trade unions and the Liberals meant that many were prepared to trust that the government had taken the right decision in the interests of the nation as a whole.[74] Its previous record on social reform made it seem unlikely that the interests of Labour would be swept aside.

The uncritical nature of Labour's support for the war was made clear during the following nine months. In April 1915 a joint statement of the NEC and PLP reiterated the party's strong support for the recruiting campaign and called for these 'endeavours to be continued until Great Britain and its allies have obtained victory'.[75] Three months later the PCTUC agreed to give their wholehearted support to the rabidly pro-war Socialist National Defence Committee in its campaign to 'counteract the influence of the anti-war party, and to declare the firm intention of the workers of England to pursue the war to a triumphant conclusion'.[76] In the preceding months the labour movement had agreed in negotiations with the government to place a moratorium on strikes, forego established protections for the status of skilled workers in the munitions industry and allow a limited amount of state direction of labour in the engineering trades. There seemed little to which some Labour leaders would not agree in support of the war. Even opposition to conscription among many Labour leaders was equivocal.[77]

Against this background, it was difficult for moderate internationalists to make their voices heard. In the following two years occasional attempts were made by Labour leaders, particularly Henderson, to re-state the alleged principles upon which the party was supporting the war.[78] Moreover, in bodies such as the BSIMF, where strong international affiliations had been developed in the pre-war period, there was growing frustration with the labour movement's passive line.[79] However, during the first three years of the war Labour never sought to impose any limits on its support for the conflict. Representatives of the Labour party, including Henderson, attended a meeting of allied socialists in February 1915, which agreed to 'resist any attempt to transform this defensive war into a war of conquest', but this stance was never officially endorsed by the party.[80] The British government was thus given a completely free hand on the war: no pressure was placed on it to establish a limited set of 'democratic' war aims.[81] This contrasted

[74] See Tanner, *Political change*, 317–24.

[75] NEC minutes, 26 Apr. 1915, LPA. The motion was passed by 24 votes to 5.

[76] PCTUC minutes, 14/15 July 1915, ibid.

[77] See Horne, *Labour at war*, 51–83.

[78] See, for example, HC, Debates lxviii.43–6 (12 Nov. 1914). See also *Report* (1916), 103; *Report* (1917), 97; and Ward, *Red flag*, 123.

[79] BSIMF advisory committee minutes, 6 Nov. 1915, 7 Apr. 16, 29 July, 6 Sept. 1916, MRC, MS 036/IMF/7/1.

[80] See G. D. H. Cole, *A history of the Labour party from 1914*, London 1948, 21–31.

[81] See NEC minutes, 24 June 1915, 30 Mar. 1916, LPA. A peace terms, 'emergency' subcommittee was established by the NEC, but this was part of the party's preparations

strongly with the situation in France where, from December 1915, French socialists insisted upon such a statement from their government.[82] It was not until the end of 1917 that the British Labour movement agreed to do the same. Only then did the compromise policy that Henderson and MacDonald had proposed in 1914 prove acceptable to a majority within the Labour movement.

for the post-war world. It was remitted 'to hold itself in readiness to take action ... when occasion [i.e. peace] arises': NEC minutes, 14, 15 Feb. 1916 and 7 Feb. 1917, LPA.
[82] See Horne, Labour at war, 305–6.

4

Thinking about International Affairs,
1914–1918

After declaring its total support for the war in October 1914, the Labour party almost completely ignored debates about international policy for the following two years. All attempts to discuss the causes of the conflict or the shape of the post-war world were resisted on the grounds that they were a distraction from the main goal – the military defeat of Germany – and probably inspired by 'pacifism'. Even the War Emergency Committee, which after 1916 began to think creatively about domestic policy, deliberately kept off international affairs for most of its existence.[1]

In contrast, among other progressive politicians and intellectuals, the war led to a fundamental reassessment of ideas about international affairs and, consequently, a period of intense creativity. In this regard, historians of the Labour party have tended to concentrate upon the ideas developed by the UDC, the organisation formed by dissenting left-wing Liberals on the outbreak of the war. It was to these ideas that Labour is said to have looked for inspiration in 1917, when the party decided to reconsider the nature of its support for the war.

Taylor's *The troublemakers*, has been extremely influential in this regard. He suggested, in his inimitable style, that 'the Labour movement under Henderson's guidance, set out [in 1917] to create its own foreign policy. Thus resolved where could it turn for ideas? Only to the UDC. The Union had staked its claim to provide an alternative foreign policy. Now it struck gold'.[2] Despite the years that have passed since Taylor's essay was written, this interpretation remains dominant.[3]

There are major problems with this view. It misinterprets and simplifies the ideological debates that took place in progressive circles in the early post-war period. It misunderstands the nature of the UDC and suggests an ideological unity to the organisation's view on the war that simply did not exist. It tends to downplay the development of ideas outside the confines of the UDC or wrongly to credit the UDC with the development of these ideas.

---

[1]   See R. Harrison, 'The War Emergency National Workers' Committee', and Winter, *Socialism.*

[2]   Taylor, *Troublemakers*, 154. See also, for example, Swartz, *Union of Democratic Control*, 147.

[3]   See, for example, Keohane 'Labour's international policy', 365, and Vickers, *Labour party and the world*, 7, 61, 74.

It misunderstands the reasons for and nature of Labour's 1917 policy change. Let us consider first the nature of the UDC and its ideological stance.

The Union of Democratic Control: its aims and ideologies

The UDC was the main organisational consequence of discussions between dissident left-wing Liberals, Labour leaders and progressive intellectuals and commentators, which began in early August 1914. It was to become, during the rest of the war, the leading critic of the government's war policy and, as a result, it and its founders came to acquire pariah status. Its meetings were regularly broken up, its speakers attacked and its leading figure, Morel, imprisoned.[4] Perhaps because of its controversial history, the Union has attracted considerable attention from historians. Its ideas, it has been suggested, while fervently rejected initially, came to be accepted first by the Labour party in 1917, and ultimately by many within the British establishment.

But what were the UDC's ideas? Did it have a single ideologically coherent stance? In investigating the functions envisaged for the UDC by its founding members, what becomes clear is that they were initially motivated as much by political as ideological considerations, and that this, together with the involvement of Morel, meant that the establishment of a unified ideological position on the war, or foreign affairs more generally, was never a major priority.

The politician who was most instrumental in the establishment of the UDC was Charles Trevelyan.[5] A junior minister in Asquith's government up to 5 August, he had resigned when Grey revealed the extent of Britain's commitment to France. As a government minister he had not been involved in any of the radicals' campaigns before the war. Indeed, he was regarded by some who had opposed Grey as a Liberal imperialist. In his letter of resignation to his constituents, however, Trevelyan argued, in traditional radical terms, that the war was unnecessary: an agreement could have been reached with Germany before it started. Germans disregard of Belgian neutrality was not a sufficient reason for Britain's involvement.[6]

Trevelyan's immediate action after resigning was to link up with the radicals in parliament. On 6 August he was elected chairman of a new parliamentary group for 'those not in accord with the foreign policy which has led to this country's intervention in the war'. The membership of this group

---

[4]   See, for example, C. P. Trevelyan to Ponsonby, 24 July 1915, Arthur Ponsonby papers, Bodl. Lib. On Morel see Taylor, *Troublemakers*, 119–22, 133–5; Spear, 'The case of E. D. Morel', 193–223; and C. Cline, *E. D. Morel, 1873–1924: the strategies of protest*, Belfast 1980.

[5]   See Trevelyan to Morel, 5 Aug. 1914, Morel papers, F6/1; Macdonald papers, PRO 30/69/1232.

[6]   See A. J. A. Morris, *C. P. Trevelyan, 1870–1958: portrait of a radical*, Belfast 1977.

was entirely predictable: it contained all those, including Ponsonby, who had played a leading part in the pre-war campaign.[7] At the same time, however, Trevelyan was spreading his net much wider. On 5 August he told Morel that 'There is a body of Liberal members united for common action on the war questions, trying to establish connection with the Labour Party … I think it more than likely that it may be an organisation which could connect with outside efforts and groups.'[8] For this reason Trevelyan also contacted George Lansbury who, as editor of the *Daily Herald*, was clearly an important contact to have. However, Trevelyan's letter indicated more ambitious aims than simple co-operation in publicising a new organisation critical of the government's pre-war foreign policy. He told Lansbury that he had resigned because 'a parting of the ways' had been reached; that although 'democracy' had been overwhelmed there was a chance that it could emerge stronger at the end of the war.[9] Trevelyan's actions after his resignation thus also had a clear political purpose. He was sounding out a broad spectrum of opinion on the left with the aim of gauging the prospects for a 'party reconstruction'. He expected the embryonic UDC to become the focus for all left-wing Liberals, eventually, he hoped, heralding the coalescence of the democratic forces in Britain in 'A British Democratic League', formed from a large body of dissident Liberals in association with the Labour party. Ponsonby gradually came to share this aim.[10] It was for this reason that the first letter to potential supporters declared that 'a dividing point has come in National history … We are anxious to take measures which may focus this feeling and help to direct public policy on broad lines which may build up on a more secure and permanent foundation the hopes which have been shattered for our generation in the last month'.[11] MacDonald was also influenced by political considerations in his early dealings with the UDC, but his hope was that left-wing Liberals could be attracted to Labour's banner.[12] Thus, Trevelyan and MacDonald, in particular, had strong, though different, political reasons for involving themselves with the Union. Morel involved himself for a different reason. He had made his name as a campaigner against secret diplomacy. He saw the new organisation mainly as a vehicle to continue and extend this campaign.

Thus, while the four main founders of the UDC were close ideologically, this was not the sole reason why they formed the new organisation. All were concerned to attract as broad a range of support as possible, either for polit-

---

[7] See *Manchester Guardian*, 7 Aug. 1914.
[8] Trevelyan to Morel, 5 Aug. 1914, Morel papers, F6/1.
[9] Trevelyan to George Lansbury, 7 Aug. 1914, George Lansbury papers, BLPES, 7/1. See also Robbins, *Abolition*, 37.
[10] See Marquand, *Ramsay MacDonald*, 172.
[11] A detailed summary of the early actions of the UDC is contained in the first minute book of the organisation's general council: UDC papers, BJL, DDC/1/1. See also Robbins, *Abolition*, 36–7.
[12] See chapter 3 above.

ical or campaigning reasons. It is in this context that the UDC's ideological stance should be understood. If support was to be maximised it was essential that the new organisation have broad appeal within the general confines of the liberal and radical tradition.

This aim was reflected in the UDC's first letter to potential supporters, which included a statement of general principles. These were, in summary, 'real parliamentary control over foreign policy'; 'When peace returns, to open direct and deliberate negotiations with democratic parties and influences on the continent, so as to form an International understanding depending on popular parties rather than governments'; and final terms suitable to ensure 'that this war will not, either through the humiliation of the defeated nation or an artificial re-arrangement of frontiers, merely become the starting point for new National antagonisms and future wars'.[13]

These objectives were little more than a rehash of traditional radical generalities with a small additional dose of socialist internationalism. Most areas of contention were skated over. No explicit position was taken on ·the causes of the war. No suggestions were made about how and when its end should be brought about. The first objective closely reflected Ponsonby and Morel's campaigns against secret diplomacy. The second reflected MacDonald's links with the socialist International.

When this letter was leaked to the press, the UDC made its first public statement. This again was ideologically vague. The central purpose of the organisation, it was suggested, was to keep 'the essential conditions of a lasting peace before the British people'. This had to take place immediately because it might not be possible when peace came to prevent 'the acts of rulers and diplomatists executing a policy in secret and finally imposed upon the peoples as an accomplished fact'.[14]

To give some idea of what the UDC regarded as 'essential conditions' for a lasting peace, a revised and more detailed set of objectives was released (*see* appendix). This manifesto was even more broadly drawn than the first draft and reflected the desire of Trevelyan and Ponsonby to offer greater reassurance to potential supporters within the Liberal party.[15] It constituted an amalgam of the main demands of liberal and radical campaigns on foreign policy: democratic control, disarmament and self-determination. The most interesting principle was the third which proposed the setting up of an 'International Council ... with such machinery for securing international

---

[13] First circular letter sent by MacDonald, Trevelyan, Angell and Morel, August 1914, UDC papers, DDC/1/1 (my italics). See also Macdonald papers, PRO 30/69/1232, and Morel papers, F6/1. On the broad appeal of the UDC's early correspondence see Clarke, *Liberals*, 169.

[14] This was to be a constant theme of the organisation's publications. See, for example, A. Ponsonby, *The Union of Democratic Control: what it is and what it is not* (UDC pamphlet xiv, 1915), UDC papers, DDC/5/95.

[15] See chapter 3 above.

agreement as shall be the guarantee of an abiding peace'. This addressed one of the major fault lines of liberal/radical debate on foreign affairs. It seemed to suggest that, in the debate between the Cobdenites and the Gladstonians on the permissible degree of intervention by Britain on the world stage, the UDC had come down in favour of the latter. Indeed, some commentators have argued that the UDC's proposal was 'a forerunner of the idea of a league of nations' and mainly on this basis claim that the UDC was a major contributor to the development of this idea during the war.[16] However, after this vague commitment in 1914 to some form of international organisation, little more was heard about it from the UDC as an organisation, or from its founders.[17] Indeed, leading UDC figures such as Morel, MacDonald and Ponsonby were to become some of most trenchant critics of the league idea, as it was eventually to emerge. The inclusion of an 'International Council' in 1914, therefore, is best understood as an attempt by the founders of the UDC to broaden their appeal to Gladstonian, as well as Cobdenite critics, of the government's pre-war foreign policy. It was part of their strategy of maximising support for the new organisation.

In its initial public statements, therefore, the UDC attempted to present itself as a body to which all those with concerns about Britain's involvement in the conflict in Europe, be they radicals, liberals or socialists, could attach themselves. Ideological purity was not the goal; it was rather to gain the maximum level of support. Despite these efforts, however, the organisation achieved only limited success. Overall, it did not attract the level of support for which its founders had hoped. Doubts about its political make-up and its forced launch ruined its chances of gaining significant backing from within the Liberal party. While many supported its aims and suggested policies, few were prepared to accept its tactics. Thus, Arnold Rowntree wrote to Morel on 5 October that 'There is no difference in policy between us … But whilst (the Government) have such tremendous burdens to carry in directing present operations I am prepared to err on the side of reticence.'[18]

However, while the level of Liberal party support was disappointing, some extremely important figures did join the organisation in its early weeks. Of these, the most significant were Brailsford, Hobson, Angell and Goldsworthy Lowes Dickinson, a Cambridge classicist, who was to play a major role in early thought about a league of nations. Their involvement greatly enhanced

---

[16] Swartz, *Union of Democratic Control*, 42. The involvement of Goldsworthy Lowes Dickinson, a member of the UDC and early proponent of a League of Nations is also used to make this argument: Vickers, *Labour and the world*, 62–3, 73–4.

[17] Only one of the UDC's wartime pamphlets dealt directly with the idea of League of Nations, J. A. Hobson's *A League of Nations* (UDC pamphlet xva, 1915).

[18] C. P. Scott's views were similar. He told Morel on 24 Sept. that 'I'm afraid I can't join … I can agree with your objects, but I sh[oul]d be apt to part company with you as to methods': Morel papers, F6/2.

the intellectual credibility of the UDC. However it also emphasised its ideological heterogeneity.

The failure of the UDC to make the political impact for which some of its founders had hoped quickly changed its nature. Increasingly, it was as a campaigning organisation that the UDC developed, the initial aim being to resist publicly the prevailing mood of jingoism and vengeance. This was reflected in the central role given to Morel. A publicist rather than a great thinker, from late 1914 it was his energy and campaigning ability that built the UDC up into a genuinely high-profile political player. However, if anything these developments made the need for an ideologically coherent approach to the issues raised by the war even less important. Morel's main aim was to release into the public domain as many opinions critical of the government's war policy as possible. This was reflected most obviously in the UDC's pamphlet campaign. As long as a pamphlet was consistent with their general policy, Morel and Ponsonby agreed, it should 'as a general rule' be passed 'with idiosyncrasies unaltered'.[19] Otherwise, Morel concluded that they might never get any pamphlets through at all. Ponsonby, no doubt, agreed. The main aim, he believed, was to teach the public as much about foreign affairs as possible: 'it understands nothing and knows nothing'.[20]

Thus the UDC was a group of individuals whose views on foreign affairs differed in important ways, but who came together on the basis of a shared general concern about Britain's involvement in the war. Indeed, it was increasingly on this matter that the organisation came to concentrate. The Union had tried on its foundation to stress its moderation: it was not 'a "stop-the-war" movement of any kind', it claimed.[21] However, this diffidence did not last long. By the end of 1915 UDC members were arguing that negotiations must end the war before a military victory decided the result. By 1917 the UDC was firmly associated with a policy of peace-by-negotiation. Indeed, by this stage of the war, it was this position rather than the organisation's four principles which largely defined it.

On all other issues, however, individual members of the organisation remained free to plough their own particular furrows and stress their distinctive approaches. The most obvious example of this was the presence of both Angell and Brailsford in the UDC. They had clashed repeatedly and fundamentally over foreign affairs in the pre-war period, but now found themselves in the same organisation. It soon became clear, particularly once ideas about the peace began to be considered, that there were a number of different ideological approaches within the organisation.

---

[19] Ponsonby to Morel, 30 Aug. 1914, ibid. F6/1.
[20] Ibid.
[21] See Robbins, *Abolition*, 38–41.

Classifying the wartime ideological groupings: the UDC radicals

Some historians have noted the catholic nature of the UDC's ideological stance, but the implications of this observation with respect to the organisation's influence on the foreign policy development of the Labour party have not been fully investigated.[22] If, however, there was no ideologically consistent UDC view on the causes of the war and the changes required in the international system to prevent its repetition, it is extremely difficult to assess the ideological influence of the organisation as a whole in any worthwhile or meaningful way. Rather, what is required is that the various ideological strands within the UDC be disaggregated, so allowing their influence to be assessed. Likewise it is also important to show how these ideological strands related and interacted with the thinking on international affairs that developed during the war outside the UDC. In this regard it is possible to identify four ideological groupings, the UDC radicals, the Gladstonian liberals, the democratic socialists and the ILP pacifists. These are not based on the organisational affiliations of their members. Rather, each grouping contains a core of individuals whose approach to the war, and/or proposals for the post-world war, were based on similar ideological assumptions, different in important ways from members of the other groups.[23]

In any exercise of this kind, there will always be individuals who are difficult to place. Hobson, for example, is one important figure whom it is difficult satisfactorily to situate in any of the groups.[24] Moreover, the placement of individuals together in a group does not mean that their views on every issue were identical. However, generally, individuals such as Hobson are the exception and the classification can be justified on the basis that it provides a valid analytical framework for Labour's foreign policy development between 1917 and 1924.

The UDC radicals included Ponsonby, Morel, MacDonald, Trevelyan and Snowden. Containing four of the five founders of the UDC, this was the dominant group in that organisation.[25] Ideologically, they were the inheri-

[22] See D. Blaazer, *The popular front and the progressive tradition*, Cambridge 1992, 72, 74, 95–6.

[23] These groupings are similar to, but not based on, Ceadel's extremely useful classification of 'pacific-isms': *Thinking about peace and war*, 109–30. However, whereas Ceadel incorporates the views of socialists, such as Brailsford, under the radical heading, this book separates out the democratic socialist strand. In this regard Ceadel underestimates the differences between the two groups, both in their overall analysis of international affairs and proposals for the avoidance of future wars. This difference was most evident in the groups' respective attitudes towards the League of Nations. See also Ward, *Red flag*, 127–8.

[24] In this regard there has been considerable debate about Hobson's ideas on international affairs and the extent to which he remained committed to Cobdenite principles. See chapter 2 n. 99 above.

[25] These four individuals were also the most active members of the UDC up to 1917: UDC minute book, UDC papers, DDC/1.

tors of the Cobdenite tradition.[26] This was reflected in their explanation of the war, their views on how it could be ended and their proposals for the peace.

The UDC radicals explained the war as a tragic diplomatic mistake for which the British Foreign Office, in particular, held a large responsibility.[27] Basing their analysis firmly on a belief in international free trade and an essential harmony of interests between nations and their peoples, they argued that it was Britain's behaviour in aligning herself too closely with France that had provoked Germany and increased her sense of insecurity.[28] The British Foreign Office, rather than attempting to negotiate with Germany, had pursued a balance-of-power policy which had led it into war. Germany's actions in July/August 1914, while reprehensible, were understandable. She was not solely to blame for the conflict.[29]

The UDC radicals blamed the failure of British diplomacy primarily on individual politicians and the British diplomatic system. In seeking to explain the war, their focus was on domestic policy rather than events anywhere else in Europe.[30] Grey was criticised, especially by MacDonald, for not pursuing a foreign policy more consistent with traditional liberal concerns.[31] However, more broadly, it was the foreign policy-making apparatus that was seen as the main problem. Too many decisions were taken in private, with no acknowledgement of the democratic will. This destabilised the international system by decreasing the general level of confidence among nations. It also represented a distortion of the popular will, which the UDC radicals, like Cobden, believed would overwhelmingly favour peace if it were fully involved in the diplomatic decision-making process. '[I]t will hardly be contested', suggested Morel in 1914, 'that if [diplomatic methods] ... are directed to secure *the real interests* of the people governed, they will be ... conducive to the preservation of harmonious relations between those peoples.'[32] Generally, this was as far as the UDC radicals were prepared to go in blaming systems and structures for the conflict. While they sometimes linked the distortion of the popular will to certain powerful groups in society, such as the landed interest, no systematic attempt was made to explain foreign policy as the product

---

[26] See Ceadel, *Thinking about peace and war*, 114–16.
[27] For Morel's own detailed explanation of his position in Aug. 1914 see Morel papers, F2/1/1–3.
[28] See, for example, Morel to Trevelyan and MacDonald, 22 Aug. 1924, ibid. F6/1.
[29] Russia was seen as particularly culpable. See, for example, Trevelyan to Morel, 9 Oct. 1914, ibid. F6/3
[30] See, for example, A. Ponsonby, *Parliament and foreign policy* (UDC pamphlet v, 1915), and E. D. Morel, *War and diplomacy* (UDC pamphlet xi, 1915). Morel's and most other UDC pamphlets can be found in UDC papers, DDC/5.
[31] See *Labour Leader*, 27 Aug. 1914.
[32] See speech to Manchester branch of UDC, 1914, Morel papers, F2/2/2 (emphasis in original). For MacDonald's views see J. R. MacDonald, *National defence: a study of militarism*, London 1917, 101–2.

of the capitalist system.[33] In this respect they differed from the democratic socialists.

Given that the UDC radicals explained the war as a diplomatic mistake, they remained firmly of the belief that it could be stopped by negotiation. Even after the conflict had started, there remained an essential harmony of interest in peace between the fighting nations, which if each nation showed good faith could be reached by reasoned discussion.[34]

The UDC radicals' explanation of the war led them to concentrate on two particular issues in the years up to 1917. First, they sought to keep the issues raised by pre-war diplomacy on the public's agenda. It was vital, they believed, to keep this debate alive, so as to show that Germany was not solely to blame for the conflict. Otherwise, a peace based on vengeance was more likely and this would inevitably lead to future wars.[35] This concern was also important with regard to the second issue upon which the UDC radicals concentrated: reform of the British diplomatic system. Foreign affairs had to be opened up to the influence of democracy. If this occurred disarmament would inevitably follow, given the pacific inclinations of the general population.

Most UDC radicals had strong associations with this demand going back a number of years, and throughout the conflict it was upon this issue that Morel and Ponsonby, in particular, concentrated.[36] However, there were differences. MacDonald, for example, while strongly of the belief that diplomacy needed to reflect the democratic will, was nevertheless doubtful that changes to diplomatic procedures would guarantee peace. In the pre-war period he had put his faith in the co-operation and growing strength of the international working-class movement to force governments to abide by the popular will. Even after the war had shown this faith to be misplaced, MacDonald continued to believe that ultimately it was only in the international socialist movement that real hope could be placed. His liberalism continued to be laced with a strong dose of working-class internationalism.

If there were some differences, however, over the exact form a more democratic diplomacy should take, there were very few differences between UDC radicals about the emerging idea of a League of Nations. They were generally extremely unenthusiastic and played little active part in the idea's detailed formulation. It was among the second ideological grouping, the Gladstonian liberals, that this idea really developed.

---

[33] See, for example, Morel to E. H. Drifill, 10 Aug. 1916, Morel papers, F/4. See also Ceadel, *Thinking about peace and war*, 114.

[34] See executive committee resolution, n.d, c.1916, UDC papers, DDC/1.

[35] See, for example, Ponsonby to Morel, 30 Aug. 1914, Morel papers, F6/1.

[36] See, for example, E. D. Morel, *The Union of Democratic Control* (UDC pamphlet xiii, 1915).

The Gladstonian liberals

This group was mainly made up of members of the Liberal party, such as Lord Bryce, L. T. Hobhouse, Willoughby (W. H.) Dickinson, Gilbert Murray and Aneurin Williams. They were the inheritors of the Gladstonian tradition on foreign affairs within the Liberal party and, as with the UDC radicals' adherence to Cobdenite radicalism, this inheritance was reflected in their explanation of the war, their views on how it could be ended and their proposals for the peace.

Unlike their Liberal colleagues who joined the UDC, the Gladstonian liberals, while initially sceptical about the war, were generally converted by Grey's speech to the House of Commons on 3 August 1914.[37] The Foreign Secretary convinced them that he had done everything he could to preserve peace but that these efforts had been frustrated by the Germans' determination on war. The war was a moral crusade against German militarism.[38] 'If we do not fight our best', warned Hobhouse, 'German militarism will sweep us away, and peace, Liberalism, and international freedom are abolished in Europe.'[39]

This belief made the Gladstonian liberals far more sceptical than the UDC radicals about the possibility of a negotiated peace. Bryce and Murray, for example, repeatedly resisted pressure from their Liberal colleagues to back the movement for more active peace diplomacy. They argued that there was little indication that Germany's view of the war had changed since August 1914 and that, for this reason, the allies had to win a military victory. Writing in 1916, Bryce emphasised that he wished 'no evil to the German people and [was] opposed to permanent hatreds', but nevertheless believed 'that for their sake and the world's sake it is necessary that the military caste in Germany should be distinctly defeated and that the people should know it'.[40] This would be made harder if a popular momentum built up for a negotiated peace.

Nevertheless, despite the Gladstonian liberals' general support for Grey's pre-war diplomacy, they still had major concerns about the way in which the pre-war international system had been managed. Indeed, they argued that it was barely managed at all and that this was the major issue that needed to be addressed if future wars were to be prevented.[41] Thus, while interna-

[37] See Clarke, *Liberals*, 166.
[38] Ibid. 169–70. Gilbert Murray was later to write a book defending Grey's pre-war diplomacy: *The foreign policy of Edward Grey*, Oxford 1915.
[39] Clarke, *Liberals*, 174.
[40] Quoted in Robbins, *Abolition*, 107. See also Clarke, *Liberals*, 172.
[41] As Ceadel suggests, 'The shock of the First world war almost instantaneously converted [liberal pacific-ists] to the view that a confederal institution was needed for the management of international relations': *Thinking about peace and war*, 111. See also G. W. Egerton, *Great Britain and the creation of the League of Nations: strategy, politics and international organisation, 1914–19*, London 1978, 19.

tional free trade was still regarded as sacrosanct, the international system was more prone to instability than pure radicals suggested. The person who took the initiative in encouraging greater thought on this problem was Golds-worthy Lowes Dickinson, one of the early members of the UDC. However, as Keith Robbins suggests, he joined the organisation 'reluctantly' and from the very start began to investigate ideas that were different from those which concerned most of the UDC radicals.[42] In this regard, he formed privately a small discussion group to draw up plans for a more permanent interna-tional organisation to prevent war. This group included Lord Bryce, W. H. Dickinson, Graham Wallas, E. R. Cross, Hobson, Angell and Ponsonby and eventually became known as the Bryce Group, after its most well-known and respected member. It met during late 1914 and early 1915 and by spring of the latter year had drawn up a proposal for a new international organisation upon which the majority of the group could agree, although, significantly, Ponsonby was a dissenter.[43] This plan, important because it was to provide the basic framework for most of the proposals made during the war, had five main features: a permanent court of arbitration for justiciable disputes; compulsory arbitration to settle disputes; a council of conciliation to be established to settle non-justiciable disputes; a moratorium on the declara-tion of war of twelve months; and 'forcible sanctions' to uphold the rules and decisions of the league.[44]

These ideas were deliberately cautious. As Lord Bryce was later to explain, the group's intention was to be as practical and realistic as possible. The proposal was thus not 'utopian' but attempted to build on those interna-tional structures and practices, such as the permanent court of arbitration in Amsterdam, which were already in place. The aim was to further develop such systems and make their use common practice in international affairs. As Bryce accepted, the plan was not concerned with the 'deep underlying causes of war'. These could 'only be gradually dissipated by the spread of intelli-gence, knowledge and goodwill'. Rather, it sought 'to provide a machinery by and through which the volume of international opinion which favours peace may be enabled to express itself, and brings its pressure to bear upon any nation in which there may [be] ... a readiness to embark on war'.[45]

Emphasis on the role of public opinion in preventing war reflected the continued influence within the Bryce Group of a Cobdenite belief in an essential harmony of interests between peoples. Hobson, in particular, stressed

[42] Robbins, *Abolition*, 49. Soon after the beginning of the war, Lowes Dickinson sent Morel an undated memorandum outlining his early ideas for a new international body. Morel was unenthusiastic. The UDC radicals' lack of interest probably explains Lowes Dickinson decision to sound out a broader range of opinion to develop the league idea. See Morel to Trevelyan, 6 Nov. 1914, Morel papers, F6/4, F6/3.
[43] See Wallas diary, Graham Wallas papers, BLPES, Box 40, 5/1/55, entries for 30 Sept., 13 Nov., 1, 22 Dec. 1914; 5 Jan., 1 Feb. 1915.
[44] James Bryce and others, *Proposals for the prevention of future wars*, London 1917
[45] Ibid. 12.

the public's role in the operation of the league.[46] He insisted that the new body should not be dominated by foreign ministers but be representative of the wider international community. Lowes Dickinson was more sceptical.[47] This issue was to become an important area of contention about the league idea within progressive circles. For UDC radicals it was a touchstone: the more the proposed league became dominated by 'governments', the less they were prepared to support it. As the Bryce Group's ideas developed over the following two years, however, the role of politicians and diplomats steadily began to increase.

The other main area of debate within the group was military sanctions. Lowes Dickinson had always envisaged that the league would have a military component, and this was ultimately reflected in the group's proposals, despite Ponsonby's strong disagreement.[48] It was agreed that the league would be 'a farce' if this power was not available: 'there would be no security against aggressive States'.[49] Thus, 'concerted measures, economic and forcible' were proposed against any member power that acted outside the rules of the league.[50] Unequivocal commitment to collective military security was to remain a central feature of the Gladstonian liberals' approach.

Early in 1915 the Bryce Group's plan was privately circulated to a broad range of politicians and intellectuals, including the Fabians, who had already begun to investigate similar ideas for themselves. Leonard Woolf, a former colonial administrator and a member of the Fabian Research department, had at the request of the Webbs produced a plan in April 1915 which was similar in many respects to the proposals of the Bryce Group.[51] It envisaged an international high court, a court of conciliation, a moratorium on declarations of war and a measure of collective security.[52] The main area of difference was over the role of governments. Whereas the Bryce Group had been reluctant to propose a scheme dominated by politicians and diplomats, the Fabians believed that it was unrealistic to propose any other type of arrangement.[53] Indeed, the plan they recommended gave predominant influence to

---

[46] See Clarke, *Liberals*, 179.

[47] Ibid. 23.

[48] Memorandum to Morel, n.d., c.1915, Morel papers, F6/4.

[49] Quoted in Robbins, *Abolition*, 53

[50] Bryce, *Proposals*, 16.

[51] Sidney Webb to Leonard Woolf, 21 Jan. 1915, Leonard Woolf papers, University of Sussex Library, IF4.

[52] L. Woolf, *International government*, London 1916. However, Woolf's proposal stressed to a greater extent than the Bryce Group the importance of the development of international law. For this reason, he also proposed the formation of an international legislature: *The framework of a lasting peace*, London 1917.

[53] See Beatrice Webb to Woolf, 17 Apr. 1915, and Sidney Webb to Woolf, 25 May 1915, Woolf papers, IE2, IF4.

the governments of the great powers.[54] On the basis of the ideas formulated by the Bryce Group and the Fabians, the League of Nations Society (LNS) was formed in May 1915 to press the case for a new international body.

The Fabians thus undoubtedly played an important role in the development of the Gladstonian liberals' attitude to the League. However, despite this period of co-operation, as the conflict continued the Fabians became increasingly interested in more ambitious schemes of international government; for this reason, they are better categorised as part of the democratic socialist ideological grouping.

The LNS gradually moved closer, as the war continued, to the mainstream of the Liberal party. It deliberately set out to influence respectable Liberal opinion and, for this reason, emphasised the moderate nature of its proposals and its distance from the UDC and the peace by negotiations group.[55] When the society held its first public meeting in May 1917, it was attended by Robert Cecil, J. C. Smuts and the archbishop of Canterbury.[56] Contacts were already being made with even more centrist Liberals close to Lloyd George, such as David Davies who had been instrumental in the formation of a rival organisation, the League of Free Nations Society, which, while proposing a similar type of body to the LNS, also argued that any league should in the first instance only be made up of the wartime allies. Germany would only be admitted after proving that she could be trusted. Despite this difference of opinion, however, it was clear to members of both organisations that their effectiveness in lobbying for a league of nations would be enhanced if they co-operated and, after lengthy negotiations, a compromise was agreed which finally allowed in 1918 a union between the two organisations in the League of Nations Union (LNU).[57] It was this body which, in the post-war period, was to take forward and develop the ideological approach of the Gladstonian liberals. It continued to argue for what it regarded as a practical and realistic league, one that was dominated by the great powers and included an explicit military component.[58]

It was the respective approaches to the league idea of the individuals associated with the UDC radicals and the Gladstonian liberals that constitutes the essential cleavage between them. Of the UDC radicals, Morel and Trevelyan took little interest in thinking about a new international structure and MacDonald and Snowden were explicitly hostile. MacDonald, in particular, was extremely doubtful whether an armed supranational structure

---

[54] There would be a weighted voting system in the council to ensure that the eight great powers (Austria, Britain, France, Germany, Italy, Japan, Russia and the USA) could not be out-voted by the smaller powers.

[55] See, for example, Willoughby H. Dickinson to James Bryce, 16 May 1917, James Bryce papers, Bodl. Lib.

[56] See Winkler, *League of Nations movement*, 55.

[57] See D. S. Birn, *The League of Nations Union, 1918–1945*, Oxford 1981.

[58] See, for example, G. Murray, *The League and its guarantees*, London 1920, and Birn, *League of Nations Union*, 41–2.

could prevent future wars. He dismissed the idea as 'quackery': it represented a concession to the view that armaments could preserve peace. He wrote of the league in 1916 that 'We cannot accept with such an amount of satisfaction as would justify us in supporting it, a proposal which employed armies to keep the peace and believes that force can be safely controlled.'[59] This was a belief to which MacDonald was to remain remarkably consistent throughout his political career. Wars could only be prevented, he believed, by disarmament and this would not occur unless diplomacy accurately reflected the democratic desire for peace.[60] New structures superimposed on the existing political system would not work. Rather what was required was 'the putting in its place a system based on democratic control [and] open diplomacy'.[61] If a league was introduced it would only be positive to the extent that it assisted in the achievement of this goal. MacDonald, however, feared that it would do little. 'In reality', he warned, 'this League will be in the hands of the men who have controlled us hitherto.'[62]

Of the UDC radicals, therefore, it was only Ponsonby who played any part in the formulation of the league idea. However, even he quickly became disillusioned. He only ever had a limited conception of a league, believing that it should build only incrementally on existing international structures and inter-governmental practices. He was suspicious even of the limited supranational features proposed by his colleagues in the Bryce Group.[63] However, it was the concept of collective military security that most turned him against the idea. 'I am quite sure', he later stated, 'that no international arrangement ought to be made which is based on a recognition of force as an instrument between nations.'[64] From an early stage in the Bryce Group's deliberations, he had decided that their ideas were not for him.[65]

However, senior members of the Labour party and in the trade unions were much more enthusiastic. Indeed there was a significant body of opinion in the labour movement which was sympathetic to Gladstonian liberalism and its backing of the war as a moral crusade against German militarism.[66] Of these, the most important figure was Henderson. Unlike many in the party, he kept a close eye on ideological developments, particularly from the end of 1916, and made clear where his sympathies lay. Thus, in response to

[59] *Labour Leader*, 14 Dec. 1916. See also Marquand, *Ramsay MacDonald*, 203–4. For Snowden's views on the League see *Labour Leader*, 27 June, 29 Aug., 17 Oct. and 5 Dec. 1918.
[60] See MacDonald, *National defence*, 101–2.
[61] See, for example, *Labour Leader*, 14 Dec. 1916 and 9 Jan. 1919. See also Marquand, *Ramsay MacDonald*, 203–4, and Taylor, *Troublemakers*, 143–4.
[62] *Labour Leader*, 14 Dec. 1916.
[63] Ponsonby to Dickinson, n.d. *c.* 1915, Willoughby H. Dickinson papers, Bodl. Lib., MS402. See also *War and Peace* (Jan. 1917).
[64] *War and Peace* (Jan. 1917).
[65] See R. Jones, *Arthur Ponsonby*, London 1989, 164.
[66] See chapters 2, 3 above.

President Wilson's early diplomatic interventions in the war in December 1916, he welcomed efforts 'to bring about a council of the league of nations … that would lay down the principles' of such an idea.[67] It was mainly at his instigation that at the Labour conference in 1917 a resolution was passed supporting the establishment of such a body, which significantly included a commitment to collective security.[68] Of all the ideas that had emerged during the war, as Henderson conceded at the public launch of the LNS in May 1917, 'none appealed to him with greater force than the proposal for a League of Nations to enforce peace'.[69] Clynes, Thomas and Shaw were also quick to associate themselves with the emerging movement and support was also evident in the broader labour movement.[70]

The democratic socialists

The democratic socialists included Fabians such as Webb and Woolf, ILP socialists, such as Brailsford, and eventually some advanced liberals, such as Charles Roden (C. R.) Buxton. Apart from its ideological differences with the UDC radicals and Gladstonian liberals, this grouping was also different in that it was not associated up to 1918 with any particular organisation.[71] Whereas the UDC radicals were most closely associated with the UDC, and the Gladstonian liberals had particular connections with the Bryce Group and the emerging league of nations movement, individual democratic social-ists figured in a variety of organisations. Moreover, even ideologically, those included in this group were more heterogeneous than the other groups, particularly in the early part of the war. Their combination into a group is justified more on the basis of their views on how the post-war world should be organised than their views about the causes of the war and the pros-pects for a negotiated peace. In this regard, the group was united by a belief that supranational economic intervention would be required to ensure the stability of the post-war international system.

The existence of an ideologically distinct democratic socialist approach to foreign affairs had been evident before the war, particularly in the work of Brailsford. His *War of steel and gold* had used Marxist and Hobsonian concep-tions of capitalist imperialism to analyse international affairs and concluded

[67] Quoted in Wrigley, *Arthur Henderson*, 109. See also R. McKibbin, 'Arthur Henderson as Labour leader', *IRSH* xxiii (1978), 79–101.
[68] *Report* (1917), 134. The motion was recommended by a number of trade unionists. It recommended that members should 'cooperate to restrain by any means possible any Government or nation' which acted in violation of international law.
[69] *The Times*, 21 May 1917.
[70] See chapter 5 below. On support for the league idea in the broader labour movement see, for example, *Railway Review*, 5 Jan. 1917, MRC, MS 127/NU/4/1/5.
[71] In 1918 it was this group that was to provide most of the members for the new Labour Party ACIQ: see chapter 5 below.

that international tensions and rivalries could not simply be explained as a failure of diplomacy, but were at least partly the result of deep-seated problems within the international structure of capitalism.[72] Absolute reliance could not, therefore be placed on the shared benefits of free trade as a guarantor of peace. This substantial step away from liberal internationalism was taken further during the war and was what most significantly distinguished the democratic socialist approach from the liberal-based strands.

It was on this basis that after August 1914 Brailsford analysed the causes of the war and developed his ideas about the prevention of future conflicts. On the causes of the war, he was closer to the UDC radicals than to the Gladstonian liberals. Germany was not solely responsible for the war: the actions of Russia in 1914, and the failure since 1900 of the other powers to accede to Germany's legitimate claims, had caused her to take offensive action. German militarism could not thus be defeated by a fight-to-the-finish because this would not remove the underlying causes of the conflict.[73]

With regard to underlying causes, however, Brailsford's analysis differed from that of the UDC radicals. Whereas they retained their Cobdenite faith in free trade and a harmony of interests, and thus blamed domestic diplomatic failings for the conflict, Brailsford was far less sanguine about the nature of international relations under capitalism. In fact, Germany and Britain's interests clashed, or, at least, this was how the German government perceived the situation. While Britain was a contented power with ready access to imperial markets and investment opportunities, Germany was a growing power, whose access to such markets was reliant, given the British empire and navy, on the goodwill of another.[74] Britain's failure to appreciate this situation and to make adequate efforts to reassure Germany had greatly exacerbated the tensions created by her hegemonic position.

However, while more enlightened British diplomacy would have eased tensions prior to 1914 the outbreak of war had shown that much more than a reform of domestic diplomatic policy-making was required to prevent future conflict. The intensity of the imperial rivalries between the powers before the war had been greater, Brailsford conceded, than even he had appreciated. Thus, while he agreed with the Gladstonian liberals that future wars could only be prevented if there was supranational management of international relations, he argued that the powers of a new international body would have to be much greater than they proposed if the source, rather than the symptoms, of conflict were to be eradicated.[75] Given that modern conflicts were caused by economic rivalries, future wars could only be prevented by

---

[72] See chapters 1, 3 above.

[73] See H. Brailsford, *Origins of the Great War* (UDC pamphlet iv, 1914), and *Belgium and the 'scrap of paper'* (ILP Labour and War pamphlet x, 1915).

[74] Idem, *A League of Nations*, 7–8, 217–24.

[75] For his views on the Bryce Group's plan see H. N. Brailsford to Leonard Courtney, n.d. *c.* Sept. 1917, Leonard Courtney papers, Bodl. Lib.

a 'world-state' empowered to internationalise the export of capital, grant colonial concessions and equitably distribute food and raw materials.[76]

The Webbs were not attracted to Brailsford's theoretical analysis of the war in 1914. As confirmed empiricists, they were more comfortable explaining the conflict as the result of German militarism. Their own proposal for a league of nations was far more limited and they had initially co-operated with the Gladstonian liberals.[77] Moreover, for much of the war, Brailsford's ideas about supranational government appeared hopelessly utopian.

However, developments in the allies' economic management of the conflict, particularly after 1917, considerably changed perceptions about the possible scope and potential of international government in the post-war world. [78] A number of inter-allied councils, such as the *Commission Internationale de Ravitaillement* and the Maritime Transport Council, were formed to co-ordinate the purchase of a wide range of commodities and decide on trading priorities in the use of shipping. By the end of the war, these were 'tending to become a general economic council for the Allies'.[79]

To many liberals these developments were worrying and unwelcome. Hobson, for example, feared that they indicated a move by the allies towards a post-war world in which Germany and her allies would be systematically excluded from world markets, and, on this basis, he persuaded the UDC to add a fifth principle to its manifesto, demanding the post-war maintenance of free trade.[80] There is little doubt that with respect to many of those supportive of the allied schemes Hobson was right to be suspicious of their motivations. To the Fabians, however, what these developments seemed to suggest was that the increased openness, evident among governing elites during the war, towards statist solutions to domestic social and economic problems, was also true in respect of their attitude towards international affairs. There was certainly evidence that this was the case: in both France and Britain, there were some politicians and government officials who believed that the inter-allied bodies 'contained elements of a new kind of economic internationalism'.[81]

---

[76] Brailsford, *War of steel and gold*, and 'The organization of peace', in C. R. Buxton (ed.), *Towards a lasting settlement*, London 1917, 151–73. There was broader, if vague support in the ILP for this type of policy. See, for example, *ILP report of the annual conference* (1915), 9, and (1919), 65.

[77] See chapter 2 above.

[78] Orde, *British policy*, 7.

[79] Ibid. 18. See also J. A. Salter, *Allied shipping control: an experiment in international administration*, Oxford 1921.

[80] See UDC papers, DDC/1/4.

[81] Orde, *British policy*, 9, 19. See also Dickinson memorandum, Dec. 1917, Willoughby Dickinson papers, MS403; R. W. D. Boyce, *British capitalism at the crossroads, 1919–1932: a study in politics, economics and international relations*, Cambridge 1987, 1–2; Trentmann, 'The strange death of free trade', 235–41; and P. Yearwood, '"On safe and right lines": the Lloyd George coalition and the origins of the League Nations, 1916–1918', *HJ* xxxii (1989), 131–55. The Fabians were also interested in these ideas because of their connec-

The Fabians' interest in these developments was confirmed by a series of articles on a league of nations that appeared in the *New Statesman* at the beginning of 1918. Written anonymously, they warned that if insufficient emphasis was given to the League's 'positive' role as a regulator of the world economy, as opposed to its 'negative' role as a body to prevent war, it would fail even to fulfil the latter function. This was because, the writer claimed, the existing conflict was due in 'a very large part' to imperial economic rivalry. Even though it was unlikely that the possession of colonies boosted economic performance, the belief that it did remained a primary influence in European diplomacy. While a 'competitive and exclusive policy with regard to overseas possessions holds sway', it was suggested, 'there can be no peace in the world'. Britain, despite its claims to be the champion of free trade, was not immune to criticism. Given the strength of her position as the possessor of the largest empire, she could not necessarily expect nations in a less favourable position to rely on her guarantees of free access. The only sure way to 'make impossible the competition for exclusive economic privileges' was for regulation by a 'supranational authority' of the economic relations of the powers in Asia and Africa. To fulfil this function, a league of nations would not only be required to act as a guarantor of free trade, but also to ensure the 'equitable allocation of tropical raw materials ... to all industrial nations'.[82]

By 1918 the Webbs were fully committed to these ideas. It was essential, Sidney argued, for example, that Labour's proposals for a league of nations were of a 'different nature' from those made by the Liberal-dominated groups.[83] International control of raw materials and food, Beatrice told Lowes Dickinson in July 1918, was 'the policy emerging as an alternative to free trade or protection'.[84] The aim was thus not the international control of all trade, but the creation of an international structure capable of supporting a stable trading system.

Democratic socialists warned that, while they shared the belief of UDC radicals and Gladstonian liberals that free trade was an essential requirement for economic reconstruction, trade would not restart automatically following the economic dislocation of the war. Many nations would be short of vital resources and would encounter problems with their currencies.[85] Moreover,

---

tion to Labour's domestic reform agenda: see, for example, 'Procedure for international labour conference', LPA, LSI 3/5/1; and Horne, *Labour at war*, 302–49.

[82] The general increase in interest in a supranational economic authority can also be gauged by the evolution of Norman Angell's thinking during the war. See, for example, his *The economic functions of the League*, London 1920.

[83] 'Procedure for international labour conference', LPA, LSI 5/3/1.

[84] Lowes Dickinson to Woolf, 4 July 1918, Woolf papers. See also 'Procedure for international labour conference', LPA, LSI 5/3/1.

[85] These ideas were later worked through by democratic socialists in Labour's ACIQ (see chapter 5 below). See, for example, 'Memorandum on international labour legislation and the economic structure of the League of Nations' and 'Memorandum on interna-

even once conditions conducive to trade had been re-established, supranational economic intervention would have to continue. Otherwise, Europe would 'drift again into the rivalries of capitalism-Imperialism-Protectionism which poisoned international relations between 1890 and 1914'.[86] In contrast to UDC radicals, therefore, democratic socialists believed that giving states a formal guarantee of their security, based on something more solid than the goodwill of other powers, was essential for future prospects of peace. However, unlike Gladstonian liberals, they did not believe a collective military security pact was sufficient. Rather, it was essential that as part of its role in settling differences and developing common interests between nations, the League of Nations should be empowered to intervene in economic affairs. By guaranteeing access to food and vital resources to all nations, the supranational authority would, they believed, remove from the international scene the main and most important source of contention between nations.

However, while some socialists moved towards an acceptance of greater international government during the war, others in the ILP responded to the conflict by emphasising their absolutist commitment to pacifism.

The ILP pacifists

Members of the ILP were represented within both the UDC radicals (for example MacDonald and Snowden) and the democratic socialists (for example Brailsford). However, there was within the ILP another important group which held different views from those of their colleagues. In this regard, the ILP was every bit as ideologically heterogeneous as the UDC. The leading members of this grouping, the ILP pacifists, were Clifford Allen, Bruce Glasier, Fenner Brockway, Lansbury, J. H. Hudson and Alfred Salter.

The defining characteristic of this group was its attitude towards war *per se*. Its members argued for a policy of resistance to the conflict based on a rejection of the instrument of war. They were pacifists in the traditional sense,[87] motivated by socialist and/or Christian ideological convictions. Salter, a Bermondsey doctor, who led the campaign for a repudiation of all wars by the ILP, did so from an avowedly Christian pacifist position.[88] Allen, on the other hand, was a socialist pacifist. 'I am a socialist', he declared in 1916. 'I believe in co-operation and not competition to the death between individuals and nations. I believe in the inherent worth and sanctity of every

tional labour legislation and the economic structure of the League of Nations', 1918, ACIQ memoranda, LPA. See also L. Woolf, *International economic policy*, London 1920, which was based on an advisory committee memorandum.
86 Woolf, *International economic policy*.
87 See Ceadel, *Thinking about peace and war*, 5–6.
88 See Robbins, *Abolition*, 80.

human personality irrespective of the nation to which a man belongs.'[89] Glasier adopted a similar approach: 'the only sound international position ... in the event of war ... is to refuse to take up arms, whatever the alleged grounds of the war'.[90]

The mixture of ethical or Christian socialism, ardent internationalism and instinctive anti-capitalism led its proponents to adopt a more explicit and unequivocal opposition to the war than either the UDC radicals or the democratic socialists. The issue upon which this opposition became manifest was compulsory military service, which would affect Allen and Brockway directly as they were young enough to be called up if conscription were introduced. Consequently, at the end of 1914, they set up the No Conscription Fellowship (NCF) to campaign against compulsion and to resist it if the campaign failed.[91]

In contrast, the UDC radicals and democratic socialists, while opposed to conscription, were much more cautious about the appropriate response. Morel, for example, warned against 'resistance ... to what has become the law of the land'. He feared that the issue would distract from the UDC's main task and, in this respect, argued that the controversy over its introduction should be used 'to force the main issue – what is the object and aim of the war?'[92]

The ILP pacifists' more explicit opposition to the war was also evident in their support, earlier than any other of the groupings, for a 'stop-the-war' campaign. They began to put pressure on the ILP leadership to campaign for peace even before the end of 1914. As editors, respectively, of the *Socialist Review* and the *Labour Leader*, Glasier and Brockway urged concerted international working-class action to bring a halt to the war. By January 1915 a 'Common Peace Programme' had been drawn up.[93] At the 1916 ILP conference the pacifists succeeded (having marginally failed the previous year) in gaining acceptance of a motion committing the party to reject all wars 'whatever their ostensible object ... even if it was nominally of a defensive character'.[94]

---

[89] A. Marwick, *Clifford Allen: the open conspirator*, Edinburgh 1964, 21. See also C. Allen, *Is Germany right and Britain wrong?*, London c.1915.

[90] *Socialist Review* (Mar. 1915). On Lansbury's pacifism see J. Schneer, *George Lansbury*, Manchester 1990, 130–95.

[91] See *Labour Leader*, 3 Dec. 1914. The NCF's statement of purpose described it as 'an organisation of men likely to be called upon to undertake military service, who will refuse for conscientious motives to bear arms, because they consider human life to be sacred, and cannot, therefore, assume the responsibility of inflicting death': quoted in Robbins, *Abolition*, 78.

[92] Morel memorandum, 6 June 1915, Morel papers, F6/4. For MacDonald's views see *Labour Leader* (1914)

[93] *Labour Leader* (Jan. 1915).

[94] *ILP Report* (1916), 53–7. For the previous year's debate see *ILP Report* (1915), 109–12, and, for following year, *ILP Report* (1917), 52–63. MacDonald and Snowden opposed the pacifist motions.

However, of all the groups identified, the ILP pacifists were to be the least influential on the development of Labour's foreign policy. They were an important presence during the war, but their success in converting Labour to any of their views was virtually non-existent.

Indeed, the Labour party showed little detailed interest before 1917 in the debates about international affairs. The association with the peace-by-negotiations movement and/or pacifism of many of the individuals involved was one reason for this. However, even discussions about a league of nations among those, such as the Fabians, who made clear their support for the military defeat of Germany, did not fully engage Labour's interest initially. While there was certainly support for this type of approach within the party, winning the war and defending, so far as was possible, Labour's pre-war gains remained the party's priority.

It was the end of 1917 before Labour finally decided to alter its policy on the war and fully engage with the wartime ideological debates. The circumstances under which this occurred and the nature of Labour's change of policy are the subject of the next chapter.

5

The Politics of the 1917 Memorandum on War Aims

The year 1917 was one of profound change. The first two-and-a-half years of the war had settled into a depressingly familiar pattern. The predictability of the stalemate on the Western Front had been mirrored by the stability of the diplomatic situation and the British home front. Any turbulence that had occurred was peripheral in that it had not threatened the *status quo* established by the end of November 1914.[1]

In contrast, in 1917, while the military situation remained static, diplomatic activity and the situation in Britain became dramatically more fluid. Much of the diplomatic fluidity was inextricably linked to international events, particularly the two revolutions in Russia,[2] while on the home front Britain witnessed the most serious industrial disruption and social discontent of the war period. Resentment grew about conscription, the increased 'dilution' of skilled labour with unskilled workers, and the worsening supply of basic provisions. All of these problems demanded a response from British politicians. They were operating in a party system already made highly fragile by the strains of the war. The prospects for fundamental change seemed immense.

However, despite predictions to the contrary, it was the political situation, rather than the social system or the government's military policy, which was forced to adapt to the pressures unleashed, encouraged or exacerbated by the developments of 1917. At the centre of these changes was the Labour party. After three years, in which its backing for the war had been almost entirely uncritical, the party appeared in August 1917 to dramatically change course. The party's leading figure in the War Cabinet, Arthur Henderson, resigned and a few days later a specially-convened conference agreed an independent set of war aims. Even more controversially, the party

---

[1] Diplomatic initiatives, particularly by President Wilson, came to nothing and labour disputes and arguments between the coalition partners were managed successfully without threat to the continued prosecution of the war.

[2] American intervention in the war in April and the first firm indication that one of the main belligerents, Austria, was investigating the efficacy of a diplomatic initiative were also important: J. Turner, *British politics and the Great War: coalition and conflict, 1915–1918*, New Haven–London 1992; V. Rothwell, *British war aims and peace diplomacy, 1914–1918*, Oxford 1971; F. S. Northedge, *The troubled giant: Britain among the great powers, 1916–39*, London 1966.

also agreed, with reservations, that Labour representatives should attend a conference of allied and enemy socialists, which neutral socialist groups were trying to arrange to meet in Stockholm. Critics of the war, such as UDC members, were delighted. The Labour party, it seemed, was finally moving in their direction. A few months later the party adopted for the first time an avowedly socialist constitution. Labour, it seemed, had become a more left-wing and independent party than the one that had entered the war.

But how dramatic was Labour's policy change on the war and foreign policy in 1917? Did it amount to a major turning-point in the party's attitude or was the change more limited? Most existing accounts have favoured the former view.[3] Dan Keohane, for example, summarises the prevailing interpretation: 'Labour's Memorandum on War Aims ... reflected the approach of the UDC. It also meant that the foreign policy ideas of the anti-war group ... were to dominate the post-war Labour Party.'[4] Various explanations for this change have been provided, but for all commentators the influence of broader international and domestic developments during 1917 has been regarded as a vital explanatory factor. In this regard, the Russian Revolution, and its effect on labour and socialist opinion throughout Europe, in combination with the growing distrust in Britain of the Lloyd George coalition, have been seen as particularly important. Thus Marvin Swartz, for example, argues that events combined to create an atmosphere where a 'Labour majority' could be found 'receptive to the foreign policy ideas of the [UDC]'.[5] This situation was brought to a head by the 'Stockholm controversy', the cause of Henderson's resignation, which involved the wartime Labour leader being refused permission by the War Cabinet to attend the meeting of international socialists in the Swedish capital. Swartz stresses the role of the UDC in taking advantage of these circumstances gradually to convert a more sympathetic Labour party to its view of the war.

Others have focused more on Henderson's role and particularly his apparent 'conversion' to an anti-war stance. Marquand, amongst others, accepts Lloyd George's view that after his visit to Russia, as a government emissary, in the summer of 1917, the wartime Labour leader caught 'revolutionary malaria' which caused him to change his view of the war. On this basis he decided to support the Stockholm conference, having previously opposed it and 'appeared to have been converted to the policy of MacDonald and the UDC'.[6] He then set about converting Labour to this view.

[3] For example, Taylor, *Troublemakers*; Cline, *Recruits*; and Spear, 'The case of E. D. Morel'.
[4] Keohane, 'Labour's international policy', 366. Of recent accounts only Ward has taken issue with this interpretation: *Red flag*, 145–6.
[5] Swartz, *Union of Democratic Control*, 147. See also chapter 1 n. 52 above.
[6] Marquand, *Ramsay MacDonald*, 220. See also Horne, *Labour at war*, 308.

Few historians of Labour's foreign policy change in 1917 have linked developments in this area with the party's constitutional reform.[7] Thus, interpretations of the latter, which have suggested that Labour's adoption of a socialist constitution in 1918 had less to do with ideology than with political strategy, have not generally been influential.[8] Only historians of Labour's constitutional change have made any explicit connections of this sort, albeit of a superficial kind. Thus Jay Winter suggests that, as part of the process that led to the constitutional reform, Labour also constructed a 'socialist' foreign policy.[9] He agrees that Henderson's trip to Russia was a catalyst for his subsequent actions, but rejects the view that he experienced an ideological conversion in Petrograd. Rather, it was Henderson's view of the appropriate political role of the Labour party that changed. After two years of 'subservience' to the War Cabinet, he became convinced that Labour had not only to adopt a more independent stance, but also had to be re-launched as a moderate socialist party, with respect to both domestic and foreign policy. This was essential if Labour was to act as a bulwark against the type of revolutionary upheaval which Henderson had experienced – and been appalled by – in Russia. On his return to Britain, therefore, the Labour leader was determined on a course that would force a break with the War Cabinet, as a prelude to the re-launch of the Labour party.

In fact, while Labour's policy change on the war at this time was significant, it did not mark a major ideological turning point with respect to the party's approach to foreign affairs: Labour certainly did not accept the views of the UDC at this time, nor construct a 'socialist' foreign policy. The events of 1917 were as much about politics as ideology. They were inextricably linked with the party's constitutional change. Labour's more independent stance on the war was mainly constructed with the aim of bringing together a party that seemed increasingly to be on the verge of splitting. In this process, Henderson's role was undoubtedly crucial, but his actions have been substantially misunderstood.

The labour alliance in crisis

Recognition of the extent of Labour's split during the war and the potential for a more permanent fracture during 1917 is essential if the party's development in that year is to be fully understood. Historians have tended to

---

[7] Vickers links Henderson's resignation to subsequent developments in Labour politics and organisation but does not elaborate: *Labour and the world*, 66–7.

[8] See, for example, McKibbin, *Evolution of the Labour party*.

[9] J. M. Winter, 'Arthur Henderson, the Russian Revolution and the reconstruction of the Labour party', *HJ* xv (1972), 753–73. Other than an acceptance of the Stockholm conference, Winter does not explain what he means by 'socialist' with respect to foreign policy.

give only cursory explanations for the Labour party's emergence at the end of the war as a generally united movement.[10] This is despite the fact that the depth and intensity of the differences in the party during the war were considerably larger than those within the Liberal party.[11] Not only was the minority opposed to the leadership's policy much greater, but the line of division followed in general terms an existing cleavage, between the unions and the ILP.[12]

At the beginning of 1917 the organisational manifestations of this split were becoming pronounced. While Ramsay MacDonald and the ILP were cementing the links of those opposed to the leadership in the United Socialist Council (USC), Henderson and the pro-war Labourites were committing themselves to a Tory-dominated government.[13] The Labour party's Manchester conference in January 1917 emphasised the divisive potential of this process. The Labour leadership's climb-down over conscription, in the face of government pressure, and decision at the end of 1916 to enter the Lloyd George coalition with the old class enemy, had created considerable unease among the party's rank-and-file. This encouraged critics of the war.[14] None the less most of the leaders of the major unions remained firm in support of the war and lined up their block votes behind the decisions taken by the Labour leadership: peace resolutions proposed by the ILP and BSP were resoundingly defeated and entry into the Lloyd George coalition was ratified.[15]

The easy passage of these resolutions showed that, while there was concern among some trade unionists about conscription[16] and the new coalition, there was no chance that this would lead to increased support among

[10] See, for example, C. F. Brand, *The British Labour party*, Stanford 1974; Howell, *MacDonald's party*, 22; Harrison, 'The War Emergency National Workers Committee'; and, more recently, Worley, *Labour inside the gate*, 7. However the extent of Labour's split is recognised by Vickers, *Labour party and the world*, 59–60.

[11] The most recent detailed study of politics in this period concludes that the split in the Liberal party was largely non-ideological: Turner, *British politics*.

[12] As McKibbin suggests, while it is not entirely accurate to describe the split in the Labour movement in this period as simply between the ILP and the unions, it is a reasonable generalisation: *Evolution of the Labour party*, 90. See also Howell, *MacDonald's party*.

[13] The United Socialist Council was formed by an agreement between the ILP and the British Socialist Party (BSP) in October 1916: *ILP report* (1917), 22–5; Marquand, *Ramsay MacDonald*, 200. For the Webbs's view of the USC see Sidney Webb to Beatrice Webb, 2 Nov. 1917, Passfield papers, BLPES, II3.

[14] NEC minutes, 27 April 1917, LPA; and PCTUC minutes, 27 Apr. 1917. Henderson received a hostile reception, with some delegates calling for his resignation from the War Cabinet: *Report* (1917), 86–8. See also Sidney Webb to Beatrice Webb, 24 Jan. 1917, Passfield papers, II3, and Beatrice Webb diary, ibid. I, unpublished entry for 3 Jan. 1917.

[15] See *Report* (1917), 125–9.

[16] See, for example, National Union of Railwaymen executive committee resolutions, MRC, MS 127/NU/1/3/3.

union bosses for the ILP's position.[17] This does not mean, however, that the unions were entirely united behind an uncritically patriotic position. There is certainly evidence of growing demands within some sections of the labour movement during the course of the war for the development of a more assertive stance on the war's purpose. This was the out-growth of the moderate internationalism evident within the trade unions before the war began. Thus, for example, the BSIMF began pressing the PCTUC from November 1915 for preliminary action in preparation for an eventual settlement of the war. In the face of a 'procrastinating' response, it called a year later for contact to be made with allied, and even neutral, trade unions in order to decide 'the main principles which should be recognised in the terms of settlement'.[18] The trade unions, it was hoped, could develop and lead 'democratic' opinion on the basis of a moderate internationalist approach.[19] However, the efforts of the BSIMF did not mean that it supported the line taken by opponents of the war. Rather, its intention was to 'control' 'pro-Germans' in the Labour party and prevent them from causing 'problems'.[20] Indeed, if anything, the hostility felt towards the ILP had increased during 1916. The ILP had become more outspoken in support of a peace by negotiation since the previous Labour conference, and the setting up of the USC was seen as an attempt to decrease the unions' influence on policy-making.[21] In the face of the ILP's open assertion of a distinct identity, a number of right-wing union bosses were prepared to act to marginalise the left. Attempts had already been made at the TUC conference in 1916 to establish a solely trade union Labour party. At Manchester, some of the unions acted to establish an even firmer grip on the party than already existed:[22] on a motion proposed by the railway clerks' union, supported by the miners' union, the conference voted to amend the procedure by which the party's executive was elected. In future, the whole conference would vote on membership of the NEC, ensuring that the unions would determine the make-up of Labour's most powerful committee through the use of their block votes.[23]

Despite this setback, ILP and UDC leaders were sufficiently encouraged by evidence of dissent at Manchester to believe that their cause was gaining ground. Since June 1915 they had hoped that opposition to conscription

---

[17] Ernest Bevin expressed concern at the conference that Labour was sharing power with a group of anti-trade union Tory lords, but also lambasted Philip Snowden's conference speech which was critical of the war: *Report* (1917), 96–7.

[18] BSIMF, advisory committee minutes, 6 Nov. 1915, MRC, MS 036/IMF/7/1. See also minutes for 7 Apr., and 29 July 1916.

[19] Ibid. 7 Apr., 1916. See also *Railway Review*, 5 Jan. 1917, MS 127/NU/4/1/5.

[20] BSIMF, advisory committee minutes, 6 Nov. 1915, ibid. MS 036 /IMF/7/1.

[21] See Marquand, *Ramsay MacDonald*, 200.

[22] See McKibbin, *Evolution*, 90.

[23] *Report* (1917), 136–8. See Sidney Webb to Beatrice Webb, 13 Jan. 1917, Passfield papers, II3.

would herald a working-class revolt against the war.[24] This they hoped would push the Labour leadership into accepting their argument for a negotiated peace. The Manchester conference seemed to indicate that discontent existed but was being inhibited by the structure of the Labour party. It was in this context that MacDonald complained to Sidney Webb in January 1917 that the 'trade unions were now a terrible incubus on Labour Party ... [T]he present organisation of the party had failed totally to represent the rank-and-file'.[25] In terms of Labour party unity, this mixture of encouragement and frustration made for an extremely dangerous situation.

Indeed, in the weeks following the Manchester conference, serious consideration was given by leading members of the ILP to the option of abandoning the Labour party altogether. Positioning himself for this eventuality, MacDonald wrote in *Forward* on 10 February 1917 that 'if a split were to come owing to the oppressive use of the block vote of some of the larger unions I would do what I could to form a new Labour combination for political purposes'.[26] There was tangible evidence that opinion in some quarters could be changing: a candidate representing the Peace Negotiations Committee achieved a creditable result in the Rossendale by-election and there were also indications that support for a more conciliatory line on the war was growing in some trade councils.[27]

For the time being, there remained a number of factors that inhibited a permanent split. The most important of these was that those critical of the war were deeply divided.[28] With little evidence of mass working-class support for their position, and only their opposition to the war uniting them, the prospects for a new party appeared bleak. Even after the mixture of hope and frustration engendered by the Manchester conference, it was a gamble unworthy of the risk.

Nevertheless, Henderson was worried. Significantly, he had opposed the railway clerks' motion at Manchester. He remained absolutely convinced

[24] See Morel memorandum on conscription, 6 June 1915, Morel papers, F6/4.

[25] Sidney Webb to Beatrice Webb, 23 Jan. 1917, Passfield papers, II3. See also MacDonald diary, Macdonald papers, PRO 30/69/1753, entry for 27 Jan. 1917. Philip Snowden was of the same opinion: HC, Debates, xc.2113–14 (20 Feb. 1917). In fact the faith expressed by critics of the war in the party rank-and-file was largely misplaced.

[26] Quoted in Pelling, *A short history*, 40. While MacDonald spent a lot of time speculating on political intrigues in his diary and with Liberal friends, it was unusual for him to make such a public utterance. See also Marquand, *Ramsay MacDonald*, 200, and Beatrice Webb diary, Passfield papers, II3, unpublished entry for 3 Jan. 1917.

[27] The PNC candidate gained almost a quarter of the vote. On the trade councils see Burgess, *Challenge of labour*, 178, and A. Clinton, 'Trade councils during the First World War', *IRSH* xv (1970), 215. See also Sidney Webb to Beatrice Webb, 23 Jan. 1917, Passfield papers, II3. The growing confidence of the leaders of the ILP and UDC was reflected in their decision to force a parliamentary debate on the government's war policy: HC, Debates, xc.1177–300 (20 Feb. 1917), and MacDonald diary, MacDonald papers, PRO 30/69/1753, entries for 12, 20 Feb. 1917.

[28] See chapter 4 above. See also Robbins, *Abolition*.

that Labour must continue to support the war, but was equally insistent that the position of the ILP must be respected. Any other approach, he feared, would fatally undermine the labour alliance. Unity, he told delegates, was the key to Labour's present strength.[29] This typified Henderson's wartime attitude. Unlike others in the Labour party's wartime hierarchy he was never the unquestioningly 'subservient' tool of government that some commentators have portrayed.[30] In fact, while it is clear that his commitment to the successful prosecution of the war increased the more involved he became in the responsibilities of its administration, it is no less true that maintaining the political effectiveness of the Labour party remained an equally important objective. Thus Henderson tried to fulfil a dual role: government minister and political leader. He tried to balance support for measures designed to increase war production with representation of the concerns and distrust felt by many unions about the government's long-term intentions, and protection of his party's the political interests. Since August 1914 his primary commitment had been to the successful prosecution of the war. However, when the long-term interests of his party were threatened he was quick to react. In this regard he was particularly concerned to prevent a wartime general election, because this posed the greatest threat to Labour's unity and influence. Thus, when in 1917 C. P. Scott, the editor of the *Manchester Guardian*, urged the government to call a poll to 'get rid of Snowden, MacDonald and other extremists who derived undue importance in the eyes of neutral States from the fact of their being MPs', Henderson was strongly resistant.[31]

Nevertheless, by the end of February 1917, the threats to Labour's unity were growing. It was not yet clear how events would develop, but it was evident that the future integrity of the party was in greater doubt than it had been at any time during the war. To this febrile atmosphere was added in March 1917 a new and potentially even more divisive new factor, the first Russian Revolution.

The Russian Revolution and Labour's war policy

The first Russian Revolution caused there to be major reassessments of the prospects for military victory in the war and the possible social and political consequences the effort to secure a victorious conclusion might involve. In government, the threat of Russia's collapse led to the renewed consideration of diplomatic initiatives to shorten the war. Outside government, far greater debate ensued on the conflict and the hopes for peace, mainly as the result of

---

[29] *Report* (1917), 136–8. See also Winter, 'Arthur Henderson', 756–7.

[30] See, for example, Winter, 'Arthur Henderson'.

[31] Quoted in *The political diaries of C. P. Scott, 1911–1928*, ed. T. Wilson, London 1970, entry for 28 Jan. 1917, 258. Scott's analysis of Snowden and MacDonald's electoral prospects was almost certainly correct.

the Petrograd Soviet's backing for a peace without annexations or indemnities. Such discussions took place in a society suffering increasingly from the hardships of three years of war, and a political system in which the strains on the integrity of the parties were already acute.

Ultimately, the changes that occurred were subtle rather than dramatic, but they provide the context within which the Labour party framed a more distinctive policy on the war. Attention must focus, in particular, on Arthur Henderson. As Labour party secretary, chairman of the PLP and a member of the War Cabinet, he was at the centre of the decision-making process in the Lloyd George government and the labour movement. Ultimately, it was his reluctant recognition that the appropriate political response in the interests of his party to the challenges posed by events in Russia could not be balanced with his role as a government minister, that provides the main explanation for the changes that occurred in Labour's attitude to the war in 1917.

Contrary to the view of some commentators, however, fear of a Russian-style working-class revolt against the war was not a major motivating factor in Henderson's actions at this time. The Russian Revolution had a hugely inspiring effect on the left, but only at its fringes was there a desire for revolutionary direct action in Britain. There was certainly increased industrial unrest during 1917, particularly in May, but this only had an indirect influence on the changes that took place.[32] Neither the strikes nor the Russian Revolution had any effect on the Labour leadership's view of the war. The NEC and the PCTUC responded to the Petrograd Soviet's demand for a peace without annexations or indemnities, which culminated in the suggestion that a meeting of the Socialist International should be held in Stockholm, with a clear rejection. Labour's NEC had long been suspicious of the motives of the 'Northern Neutrals' (the Dutch-Scandinavian Committee of the International which had encouraged the conference) and dismissed the Stockholm idea, as they had rejected all efforts to revive the International earlier in the war. The NEC would only agree to a meeting of allied socialists.[33] The PCTUC was not interested in a 'peace conference'.[34]

These decisions were a major disappointment to critics of the war. To the UDC, for example, the Russian Revolution seemed to offer a great opportunity, and Morel was quick to associate the organisation with the demands of the new Petrograd Soviet.[35] It was hoped that the call for a democratic peace would focus fresh attention on the UDC's demands for a government

---

[32] On the May strikes see J. Hinton, *The first shop stewards movement*, London 1973, 196–212; Waites, *A class society*, 208–10; and T. Wilson, *The myriad faces of war: Britain and the Great War, 1914–18*, Cambridge 1986, 519–30.

[33] NEC minutes, 6 Mar., 16 May 1917, LPA.

[34] PCTUC minutes, 6 June 1917, LPA.

[35] See E. D. Morel, *Free Russia and the Union of Democratic Control* (UDC pamphlet xxxvii, 1917).

statement on war aims, as a preliminary to a negotiated peace.[36] MacDonald wrote in his diary that 'If Russia will keep democratic they could now end the war very shortly.'[37]

With their hopes raised to such a large extent, MacDonald and his colleagues watched with increasing frustration as the Labour party failed to respond to the promptings of Russian and international socialists.[38] The divisions in the party, strengthened by the events of early 1917, were further exacerbated. The BSP and ILP decided that it was no longer prepared to allow the Labour leadership to set the agenda. A joint meeting of the two organisations decided that the USC would inititate contacts with the International independent of the NEC.[39] An independent labour convention on the Russian situation was also called with the aim of focusing attention on the prospects for peace opened up by the Russian Revolution.[40]

Paradoxically, however, despite the growing pressure from the ILP and the UDC, it was the War Cabinet that did most to keep alive Labour's interest in the Stockholm Conference. Concern was growing among some Cabinet ministers about the implications for the war effort of the possible collapse of Russia. Lloyd George and Robert Cecil, in particular, feared that if a British delegation did not attend Stockholm, the German representatives would be free to 'impress on the Russians that the British Empire and France were alone in the way of peace'.[41] Henderson was ambivalent about – if not openly hostile to – these ideas.[42] Nevertheless, British attendance at Stockholm was agreed by the War Cabinet and, in desperation, it was also decided that Henderson should go to Moscow to replace the British ambassador, George Buchanan.[43] Henderson's presence in Petrograd, it was felt, would exercise a 'powerful influence on the democratic elements which now predominate[d] in Russia, to pursue the war with energy'.[44]

---

[36] MacDonald diary, MacDonald papers, PRO 30/69/1753, entry for 26 May 1917.

[37] Ibid. entry for 2 Apr. 1917. See also 2, 9 May 1917, and for similar views expressed by Charles Roden Buxton, Swartz, *The Union of Democratic Control*, 152.

[38] See MacDonald diary, MacDonald papers, PRO 30/69/1753, entry for 9 May 1917.

[39] Ibid. entry for10 May 1917; NEC minutes, 16 May 1917, LPA. See also MacDonald diary, MacDonald papers, PRO 30/69/1753, entry for 16 May 1917.

[40] This convention eventually met in Leeds on 6 June 1917. It was organised by the USC and Lansbury's Herald League: Hinton, *The first shop stewards*, 201; Marquand, *Ramsay MacDonald*, 208–9; and 'The international and peace; a call for action', June 1917, ILP papers, ILP1, NAC.

[41] War cabinet minutes, 21 May 1917, TNA, CAB 23/3. See also Beatrice Webb diary, Passfield papers, I, unpublished entry for 20 Apr. 1918, and Turner, *British politics*, 204–9.

[42] See Leventhal, *Arthur Henderson*, 220.

[43] A delegation of pro-war trade unionists to Russia had failed to make any impact: George Buchanan to Charles Hardinge, 3 Apr. 1917, Charles Hardinge papers, Cambridge University Library, HP31; PCTUC minutes, 30 May, 6 June 1917, LPA; NEC minutes, 18 Apr. 1917, LPA. See also Buchanan to Hardinge, 7 May 1917, Hardinge papes, HP31.

[44] War cabinet minutes, 21, 23 May 1917, CAB 23/3. It is also clear that members of the

Henderson in Russia

Henderson's experiences in Russia played a major role in convincing him that changes had to be made in Labour's attitude to the war. He was not, however, 'converted' to socialism or 'radicalised' by the trip.[45] He did not , as Lloyd George later claimed, catch 'revolutionary malaria'.[46] Rather, he came to believe that the forces unleashed by the Russian Revolution threatened not only the war effort, but also the long-term interests of the international socialist movement and the Labour party, as he wished to see it develop. These forces demanded a response, but Henderson did everything in his power to limit the extent and implications of the changes required.

When Henderson left for Moscow, he was extremely sceptical about the usefulness of the proposed conference in Stockholm. His task was to bolster the Provisional Government and, on his arrival, he made every effort to support Buchanan in pressing the view that Russia should continue a 'vigorous prosecution of the war'.[47] At the end of June he thus rejected a formal invitation to the conference from the Petrograd Soviet. It was informed that British Labour's policy on the war, agreed at the Manchester conference, remained unaltered.[48]

While travelling around Russia in the following month, however, Henderson's views began subtly to alter. The political, social and economic chaos he witnessed convinced him that Russia's continued participation in the war had virtually to be written off. After a particularly chaotic trip to Moscow, he wrote a long telegram to Lloyd George outlining his conclusions. This merits close attention for the light it throws on the way in which Henderson's views had changed and the extent of – and reasons for – these changes. The ideas he expressed in the telegram were to be the basis for many of his actions during the following six months. He wrote:

> [The] conclusion which I draw from the month's observation is that Russia can no longer be regarded as an effective ally ... [W]e must make it our aim to continue the struggle alone with France and America carrying Russia with us as an inert partner ... There are two influences in particular about which we must be on our guard. One is any appearance of coldness or neglect in our dealings with the Provisional Government ... The other is effect [sic] on

War Cabinet did much to encourage a planned trip by MacDonald to Russia: MacDonald diary, Macdonald papers, PRO 30/69/1753, entries for 29 May, 5, 7 and 8 June 1917, and MacDonald to Robert Cecil, n.d., PRO 30/69/1161. See also Marquand, *Ramsay MacDonald*, 209–14.

45 See Winter, 'Arthur Henderson', 770.
46 D. Lloyd George, *War memoirs*, ii, London 1934, 1127.
47 See Hardinge papers, HP31. See also G. Buchanan, My *mission to Russia and other assignments*, ii, London 1923, 147, and Wrigley, *Arthur Henderson*, 115–16.
48 See NEC minutes, 20 June 1917, LPA, and D. Kirby, 'International socialism and the question of peace: the Stockholm Conference of 1917', *HJ* xxv (1982), 709–16.

our own people of extremist propaganda. There are two currents of opinion here as to the means of influencing Western Allies in the direction of what is called generally peace but in truth would be a general surrender. One is for direct action on western proletariat to provoke uprising against capitalism and war together. The other is for constitutional action by first converting Labour and Socialist parties and then trusting to pressure they will exercise on their governments. Differences correspond to methods of Bolshevik and Menshevik in domestic politics here and fundamentally to distinction between agitator and idealist in all countries. Against this I see only one defence and that *is serious review in concert with France and America of our own war aims and reasoned exposition to our people of concrete meaning of reparations and security which we have declared to be our objects in this war.* Such a course together with a frank exchange of views with Russian representatives at conference proposed by Minister of Foreign Affairs for August would make it possible for us to consolidate our policy and if present government remains in power here I should not despair of [reaching] real unity of aim in spite of [divergent] formulas.[49]

Henderson had concluded that the greatest threat to the allies' war effort was no longer the military withdrawal of Russia, which was inevitable, but the prospect of a more extreme left-wing government in Russia encouraging pacifistic and revolutionary tendencies throughout Europe. At this stage he still believed that the idea of an inter-governmental conference, involving the Provisional Government, to review war aims would be sufficient to address this threat. By the middle of July, however, he was convinced that the pressure on the Provisional Government had become so great that outright rejection of the Stockholm conference was no longer appropriate.

However, for Henderson, these observations also had major implications for the political situation in Britain. It was no longer the war effort alone that was at risk. The future unity of international socialism and the British Labour party was also imperilled. European labour movements were already deeply divided on the war. The prospect of increased pressure for a general peace from the government of an ally had potentially devastating implications. Eight days before he had left Britain, Henderson had witnessed at first hand the extent to which divisions in the Labour party were escalating. His perception must have been that the threat to Labour's unity was becoming acute. News of the USC's Leeds convention would have strengthened this perception.[50] Henderson must have doubted whether it would survive intact the divisive influence of a Russian government pledged wholeheartedly to a

---

[49] Henderson to Lloyd George, 1 July 1917 (arrived 2 July), TNA, FO 371/2997 (my emphasis).

[50] Beatrice Webb wrote in her diary after the convention: 'We fear that it is only one among many signs that the Labour movement after the war will break into internecine struggles which will eliminate it as a force in national politics': Beatrice Webb diary, Passfield papers, I, unpublished entry for 7 June 1917. See also Ward, *Red flag*, 143–4.

peace by negotiation. There seemed a real prospect that European socialism might split along Russian lines, with moderate reformist parties opposed by revolutionary movements on their left.[51] The overall effect of his experiences in Russia, when combined with the political situation he had left behind in Britain, convinced Henderson to change his mind and support the Stockholm conference.

Nevertheless Henderson remained determined not to undermine the war effort. His main aim was, rather, to ensure that the socialist and labour movements continued to support, or at least not actively oppose, the conflict in the face of growing pressure from the radical left for a general peace. To this end he wanted to minimise the extent of the policy change that was required. Thus, with respect to Stockholm, he was only prepared to accept the conference if its mandate was strictly controlled. It was to be less a negotiation than a statement of democratic war aims by the allied socialists. This, in turn, Henderson hoped, might lead to a similar statement by the allied governments. This strategy coincided with Henderson's perception of Labour's party political interests. He had always sought to preserve Labour's unity while ensuring that the party openly supported the war. The controversy over the Stockholm conference posed the greatest threat to this policy, but by supporting the conference, while working to prevent it becoming the start of a socialist campaign for a peace by negotiation, he still believed that he could preserve this twin strategy intact. He had certainly not, as Winter argues, determined on resignation when he returned home. Indeed, he feared that resignation would be both militarily and politically damaging: a high-profile government resignation on such a sensitive issue would cause instability and undermine the war effort. It would also suggest that Labour had turned against the war. Moreover, he had no reason to believe that his change of mind over Stockholm was inconsistent with his continuing membership of the War Cabinet. Lloyd George and Cecil, after all, had supported Labour's attendance in May.[52]

However, what Henderson had failed to realise was that the balance of political power and opinion had changed substantially while he had been away. During June and July pessimism about the war, which had done much to encourage the renewed diplomatic activity, had dissipated greatly. Meanwhile the Unionists' position in government had strengthened. They were determined to reverse any momentum for an 'early and inconclusive peace'.[53]

[51] Kirby has suggested that the Stockholm conference constituted 'the first round of the struggle which was to lead to the final splits in international socialism of the immediate post-war years': 'International socialism', 711.
[52] As Leventhal suggests, Henderson left Britain believing that Lloyd George was 'pro-Stockholm': *Arthur Henderson*, 220.
[53] See Hardinge to Lord Bertie and Rodd, 31 July 1917, Hardinge papers, HP31, and Turner, *British politics*, 220.

On Henderson's return to Britain, enormous pressure was thus put upon him and Lloyd George explicitly to repudiate the Stockholm idea.[54] Henderson resisted. He sought to maintain both his support for Labour's attendance at Stockholm and his position in the War Cabinet.[55] In adopting this position, he appears to have thought that ultimately Lloyd George would back him rather than risk his resignation,[56] and, indeed, the prime minister made considerable efforts to find a compromise formula that would satisfy both the Unionists and the Labour leader.[57] Gradually, however, as the pressure from Unionists increased, Lloyd George withdrew his support for Labour's attendance at Stockholm.[58]

Even then Henderson made no move to resign. Nor is there any reliable evidence that he had accepted the government's decision.[59] In fact he did everything he could to ensure that a special Labour conference on 10 August, called by the NEC on Henderson's return from Russia, voted in favour of Stockholm.[60] He remained convinced that outright rejection of the Stockholm conference would be disastrous for the Labour party and international socialism. It was in these terms that he sold the idea to the party. His speech skilfully attempted to reassure those who feared that support for Stockholm would undermine the war effort. Henderson reiterated his absolute support for the military defeat of Germany. He was not seeking to 'supplant' the military effort, he told the conference, only 'supplement' it with the 'weapon of diplomacy'. The most revealing part of the speech was the final paragraph. He pleaded:

[54] See, for example, War Cabinet minutes, 26 July 1917, CAB 23/3.

[55] Ibid. Henderson offered his resignation on 26 July, but with Lloyd George absent in France and with Cecil's support, must have calculated that there was little chance that it would be accepted.

[56] Despite claiming otherwise in his memoirs, Lloyd George certainly gave no immediate indication to Henderson that his views on Stockholm had changed: Lloyd George, *War memoirs*, 1900–1. See also war cabinet minutes, 26 July 1917, CAB 23/3, and *Thomas Jones: Whitehall diary*, ed. K. Middlemas, i, London 1969.

[57] War Cabinet minutes, 1 Aug. 1917, CAB 23/3. Lloyd George and a number of his colleagues were anxious not to lose the leading Labour member of the War Cabinet given the still volatile industrial situation and fears of a growing momentum for peace.

[58] See War Cabinet minutes, 8 Aug. 1917, ibid; Turner, *British politics*, 208; and Leventhal, *Arthur Henderson*, 70.

[59] Turner argues that Henderson misled the War Cabinet by suggesting that he would change his mind on Stockholm and urge the Labour party not to attend at the conference on 10 August. However, it is not clear what his evidence is for this assertion: *British politics*, 208–9. See also Winter, 'Arthur Henderson', 76, and Beatrice Webb diary, Passfield papers, I, unpublished entry for 12 Aug. 1917.

[60] At the NEC on 9 August, Henderson was instrumental in fighting off a determined challenge by opponents of Stockholm to reverse the recommendation to attend that was due to be presented to the following day's conference: NEC minutes, 9 Aug. 1917, LPA. See also War Cabinet minutes, 8 Aug. 1917, CAB 23/3.

Let us remember poor Russia and if we cannot give the newest democracy all she asks, I beseech you not to give her an entire point blank refusal. Of this I am convinced, and I want to say this with all seriousness and deliberation of which I am capable, that if we to-day representing as we do the great British Labour and Socialist Movement, determine for the whole period of the war not to use the political weapon to supplement our military activities, not only shall I regret it, but *I venture to predict that you as a movement will regret it hereafter.*[61]

The threat posed to the successful prosecution of the war by allowing the Stockholm conference to take place was far less than that posed to the future of the Provisional Government if it did not meet. The fall of the latter, Henderson was explaining, would have dangerous implications for the unity of the international and domestic socialist movement, thereby threatening the war effort and Labour's future prospects. The conference accepted Henderson's argument by a large majority. Nevertheless, there continued to be considerable unease about Stockholm, as was indicated by the conference's refusal to allow the ILP to send a separate delegation. This meant that another conference had to be arranged.[62]

Henderson's speech conflicted directly with the decision taken by the War Cabinet on 8 August, but he seems still to have believed that Lloyd George would not sack him.[63] He was wrong. Lloyd George had lost patience with the Labour leader and forced his resignation.[64]

The trade unions and Henderson's new policy

Henderson's resignation meant that the strategy that he had been pursuing since returning from Russia had at least partially failed. He had hoped to bring about a change in Labour's policy on the war, as part of its attendance at Stockholm, without a change in its relationship with the government. Attending the conference and taking a more independent line on war aims, he believed, would be sufficient to resist the divisive forces emanating from Russia which threatened the unity of the Labour party. At the same time, so long as Labour remained associated with the War Cabinet, this would ensure that it did not become too closely associated with critics of the war such as the ILP and UDC.

---

[61] Quoted in P. Stansky (ed.), *The left and the war: the British Labour party and World War One*, New York 1969, 229 (my emphasis).
[62] The invitation to Stockholm stated explicitly that minority parties should be able to attend.
[63] For a possible explanation of Henderson's confidence in this regard see *Whitehall diary*, entry for 10 Aug. 1917. See also HC, Debates, xcvii.909–34 (13 Aug. 1917), and Leventhal, *Arthur Henderson*, 69.
[64] *Whitehall diary*, entry for 29 Aug. 1917.

Nevertheless, despite this partial failure, Henderson was anxious to main-tain intact as much as was possible of this strategy. Labour must continue to be seen to support the war and not break all its connections with the government. The other Labour ministers should, therefore, remain in the coalition.[65] At the same time, the party should not be seen to bow to Lloyd George's pressure on Stockholm. It would continue with its planning for the conference on the same basis as previously, and proceed with the publication of an independent statement of war aims.

Indeed, Henderson's determination to press on with this strategy was, if anything, increased by the circumstances surrounding his resignation which had confirmed him in the belief that Lloyd George was a captive of the right, that his split from the Liberal party was unlikely quickly to be resolved and that the coalition government was likely to fight the next general election as a unified force.[66] In these circumstances, the need for Labour to unify and strengthen its position became even greater. It was these concerns that, as historians of Labour's constitutional change have noted, were to lead to the formulation of a new party constitution.[67] However, the construction of a more independent line on the war was also a central part of this process.[68] In this regard, the central aim had always been to unify the party against the divisive effects of peace propaganda from Russia. However, increasingly, the policy took on a broader political purpose. It also became part of an audacious attempt by Labour to widen the base of its coalition of support. The MOWA was particularly important, in this regard, because it showed that Labour was thinking seriously for the first time about an issue outside its normal concerns. Labour was seeking to show that it was a fully independent party, with the potential to become a genuine competitor for power; that it, rather than the Liberal party, should henceforward be considered as the dominant progressive party in British politics.

The problem for Henderson was opinion within the trade union move-ment. Certainly this had become more fluid during the course of the year, and there is clear evidence for a growth in support during the summer of

---

[65] See *Labour Leader*, 31 Jan. 1918.

[66] Henderson told the Webbs that 'he had apparently become aware for some time that he was a mere hostage for the good behaviour of labour and he had no say in policy': Beat-rice Webb diary, Passfield papers, I, unpublished entry for 22 Aug. 1917 (passage inserted in May 1918). He later confided to MacDonald that Lloyd George was attempting to entrench the coalition as 'a new party': MacDonald diary, MacDonald papers, PRO 30/69/1753, entry for 9 Sept. 1917. See also Turner, *British politics*, 253–333.

[67] See McKibbin, *Evolution of the Labour party*, 247; Winter, 'Arthur Henderson', 770–3; and Worley, *Labour inside the gate*, 13.

[68] In a conversation with Thomas Jones immediately after his resignation, Henderson said 'he would do all he could for the war, but would try to develop some form of criticism of the government's policy and, after the war, attempt to re-cast Labour representation in some way as to bring in a larger infusion of the non-trades unionists': *Whitehall diary*, entry for 29 Aug. 1917.

1917 for the more critical line that Henderson was proposing. Thus, for example, the executive committee of the National Union of Railwaymen received correspondence at this time from 'numerous branches asking the Committee to take action in favour of national peace'. In response, a motion calling for a special meeting to ascertain members' views on bringing 'this terrible war to a speedy and honourable termination' was only narrowly defeated.[69] Similarly, while the executive committee of the London Society of Compositors expressed itself in August 1917 as against any 'proposals or declarations that may be construed as conditions upon which the British Labour Party would be prepared to press for the settlement of the war', this statement was only agreed on the deciding vote of the chairman.[70]

Overall, however, and contrary to many existing accounts, many trade unionists remained extremely reluctant to consider a change of policy on the war; and even those that were remained determined to resist any policy that might be perceived as an acceptance of the views of the ILP or the UDC.[71] At the 10 August conference the balance of opinion had tilted in favour of the Stockholm conference and an independent statement of war aims, mainly on the basis of Henderson's reassurances about the party's continued support for the conflict, but also in the belief that the Stockholm idea was, at least partially, accepted by the government. The prime minister's subsequent direct repudiation of Stockholm, and Henderson's resignation, significantly altered the balance of forces within the Labour movement.[72] Those wishing to minimise the change in Labour's position began to reassert themselves. At a joint meeting of the NEC and PLP on 14 August, members of the latter made clear their displeasure at the events of the previous two weeks and succeeded in ensuring that they would be fully involved in re-drafting the statement on war aims.[73] Growing unease in the party was confirmed at the second special conference on Stockholm, at which support for the initiative declined dramatically and the exclusion of the minority parties was confirmed.[74] The divisions in the party began to re-open.[75] This situation was

---

[69] National Union of Railwaymen, executive committee resolutions, MRC, MS 127/NU/1/3/1–2.

[70] London Society of Compositors, executive committee minutes, 14 Aug. 1917, ibid. MS 28/CO/1/1/14/1..

[71] See *Railway Review*, 5 Jan. 1917, ibid. MS 127/NU/4/1/5.

[72] See PCTUC minutes, 25 July 1917, LPA. The PLP questioned the right of the NEC to make international policy: NEC minutes, 9 Aug. 1917, LPA.

[73] The minutes record that 'It was pointed out that the Memorandum was the work of a sub-committee who were not agreed upon all its terms, that it had not been endorsed by the Executive Committee, but had been submitted to the special conference as a satisfactory basis for discussion and amendment': NEC minutes, 14 Aug. 1917, LPA. Sidney Webb believed that the 'bulk of Labour MPs' and 'the Labour ministers' were against Henderson: Sidney Webb to Beatrice Webb, 13/14 Aug. 1917, Passfield papers, II3.

[74] The Stockholm motion was passed by only 3,000 votes. The miners' union, among others, had changed their view.

[75] Beatrice Webb diary, Passfield papers, I, unpublished entry for 22 Aug. 1917.

confirmed when a conference of allied socialists met in London a week later. Called for the purpose of preparing a joint policy statement on the war for the Stockholm conference, it became a 'fiasco', with the pro-war sections in one room and the minority parties and the Russian delegation in another.[76]

It was increasingly clear that if a new independent policy was to be agreed this would only occur with the full engagement of the trade union wing of the party. Even those in the trade unions who supported Henderson's new approach felt that the unions needed to exert more control on the process of policy change. Thus, for example, the BSIMF, which had been pressing the PCTUC on this issue since 1915 now felt that 'the flow of events was carrying them onward almost in spite of themselves ... they were being led or otherwise driven instead of leading democratic thought and action'.[77] It was in this context that at a joint meeting between the NEC and the PCTUC a compromise on the twin issues of the Stockholm conference and war aims was hammered out. This was based on resolutions passed by the TUC's annual conference of the previous week which had agreed that the idea of an international conference was good in principle, but that such a meeting should not take place immediately.[78]

The NEC's acceptance of these conditions was a victory for those who wanted to limit Labour's change of stance on the war, a victory that was further secured when a joint meeting of the NEC and PCTUC on 16 September agreed that the latter's increased influence on Labour's international policy should be institutionalised: a joint international committee (JIC) was set up with equal representation of Labour and TUC executives. Its remit was to oversee the final drafting and amendment of the MOWA.[79]

The Memorandum on War Aims and a policy for peace, 1917–18

It was to the TUC, therefore, not the UDC that Labour was ultimately beholden for its new policy on the war. Indeed, given this situation, special efforts were made to ensure that ILP moderates, such as MacDonald, did not become disillusioned by the continued caution of the Labour movement.[80] MacDonald generally co-operated. He '[d]ecided to let war aims [memo-

---

[76] See MacDonald diary, MacDonald papers, PRO 30/69/1753, entry for 28 Aug. 1917; Henderson to MacDonald, 18 Sept. 1917, ibid. PRO 30/69/1161; Beatrice Webb diary, Passfield papers, I, unpublished entry for 1 Sept. 1917. See also Wrigley, *Arthur Henderson*.

[77] BSIMF, advisory committee minutes, 6 Sept. 1917, MRC.

[78] *Report* (1917).

[79] NEC minutes, 26 Sept. 1917, LPA. The members of the subcommittee were F.W. Purdy, MacDonald, Sidney Webb, Henderson, George Wardle, Will Thorne, J. Ogden, J. Hill, J. McGurk and C.W. Bowerman. See also NEC minutes, 14 Nov. 1917, LPA.

[80] Henderson to MacDonald, 18 Sept. 1917, MacDonald papers, PRO 30/69/1161.

randum] go through as an attempt to state the position in a way which is on the whole satisfactory'.[81]

The completed MOWA, which was eventually presented to a specially convened conference in December, had been contemplated and amended by three meetings of the JIC. It had also been amended by the PCTUC and the NEC. It was thus a document into which the pro-war elements in the party had had a major input. After three years of war, they had decided to accept the publication of a moderate internationalist set of war aims, so long as Labour's continued support for the war was clearly reiterated.

However, the memorandum was also an intensely political document, intended to reunite the Labour party on the war and to help widen the base of the Labour coalition. The document was thus a compromise between the different ideological groupings in the Labour party in which all were given some encouragement. It was also meant to appeal to potential supporters outside the party.

On the central issue, however, the document represented a clear victory for supporters of the war. It did not commit Labour to a peace-by-negotiations policy. Publication was accompanied by a firm re-statement of Labour's continuing support for the conflict; and while the memorandum stated that the establishment of a lasting peace was the party's primary aim, it was only concerned with how peace could be maintained once it had been achieved. This stance was emphasised by Henderson at the December 1917 conference called to consider the re-drafted MOWA. He stated that:

> We all of us recognise that the evil effects of Germany's policy of aggressive militarism and world domination must be destroyed, [but] if the workers are to be called upon to make further sacrifices they must secure definite assurances that such sacrifices are essential to the winning of an honourable and righteous peace. To make this claim does not signify 'hands up'; it is not to exhibit the white feather, [but] if the struggle has to continue it must only continue for principles and for ideals and not for conquest.[82]

This was an unequivocal defeat for the UDC and ILP. A negotiated peace had been the declared policy of war critics since 1915. Within the UDC, it had increasingly taken precedence over the five official propositions of the organisation. The Labour party had thus rejected the war critics' central proposition, that a lasting peace could only be secured if the existing conflict was brought to an end by negotiation.

However, while this was a defeat for the UDC and ILP, and reassured the trade unions, critics of the war were nevertheless given sufficient encourage-

---

[81] MacDonald diary, ibid. PRO 30/69/1753, entry for 27 Dec. 1917. See also *Socialist Review* (Apr./June 1918).
[82] *Report* (1918), appendix, and p. 26 for Purdy's address as chairman. See also *Report* (1918), 196.

ment by the document to reassess their relationship with the Labour party. The very fact that Labour's policy had changed at all convinced some that the party would inevitably move further.[83] Moreover, the content of the document encouraged this hope among UDC radicals and democratic socialists.

UDC radicals were encouraged by the MOWA's commitment to 'the suppression of secret diplomacy', 'the placing of foreign policy, just as much as home policy, under the control of popularly elected Legislatures' and the requirement that foreign ministers in every country be made responsible to their legislatures. These proposals were all entirely consistent with the UDC radicals' views and the ideological assumptions upon which they were based. The document also gave some encouragement to the democratic socialists, in that limited support was given to the idea of international co-operation to manage the post-war world economy. The memorandum declared that 'in view of the probable world shortage after the war of exportable foodstuffs and raw materials and of merchant shipping, systematic arrangements should be made on an international basis for the allocation and conveyance of the available exportable surpluses of these commodities'.[84]

Despite these concessions, however, it is difficult, even with respect to the MOWA's proposals for the post-war world, to regard the document as indicative of a general shift by Labour towards the positions of the war critics, particularly the UDC radicals. This is because the most important feature of the document was the central place given to a league of nations based on the approach of the Gladstonians. The document envisaged the establishment of an international high court, a council of conciliation and an international legislature, and an agreement among the members to submit all their disputes to the new bodies for arbitration. UDC radicals had major problems with the concept of a league, but even with regard to their more specific concerns about the role of professional diplomats in the supranational authority the document made few concessions.[85] It envisaged the international legislature having a limited role initially, with international legislation developing gradually 'as may prove possible'.[86] Labour, it seemed, had accepted that the new league was likely to be a league of 'governments' rather than 'peoples'.[87] Moreover, no mention was made of economic interventionist powers in line with the ideas of the democratic socialists. While the document indicated

---

[83] See, for example, Trevelyan to Ponsonby, 12 Aug. 1917, Ponsonby papers, MS 666.

[84] Labour party, *Memorandum on war aims*, London 1918.

[85] For the UDC radicals' continued concerns about the league idea after the acceptance of the MOWA see *Labour Leader*, 17 Oct., 5 Dec. 1918.

[86] A copy of the memorandum is in Stansky, *The left and the war*, 318–26.

[87] Henderson sometimes paid lip-service to the idea of a 'League of Peoples', but always made clear that the post-war structure was only likely to be a 'first step' in the direction of this long-term goal: for example, Henderson, *League of Nations*, 8.

some support for greater international economic co-operation, no explicit link was made between this proposal and a league of nations.[88]

Moreover, the league envisaged by the memorandum included an element of collective security, a policy to which UDC radicals were utterly opposed. It was suggested that all members would 'make common cause against any state which fails to adhere' to the compulsory arbitration stipulations of the new body. A firmer commitment had been made in an earlier draft presented to Labour's August 1917 conference, which was more explicit on the military component. Moreover, in a further draft of the memorandum, later agreed by a meeting of inter-allied socialists in February 1918, an even firmer commitment to collective security was made. This stated categorically that 'all nations will have to make common cause, *by using any and every means at their disposal, either economic or military*, against any State or States refusing to submit to the arbitration award, or attempting to break the world's covenant of peace'.[89]

The ideological influence of the UDC radicals on Labour's MOWA was thus only partial and certainly not predominant. Nor were the emerging ideas of the democratic socialists particularly well represented. Certain radical shibboleths were accepted by Labour, and nods were made towards emerging ideas on international government, but many of these proposals were uncontroversial. Most progressives could agree that greater democratic control of diplomacy would be a good thing, but, unlike the UDC radicals, Labour argued this was insufficient by itself. The interventionist stance of the democratic socialists was more controversial, given its implications for free trade, but Labour had only very partially endorsed such an approach. Overall the main influence on Labour's new policy was the Gladstonian liberal strand of thought.

The predominance of these views should not come as a great surprise. Moderate internationalist attitudes were common among a significant section of the wider labour movement in the pre-war period, and these were not entirely swept aside by the patriotic upsurge created by the outbreak of war. There were some in the party who had always regarded the war as a moral crusade against German militarism. It was this position which was more explicitly stated in 1917.[90]

This was to become increasingly apparent when, in the final year of the war, Labour's moderate leadership outlined in more detail their thinking

---

[88] This implied that any such management would continue to be handled by the inter-allied bodies established during the war, rather than supranationally through a new international organisation.

[89] Labour party, *Memorandum on war aims* (my emphasis).

[90] In this regard, the disaffiliation of the pro-war British Workers League and formation of the National Democratic Party after the passage of the MOWA is illustrative: R. Douglas, 'The National Democratic Party and the British Workers League', *HJ* xv (1972), 533–52, and J. O. Stubbs, 'Lord Milner and patriotic labour, 1914–1918', *EHR* lxxxvii (1972), 717–54.

on the nature of the final peace settlement. During this period Henderson, Clynes, Thomas and Shaw (an increasingly important figure) sought, with the support of moderate internationalists in the trade unions,[91] to translate the 'centrist' line on the war into a 'centrist', moderate internationalist policy on the peace, which reflected the fact that the war had been supported as a moral fight against German militarism.[92] Thus, even after victory had been secured, measures would be needed to ensure that German militarism was 'wholly and finally' dismantled. Germany should be treated fairly in terms of trade, but Henderson, for example, insisted that Labour was not willing 'to condone the brutality of the enemy, [nor] leave her with all her powers of mischief unimpaired'.[93] As Clynes told the House of Commons, the party was 'conscious that the crime of the German government was a colossal one'.[94] Even after Germany's defeat and the republican revolution of the SPD, Henderson and many others in the Labour party were unconvinced that the German people had rejected militarism. Henderson, in particular, was suspicious of the SPD and noted in August 1918 that '[m]uch educational work has yet to be done before the German people will be ready ... to approach all the problems of peace in the interests of humanity and world democracy'.[95]

Continued emphasis by Labour moderates on German militarism led them to accept the need for a military component in a league of nations. The fact that a nation had considered it to be in her interests to go to war, reduced faith in free trade and international conciliation as guarantors against future conflict. The role of moderate internationalists was to ensure that the enduring fear of German power did not lead to the return of a balance of power policy. In the longer term it was hoped that a league of nations would create a new spirit of international co-operation between peoples, but it was not assumed that this situation already existed. Henderson explained in the last months of the war that the '[t]he question of security', was central to any proposal for a league. It was 'an essential condition' of any practical scheme that the new body was allowed to use '*any and every means at its disposal, economic or military*, in order to compel the offending nation to keep the world's covenant of peace'.[96] Thomas held similar views. He was

---

[91] See, for example, BSIMF advisory committee minutes, 6 Sept. 1917, 9 July, 6 Sept. 1918, MRC, MS 036/IMF/7/1.

[92] *Report* (1918), 196–9, 204–5.

[93] Ibid. 42. This policy was also reflected in Labour's 1918 election manifesto: *British general election manifestos, 1918–1966*, ed. F. W. S. Craig, Chichester 1970, 5–6.

[94] HC, Debates, cxviii.960 (21 July 1919).

[95] 'Memorandum on replies from socialist parties of the central powers to the memorandum on war aims', Aug. 1918, NEC minutes, LPA. For similar concerns expressed by Thomas see speech at Berne Conference (1919), LPA, LSI 6/137. See also BSIMF advisory committee minutes, 1 Nov. 1919, and 5 June 1920, MRC, MS 036/IMF/7/1.

[96] See Henderson, *League of Nations*, 9–10 (my emphasis).

a founder member of the League of Free Nations Society, which particularly emphasised the security function of international co-operation.[97]

Thus Labour's policy on the war and its general approach to foreign affairs did change in 1917. After three years, during which it had provided virtually uncritical backing for the government, Labour finally placed explicit limits on this support. The party stated categorically for the first time that it supported the war only to the extent that it was conducted as a genuine fight for democratic principles. More generally, 1917 was also the first time that the party as a whole seriously contemplated in any detail the wider issues raised by foreign affairs: a policy had been constructed that had the full endorsement of the wider Labour movement.

This policy change did not take place because of pressure from below among Labour's main working-class constituency, of which there was little. It was concern about political, rather than social, upheaval that was most important. Henderson became convinced that, if moderate supporters of the war on the left did not adopt a more independent approach to the conflict, the entire movement could fracture in the face of an intense peace propaganda emanating from Russia. In Britain, the labour alliance which had been the bedrock for the growth of labour as a political force since 1900 would be torn apart and the Labour party's political progress would be halted.

Henderson made every attempt, however, to minimise the shift in policy that was necessary to prevent this split occurring. He did not want Labour to back a peace-by-negotiations policy. Such an approach was not consistent with his views on the conflict, nor did he believe that it was in the political interests of the party. It was also strongly opposed by the trade union movement. Thus, while ideas associated with UDC radicals and democratic socialists were represented in the MOWA, they were not dominant. Their inclusion was necessary both to bring the party back together, after the ever-worsening divisions of the previous three years, and in an attempt to attract as broad a range of support as possible to Labour's standard. The MOWA was thus part of an attempt to shore up and expand the Labour party's electoral base, to protect the party against Lloyd George's political plans and to take advantage of the split in the Liberal party. To this end, with respect to foreign affairs at least, Labour situated itself firmly within the Gladstonian liberal ideological tradition.

Henderson's strategy was extremely successful in the short term. In combination with the other important changes that took place at this time, Labour's new approach to the war ensured that by the beginning of 1918 the threats of a split had receded and the party was beginning to be feted, in influential circles, as the up-and-coming party – a real competitor for power

---

[97] See Winkler, *League of Nations movement*, 73. For Clynes's view see HC, Debates, cxviii.961–2 (3 July 1919).

in the post-war world.[98] However, such optimism was short-lived. When, with the sudden collapse of Germany in the autumn of 1918, the party had to respond to the Versailles peace settlement, the ideological differences that had been masked by the eclecticism of the MOWA were again brought into focus.

---

[98] See Beatrice Webb diary, Passfield papers, I, unpublished entries for 10 Jan., 27 Feb. 1918, and Robbins, *Abolition*, 151.

6

Labour and the Peace, 1918–1921

Germany's apparently rapid collapse in the autumn of 1918 was the result of both its ill-judged offensive of the previous March, and a series of allied offensives in the summer in which the tactical lessons, learned in the previous four years, were finally used to good effect.[1] On 4 October President Wilson was formally asked by the German High Command to bring about a cease-fire on the basis of his 'fourteen points'. Within five weeks, the *Kaiser* had abdicated and the armistice had been signed. By May 1919 the allies had agreed between themselves at Versailles a harsh peace treaty, which nevertheless included the establishment of a League of Nations. This treaty was presented as a *fait accompli* to the central powers for their agreement. On 28 June 1919 it was signed by Germany.

The nature of the political debate on foreign affairs had dramatically changed: rather than proposals, ideals and speculations, it was the post-war settlement as it had actually been agreed and the structure of the League of Nations as it existed that now provided the framework for discussion. The main questions for progressives became the extent to which the fundamentals of the post-war settlement could be accepted. To what extent could any necessary changes be made by incremental reform? In answering these questions, the responses of individuals and organisations were bound to be influenced by the way in which they had interpreted the events of the previous four years.

The Labour party remained a firm, if increasingly critical, supporter of the war throughout its entire course. This remained the situation up to the end of the war.[2] But did this policy change with the coming of peace? Was Labour so appalled by the Versailles Treaty that, retrospectively, it finally accepted the arguments of the war critics? Most historians suggest that it did. The harshness of the peace treaty and, more important, the entry into the party of former members of the UDC, it is argued, firmly entrenched the views of the organisation in Labour party policy.[3] During this period, according to A. J. P. Taylor, a 'marriage' took place between the UDC and the Labour

---

[1] See J. M. Bourne, *Britain and the Great War, 1914–1918*, London 1989, 85–101.
[2] Labour's efforts to bring about an exchange of views between allied and enemy socialists showed that substantial differences existed, much to the chagrin of the ILP. See, for example, NEC, JIC minutes, 11, 24 July 1918, LPA; and *Labour Leader*, 28 Mar., 4 Apr., 6 June, 4, 18, 25 July, 22 Aug. 1918.
[3] On the entry of ex-Liberals and others into the Labour party in the early post-war period see Cline, *Recruits*, and Dowse, 'Entry of the Liberals'.

party; they were 'one so far as foreign policy was concerned'.[4] Henry Winkler concurred: 'The influence of the [UDC] on the Labour movement in the early post-war years would be difficult to exaggerate.'[5] The party institution through which most historians argue that the ex-Liberal UDC recruits, and their sympathisers in the ILP, exerted their influence was the ACIQ, set up in January 1918.[6] This institutionalised the ideological conversion of Labour's foreign policy because the new committee came to be dominated, particularly in its early years, by leading members of the UDC.[7] It became, according to Miller, 'almost a continuation of the UDC'.[8]

There are, however, some important areas of disagreement in the literature with respect to the influence of groups other than the UDC, and the timespan within which the UDC's influence was at it greatest. Winkler, for example, argued that the ILP also remained an important force at this time, particularly in the constituency parties; and both he and Catherine Cline suggested that Clynes and Henderson argued (with limited success) for a more moderate policy on the post-war settlement during this period. On the role of the trade unions, however, they differ. Winkler suggests that 'the bulk of the trade union leadership remained much closer to the radicalism of the ILP and the UDC than to the [moderates]', a view that is directly contradicted by Cline.[9]

With regard to the timescale of the UDC's influence, most historians agree that Labour's 1924 period of government was an important turning-point. It is generally accepted that the foreign policy pursued by MacDonald, as Foreign Secretary, differed in important respects from that proposed by Morel and his colleagues, and apparently supported by the party in the early post-war period. However, there is disagreement on the reasons for this decline in influence. It was only after their first experience of government in 1924 that Winkler detected any 'real shift' in Labour's position.[10] After this 'education in the realities of international politics', it adopted a more moderate policy closer to that followed under the second Labour govern-

4 Taylor, *Troublemakers* 160–1.
5 Winkler, 'Emergence', 249. He stood by this view in his later work: *Paths*, 17. See also Berger, *British Labour party*, 229; Cline, *Recruits*, 69; Dowse, 'Entry of the Liberals', 87; Horne, *Labour at war*, 308; Naylor, *Labour's international policy*, 3–4; K. Robbins, *Politicians, diplomacy and war in modern British history*, London 1994, 255; Spear, 'The case of E. D. Morel'; Vickers, *Labour and the world*, 74–5; and, for a slightly different view, Blaazer, *Popular front*, 105–21, 129–33.
6 Taylor, *Troublemakers*, 154–5; Winkler, 'Emergence', 248; Cline, *Recruits*, 69–70.
7 Taylor, *Troublemakers*, 154.
8 Miller, *Socialism and foreign policy*, 83.
9 See Winkler, 'Emergence', 252, and Cline, *Recruits*, 74.
10 Winkler does, however, suggest that the party's attitude towards the League of Nations gradually became more positive from 1920 onwards, a view he emphasised a little more strongly in his later work: 'Emergence', 255; *Paths*, 92–123.

ment in 1929–31. Only Cline detects any indication of a major change in Labour's policy before 1924. Greater sympathy began to be shown from 1923 for French security concerns and, consequently, the idea of collective security through the League of Nations gained more support. This 'startling' change of policy, she suggests, was to form the basis for Labour's foreign policy in 1924.[11] However, she can provide no real explanation for why it occurred.

In fact, as this chapter will argue, the extremism of Labour's reaction to the post-war settlement has been exaggerated. To a considerable extent the party maintained in the peace the more mainstream position it had adopted during the war. There are two main reasons why such misinterpretations have occurred. First, the peacemaking policies of the various individuals and groups on the centre and left of British politics have been too imprecisely defined. Catherine Cline, for example, cites the fact that Labour party conferences 'called annually for the revision of the Treaty of Versailles' and 'enthusiastically received … proposals for disarmament', as evidence that the position proposed by UDC radicals on the post-war settlement had been accepted.[12] The use of terms such as a 'Wilsonian peace' by different individuals and groups has also been seen as an indication of a general agreement on foreign policy. What this type of approach ignores is the different ways in which the various groups understood these terms, variations that were not just of detail, but were related to fundamental differences in ideology. Second, vocalism has been confused with influence. Insufficient allowance is given for the chaotic nature of Labour politics between 1918 and the end of 1921. This situation was the result both of organisational problems within the party and the radicalised nature of the post-war world to which it had to respond. Together, these factors made the party much more difficult to manage, and rendered policy co-ordination an almost impossible task. They gave critics of the war greater opportunity to voice their views, because they reduced the political salience of the post-war settlement for many in the party. Those who had opposed Labour's moderate wartime stance sought to take advantage of these circumstances to convert the party to their position. Ultimately, they were unsuccessful and by 1921 their chance had gone.

The search for a 'Wilsonian peace'

The action of the German High Command in involving President Wilson in the negotiation of the armistice at the end of September 1918 is significant. Many progressive politicians and commentators were later to argue that a 'Wilsonian' peace was promised in October 1918, only for this promise to

---

[11] Cline, *Recruits*, 85. See also Naylor, *Labour's international policy*, 4.
[12] Cline, *Recruits*, 84.

be broken at Versailles in 1919. Labour was frequently to compare the 1919 treaty unfavourably with the armistice agreement. What, therefore, was the nature of the armistice, its relationship to the final peace settlement and the influence on both of Wilsonian principles?

Wilson had outlined his principles for a 'democratic peace' – the fourteen points – in January 1918. These had included commitments to open covenants of peace, openly arrived at; absolute freedom of navigation upon the seas; the removal, as far as possible, of all economic barriers; the reduction of national armaments to the lowest level consistent with domestic safety; a free, open-minded adjustment of all colonial claims; and the formation of a 'general association of nations'. This vague list left substantial room for debate, both about the exact meaning of the term 'a Wilsonian peace' and its precise implications. However the term was understood, moreover, it is clear that even before the armistice agreement the allies were beginning to move away from the fourteen points. On hearing of the Germans' request for peace, both France and Britain insisted that Wilson's ideas could not constitute the sole basis for the conclusion of the war. The French demanded that Germany accept responsibility 'for all the damage done to the civilian population of the Allies and their property by [her] aggression'.[13] The British claimed the continued right to impose a naval blockade upon their erstwhile foe, thus contravening Wilson's stipulation about the freedom of the seas.[14] These reservations were included in the armistice that was eventually signed. That agreement's tough provisions with regard to the German army also indicated that the final peace conditions that the allies would propose would be harsh.[15]

The retreat from Wilsonian principles in the construction of the peace settlement thus began well before the allies met at Versailles in the early months of 1919, and continued in tandem with negotiations for peace. Britain was 'already instinctively reverting to [her] traditional balance of power stance': German power needed to be weakened to an degree which would limit the threat posed to Britain's global interests, but at the same time not place France in a dominant European position.[16] She was also determined to gain some financial compensation, having underwritten much of the allies' war effort and borrowed heavily from the US. The French, on the other hand, having been invaded twice in the previous fifty years, were obsessed with security. They were also determined to gain international assistance for the reconstruction of their devastated northern regions.

---

[13] The fourteen points called for the 'restoration' of all occupied areas, but Wilson was adamantly opposed to indemnities. Too great a demand for compensation would also contravene his call for the removal of economic barriers to trade.
[14] See R. Henig, *Versailles and after, 1919–1933*, London 1984, 10–12, and S. Marks, *The illusion of peace: international relations in Europe, 1918–1933*, London 1976, 2–3.
[15] See Henig, *Versailles*, 12. See also C. Fischer, *The Ruhr crisis, 1923–1924*, Oxford 2003.
[16] Marks, *Illusion*, 11.

Germany was thus not treated at Versailles as a partner in the creation of a new international order, as some supporters of Wilson had hoped, but as a defeated foe. An essential purpose of the Versailles settlement was to reduce or control her economic and military power. She was stripped of one tenth of her pre-war territory, including Alsace-Lorraine, which was transferred back to France without a plebiscite. Moreover, the Saarland was ceded to the new League of Nations for fifteen years, with the French given control of its coal mines during this period. Germany was also stripped of her colonies. The sections of the treaty that dealt with disarmament were aimed exclusively at Germany. She was largely disarmed; her military establishment was drastically reduced; and the Rhineland was to be temporarily occupied and permanently demilitarised. Economically, Germany was forced to grant 'most favoured nation status' to the allies; custom controls were imposed; and restrictions were placed on her domestic economic policy. Moreover, she was to meet the bill for the allies' occupation of the Rhineland.

Most important of all, however, was the reparations issue. While the Germans were not made to pay a general indemnity, the meaning of 'reparation' was interpreted broadly, mainly at the insistence of the British, to include such dubious items as war pensions and separation allowances. Moreover, due to the allies' inability to reach an agreement, no final figure was set, which seemed to suggest that Germany was being asked to sign a 'blank cheque'.

Nevertheless, while the Treaty of Versailles was undoubtedly harsh, the traditional view that it was simply a vindictive peace settlement, constructed by the allies with the sole intention of taking advantage of Germany's temporary weakness in order to gain permanent economic and military supremacy, has largely been reassessed, in the light of more recent scholarship.[17] Nowadays, it is generally agreed that, while the treaty was severe, 'it is amazing that it was not more so ... considering how thoroughly Germany had lost a long and bitter war'.[18] Wilson's determination to secure a 'just peace', and a French policy that in parts was more enlightened than is often suggested, ensured that the treaty was less punitive than it might have been. Thus, no attempt was made to dismember Germany, her territorial losses were relatively slight given France's continuing security concerns and she was not forced to pay general indemnities to the allies as a punishment for aggression. With regard to financial clauses of the treaty, intense debate continues about the scale and feasibility of the reparations demanded of Germany.[19] However, it is now generally agreed that, despite Keynes's fervent objections, the allies did not entirely ignore economic considerations in constructing

---

[17] See, for example, Boemeke, Feldman and Glaser, *Treaty of Versailles*, 1–4.

[18] Marks, *Illusion*, 11. See also, for example, M. Trachtenberg, *Reparations in world politics: France and European economic diplomacy, 1916–1923*, New York 1980, and Orde, *British policy*.

[19] See, for example, Boemeke, Feldman and Glaser, *Treaty of Versailles*.

the treaty; the size of the bill that Germany was eventually asked to pay has been overrated; the practical and economic difficulties caused by reparations can be exaggerated;[20] and they were not the only cause of Germany's financial problems in the early 1920s.[21]

Moreover, the Versailles negotiations also led, mainly on Wilson's insistence, to the setting up of the League of Nations. This was not entirely in accord with the structures proposed by liberal groups during the war, but nevertheless was close enough to offer hope. It consisted of a council, an assembly, a secretariat and a permanent court of international justice.[22] The council was the most important body. Its main task was to settle by mediation all non-justiciable disputes between member nations. Where this failed, the League was able to operate a limited form of collective security: various sanctions were made available under the League's covenant to guarantee members against external aggression and enforce the council's decisions on disputes. Any state which resorted to war in disregard of the League's procedures would face financial and economic penalties and, in such cases, it would be the duty of the council 'to recommend ... what effective military or naval force the Members of the League shall severally contribute to the armed forces to be used to protect the covenants of the League'.[23] On more general matters of members' security, the council was also given a duty to formulate plans for a 'reduction of national armaments to the lowest point consistent with national safety and the enforcement of common action of international obligations'.[24]

Nevertheless, there were some aspects of the new League that caused problems for all those with progressive views. Of these the most important were the domination of the council by the governments of the allied great powers and its almost complete operational independence from the more representative assembly, and the exclusion of the defeated nations until they could provide solid proof that they intended to abide by international agreements. Most progressive commentators and politicians agreed that these were unattractive features of the new body. The main debate in the early post-war years concerned the extent to which the new structure could be improved by incremental reform. The Gladstonian liberal LNU generally gave the body an enthusiastic welcome, despite its obvious flaws. The reaction of the UDC radicals, democratic socialists and Labour party was another matter.

---

[20] It is probably on this issue that debate remains most fierce: S. Marks, 'Smoke and mirrors: in smoke-filled rooms and the Galerie des Glaces'; N. Ferguson, 'The balance of payments question: Versailles and after'; and G. D. Feldman, 'A comment', all in Boemeke, Feldman and Glaser, *Treaty of Versailles*, 337–70, 401–40, 441–7;

[21] J. M. Keynes, *The economic consequences of the peace*, London 1920.

[22] See A. Zimmern, *The League of Nations and the rule of law*, London 1936, 497–511.

[23] Ibid. article 16.

[24] Ibid. article 8.

While it is clear that the influence of Wilsonian principles on the peace-making process declined from the moment it began in October 1918, there were nevertheless still some aspects of the post-war settlement that progressive supporters of the American president could welcome. The extent to which an individual or group did so, rather than concentrating on those features less consistent with Wilsonian principles was largely determined by where they had stood on the war itself.

Labour's response to the Versailles settlement

The Labour party might have been expected to have concentrated on the more positive aspects of the peace settlement. It had backed the war in 1914. It had consistently refused to endorse a policy of peace by negotiation. It had shown itself, in its proposals for the post-war world, to be closest ideologically to the moderate Gladstonian liberals. However this is not the way in which Labour's policy on the peace has been interpreted by historians. They suggest that the party adopted an absolutist stance due to the influence of UDC members, whose numbers in the party increased from 1918.

It is certainly the case that Labour moderates were disappointed with some aspects of the post-war settlement. Nevertheless, there were important differences in their views in comparison with those of critics of the war. In fact, Labour moderates sought to maintain the mainstream approach to the peace constructed in the final year of the war. The Versailles Treaty was not unequivocally condemned. Indeed, Clynes praised it as the 'work of men who, in the circumstances which surrounded it, must have acted with motives of the highest patriotism and with the highest and noblest considerations for human government'.[25] Generally, however, the tone was one of moderate criticism. Moderate internationalists at the top of the party and the trade unions focused on those aspects of the treaty that appeared to go beyond the necessary precautions needed to ensure the destruction of German militarism, and which seemed motivated by a spirit of vengeance.[26] In this regard, treaty stipulations that went further than the armistice agreement were particularly criticised. Thomas summarised the PLP's position. He told the Commons that 'I want reparation … [but] I do not want to see us carried away by passion, bitterness or hatred, or by our own personal feelings, forgetting that we can create a situation that will render peace permanently impossible.' Nevertheless, he believed, it was vital, that 'nothing should be said that would encourage the enemy not to sign the peace terms'.[27] Henderson

---

[25] HC, Debates, cxviii.965 (21 July 1919). See also *The Times*, 29 Apr. 1919.
[26] For trade union comment on the peace see BSIMF, advisory committee minutes, 6 Mar. 1920, MRC, MS 036/IMF/7/1, and *Railway Review*, 8 Nov. 1918, MS 127/NU/4/1/6. See also *Report* (1920), 62.
[27] *The Times*, 15 May 1919, and also 4 Nov. 1918.

was equally insistent in this regard. He told a German press agency that 'it would be better for Germany to accept an unsatisfactory peace than by rejecting peace conditions to create a situation the effect of which could not be foreseen'. Reflecting his own continued concerns about the erstwhile enemy, he suggested that 'there was still great mistrust of the sincerity of the democratic conversion of Germany'. He continued: 'The best way for Germany to achieve a rapid consolidation of the situation, a sensible policy and economic reconstruction was to remove the strong distrust which still prevailed in Entente countries by accepting peace and, for the rest, to rely upon the democracies of the Western powers to secure her just demands.'[28] Labour moderates viewed the League of Nations as a beacon of hope, despite its obvious flaws, a view shared by most moderate progressives. The mere fact that it had been set up was seen as a positive sign. Clynes, in particular, proposed that Labour should give its wholehearted support to the new body, even if it was not ideal in its present form. In the House of Commons he aligned himself strongly with Robert Cecil, the Conservative advocate of the League and leading member of the LNU. The new body was 'a great international world organisation for future times', he suggested. 'It now had its defects ... [but] what kind of new organisation or machinery could be made to be perfect in its initial stages.'[29]

This 'constructive' approach to the post-war settlement was maintained by Labour moderates during the following two years. Like most mainstream progressives, their views on the peace became more critical, as the continuing failure of European governments to resolve the reparations dispute and agree an international programme of economic reconstruction exacerbated international and domestic instability.[30] However, within all the party's main institutions, they continued to argue strongly against an absolute rejection of the Versailles treaty and the League of Nations.

Even when criticising the post-war settlement, they concentrated on specific aspects, rather than the entire Versailles agreement. Thus, Shaw told the 1920 Labour conference, for example, that the document was '*in certain of its clauses* a direct violation of the terms on which the Armistice was arranged ... and that *certain of the clauses* were calculated ... to defeat their own object'.[31] Given that the armistice itself imposed harsh terms, this was far from being a 'pro-German' argument. Labour moderates continued

---

[28] *Manchester Guardian*, 29 Apr. 1919. Henderson's rhetoric on the treaty sometimes varied according to his audience and the immediate political context, but in internal party debates he remained firmly in the moderates' camp throughout the period: see, for example, *The Times*, 23 June 1919.

[29] HC, Debates, cxviii.961–2 (21 July 1919).

[30] On the Asquithian Liberals during this period see K. O. Morgan, *Consensus and disunity: the Lloyd George coalition government, 1918–1922*, Oxford 1979, 192–212.

[31] *Report* (1920), 132 (my emphasis). Henderson expressed similar views: HC, Debates, cxviii.697 (17 Nov. 1919). Shaw's support for the armistice agreement in itself made his views very different from those of the UDC.

to argue that Germany should pay reparations and that precautions against the re-emergence of militarism should remain in place.[32] 'A point may be reached', Clynes was even prepared to accept in March 1921, 'where measures of force, possibly economic measures of force, will have to be applied.'[33]

This response to the peace settlement contrasted strikingly with that of critics of the war. Of these, the UDC radicals were the most uncompromisingly hostile. Their approach had always been based on the view that Germany was not solely responsible for the conflict. On this basis, there was less reason for Germany to be singled out for special treatment once peace arrived. She should, for example, pay only a proportionate amount for the damage caused by the war, and receive compensation for the colonies she had lost. No special measures were required to prevent the revitalisation of militarism in Germany; instead there should be universal disarmament. Any approach significantly different from this would suggest an enduring militarist and protectionist spirit among the victorious governments, indicative of a desire to use Germany's temporary weakness to gain a permanent economic and military advantage. It would also create a burning resentment among the German people, thus making future conflicts more likely. These views were reinforced by Germany's acceptance of the stringent armistice and the 1918 republican revolution.[34]

Given this approach, the UDC radicals' response to the peace was one of outrage. Morel, for example, described the treaty as 'a great international tragedy'. Its 'deliberate purpose … disclosed in every section', he asserted, 'is that of encompassing the utter ruin of a great people'.[35] The broad interpretation of reparations would 'rightly' kindle 'a passionate fury … in the breasts of 80 millions of Germans'. The treaty perpetuated the 'fundamental falsehood of the war', the 'legend of … France as the eternally persecuted victim of an intolerant neighbour'.[36] MacDonald was no less forthright. He described the treaty 'as an act of madness unparalleled in history'.[37] Within UDC radical circles, therefore, it quickly became accepted that the treaty should be utterly condemned.[38] Its complete revision, suggested Ponsonby, should be 'the foremost plank in the policy of any party who understands that the welfare and security of this country depends on real European peace and the strengthening of the bonds of internationalism'.[39]

---

[32] See HC, Debates, cxxxix.743 (10 Mar. 1921). See also *Report* (1921), 180–1.

[33] HC, Debates, cxxxix.2040 (18 Mar. 1921).

[34] See *The UDC* (Mar. 1919).

[35] Ibid. (June 1919).

[36] *Labour Leader*, 22 May 1919.

[37] Ibid. See also MacDonald diary, Macdonald papers, PRO 30/69/1753, entry for 8 May 1919.

[38] For example, Snowden was strongly critical of the Labour party's more considered reaction to the peace treaty: *Labour Leader* 15 May 1919.

[39] *Labour Leader*, 5 June 1919. See also Pethwick Lawrence in *The UDC* (Jan. 1919).

On the League of Nations too, the UDC radicals' response was much less favourable than that of the Labour moderates. They had always been more sceptical than the Labour leadership about the league idea but the nature of the structure established in 1919 greatly increased this scepticism. In this regard, the main problem with the new body was the dominating role played by the League Council. Democratic control remained the priority and it seemed that a League, dominated by the politicians and diplomats of the great powers, would not advance this cause.[40] MacDonald, in particular, was scathing. It would be better 'if there was no League at all and each national parliament remained solely responsible for foreign policy'. The new organisation, he continued, was merely a means 'by which officialdom, diplomacy, government and executives, discredited by the war ... [could] entrench themselves behind the walls of international authority'.[41] The League's limited element of collective security, therefore, which was dubious in itself, turned the organisation into a form of 'armed bureaucracy'. Moreover, it was an 'armed bureaucracy' that was, given the exclusion of the defeated powers, directed against the former enemy. On these grounds Snowden argued that 'Some people who share our views about the iniquitous character of the Treaty regard the League of Nations as a means by which to change its most objectionable features. This hope we regard as wholly without foundation. The covenant of the League of Nations is an instrument for the execution of the Treaty.'[42] There remained much, therefore, that separated Labour moderates from critics of the war when the Versailles Treaty was released. But whose views were in the ascendant? Labour entered the post-war period with a centrist policy on the peace. To what extent did critics of war succeed in overturning this once the nature of the peace settlement became clear, and how might such a conversion have been achieved?

Policy-making in the Labour party 1918–22

The entry of ex-Liberal members of the UDC into the Labour party is an important element in the traditional explanation of the party's policy on the peace. However, this development and its significance needs to be investigated in more detail. There is no doubt that there was such an influx in the early post-war period, albeit that its extent is sometimes exaggerated, but to what extent were these new members able to exert an influence over

---

[40] Morel told a meeting in Glasgow on 23 Nov. 1918 that the 'UDC's competence' was restricted to 'the abolition of secret diplomacy by *our* government, and the democratisation of *our* foreign office and *our* diplomatic service': *The UDC* (Jan. 1919) (emphases original).

[41] Ibid. 27 Feb. 1919.

[42] Ibid. 12 June 1919. See also 20 Feb. 1919, 'The ILP and the League of Nations', n.d. c. Feb. 1919, ILP papers, NAC4.

Labour's foreign policy-making process? It is not sufficient to rely on the fact that various individuals associated with the UDC were vocal; it is also necessary to show that they held positions of executive power within the policy-making apparatus of the party, or could exercise substantial influence over those who did.

When the situation is analysed on this basis, the political weakness of the former Liberal members, and their sympathisers, in the early post war period becomes apparent. Their significance in all Labour's most important institutions was either non-existent or small. With respect first to the PLP, most of those who had had parliamentary seats lost them in 1918, a fate which also befell their supporters in the ILP, such as MacDonald, Snowden and Jowett. The new PLP was thus dominated by trade unionists, most of whom had remained supporters of the war throughout, and some of whom were closely associated with Lloyd George.[43] It was led by a 'dull' miner, William Adamson, but it was generally accepted that Clynes and Thomas were the powers behind the throne. They and some of their colleagues had strong views of their own on international affairs, mainly based on a Gladstonian internationalist approach. Neither they, nor the PLP in general, was prepared to hand over policy development to a group of ex-Liberal intellectuals, who had only recently joined the party, and whose views had been consistently repudiated over the previous four years.[44]

The situation with respect to the NEC was only slightly better for critics of the war. MacDonald, Snowden and Jowett retained their membership, despite the ending of the sectional principle of election in 1917,[45] and this ensured that the views of critics of the war were heard. However, they were very much in a minority. Moreover, with respect to the foreign policy-making role of the NEC, the formation of the JIC in 1917 had seen the PCTUC incorporated into the central policy-making process of the party. This remained the case in the post-war period and ensured that, potentially, the trade unions retained a major input into the foreign policy decisions of the Labour party.[46] This did not inevitably mean that patriotic views predominated, but as Ross McKibbin has suggested, 'the PCTUC ... elected in 1918 was at least as patriotic as any elected before it, and perhaps slightly more so'.[47]

---

[43] C. Howard, 'Henderson, MacDonald and the leadership of the Labour party, 1914–1922', unpubl. PhD diss. Cambridge 1978, 224.

[44] See Beatrice Webb diary, Passfield papers, I, unpublished entry for 14 Jan. 1919.

[45] See Howell, *MacDonald's party*, 56–7, 237, 239.

[46] On the trade unions input into the policy process see, for example 'Trade Union Congress, peace treaty revision', MRC, MS 292/940/3–5, and TUC international committee minutes, Trades Union Congress, MS 292/901/1. The JIC was re-named the National Joint Council.

[47] McKibbin, *Evolution of the Labour party*, 103. As McKibbin points out, the election of Havelock Wilson, a wartime super-patriot, was particularly significant in this respect.

Party leadership remained in the hands of Henderson in 1919. He was the architect of the centrist position on the war and, while anxious to safeguard the place of critics of the war in the party, he remained firmly of the belief that Labour's policy should primarily reflect the concerns and interests of the trade unions.

Critics of the war therefore had barely a foothold in any of the Labour party's most important institutions in 1919. The only body that was not dominated by pro-war trade unionists was the new advisory committee, and it is through this that previous commentators have suggested that UDC radicals were able to exert their influence.

There are two major problems here. First, the argument is based on the notion that the three other party institutions were prepared to defer to the advisory committee on matters of foreign affairs. Given the suspicion with which intellectuals were viewed within the party this seems unlikely and the circumstances under which such deference might have occurred have not been explained.[48]

The second problem concerns the composition of the advisory committee. Analysis of its attendance records shows that, while members of the UDC were represented, they rarely made up a majority and those who were represented were generally democratic socialists, rather than radicals.[49] The overwhelmingly dominant individual in terms of attendance was Leonard Woolf, who was not a member of the UDC at all.[50] Not only did he attend more meetings throughout the period than anyone else, he also chaired a large proportion of them. Sidney Webb was also a regular attender during the first two years of the committee's existence. There were many other members who had never been members of the UDC and were not sympathetic to its views.[51]

Moreover, it is also important to appreciate that, from November 1920, great efforts were made to open the committee's meetings to Labour MPs.[52] Many members of the PLP who subsequently attended had been supporters of the war and had no connection with the UDC. Of these, Tom Shaw was

[48] On Labour and intellectuals see ibid. 100–6.
[49] ACIQ minutes, LPA, LSI.
[50] There appears to be some confusion over Woolf's relationship with the UDC. Horne suggests that he was a member, as does the editor of his letters, Frederic Spotts. However, there is no evidence for this view in Woolf's letters or in his autobiography. Moreover, no evidence for Woolf's membership of the UDC was found in the organisation's archive. This and the ideological differences between Woolf and leading UDC members suggest that he was not a member: Horne, *Labour at war*, 308; *The letters of Leonard Woolf*, ed. F. Spotts, London 1989, 412n.; L. Woolf, *Beginning again, 1911–1918*, London 1964, and *Downhill all the way, 1919–1939*, London 1967.
[51] These included some notable intellectual figures, such as David Mitrany, later a theorist of supranational development, Alfred Zimmern, a former adviser on the League of Nations to the Lloyd George government, and the historian, Arnold Toynbee.
[52] ACIQ minutes, 19 Nov. 1920, LPA.

the most important. He became chair of the committee and was later considered by some to be a potential Labour Foreign Secretary.[53]

In comparison, the involvement of UDC members with the advisory committee was limited. Only Norman Angell, of the founding members of the organisation, was present on a regular basis between 1918 and 1923. Morel and Ponsonby only attended eleven out of the ninety-nine meetings held during this period; between 1918 and the summer of 1922 they attended none. They only began to attend after they had been elected as Labour MPs at the 1922 general election. This suggests that they had not previously been invited.[54] MacDonald, on the other hand, was only a very intermittent attender during the whole period, while Trevelyan did not attend a single meeting until 1923.[55] The members of the UDC who, together with Angell, were most in evidence during this period were Brailsford and the Buxtons – Charles, Noel and Dorothy – although after 1921 Brailsford's involvement began to decline. In terms purely of personnel, therefore, the advisory committee was more than just a continuation of the UDC within the Labour party.

While the absence of leading UDC radical figures has been noted by some historians, its significance has been dismissed. Thus, Taylor, for example, claims that, while Morel was absent, his views and thus the ideology of the UDC 'set the tone' for the committee's proceedings.[56] However, the UDC did not have a single ideology based on the views of Morel. Important ideological differences existed among its members on post-war international relations and the value and purpose of a league of nations. The fact that the only members of the UDC who joined the advisory committee in its early years were democratic socialists, when combined with the Fabian influence on the new body, makes it extremely difficult to maintain the traditional interpretation of the committee as overwhelmingly dominated by the views of Morel.[57]

Given their generally weak position in the policy-making structures of the Labour party, therefore, what critics of the war required in order to challenge the moderates' policy was a broader shift of opinion within the movement. No real challenge to Labour's centrist position on the peace was

---

53 *The political diary of Hugh Dalton, 1918–40*, ed. B. Pimlott, London 1986.

54 This view is confirmed by P. Clarke, 'The progressive movement in England', *TRHS* xxiv (1974), 159–81. After 1921 all MPs were invited to attend the advisory committee's meetings.

55 Of the other UDC members, Goldsworthy Lowes-Dickinson, the Cambridge academic and member of the Bryce Group, was also a regular, if intermittent, attender.

56 Taylor, *Troublemakers*, 155. Cline and Winkler similarly conflate the ideas of Morel with the ideology of the UDC: Cline, *Recruits*, 71–81; Winkler, 'Emergence', 249.

57 The one party institution in which UDC radicals were strong was the Labour press. All the main left-wing papers and journals of the time (*The Daily Herald*, *Labour Leader*, *Socialist Review* and *Forward*) were either edited by UDC radicals or sympathetic to their arguments. Moreover, the UDC also had its own newspaper, edited by E. D. Morel. Winkler's *Paths*, in particular, is weakened by its over-reliance on this source.

possible unless the stranglehold that pro-war trade unionists had exerted on foreign policy development during the previous five years was broken. In fact a general shift of opinion in this direction did occur within the Labour movement in the early post-war period. However, its effect on Labour's attitude towards the peace was not as clear-cut as critics of the party's previous policy might have hoped.

Labour, direct action and the peace

Between 1919 and 1921 Britain and Europe saw a significant upsurge in extremist politics on the left. To a large extent, in Britain at least, this trend was not directly attributable to the peacemaking process. It nevertheless had a growing influence on perceptions of the post-war settlement within the Labour party. In particular, it was largely responsible for the development of a retrospective scepticism about the war within the party, which allowed those who had opposed the conflict to gain a more sympathetic hearing. In Europe these events led to a division in the International Labour and Socialist movement, which greatly complicated British Labour's relationship with its European partners, with further consequences for the development of the party's policy on the peace.

Domestically, this trend in left-wing politics was caused by the combined effect of militant trade unionism, which had gained a toehold in the labour movement in the last eighteen months of the war, and the policies pursued by the first post-war government.[58] The former had left a legacy of militancy among important sections of the trade union movement, which, although supported only by small minorities on the executive committees of the TUC and Labour party, represented a growing force in the party.[59] With regard to the first post-war government, it soon became clear that, despite the use of the coupon at the 1918 election, Lloyd George had become the captive of the Conservative party.[60] As Keith Jeffery has shown, a militarist spirit thus seemed to pervade the early post-war years, an impression that was strongly reinforced by the Lloyd George government's policies in Ireland and India, where nationalist movements were forcibly faced down.[61]

The result was a period of intense social and industrial unrest in the early post-war years.[62] This situation was greatly exacerbated by the government's

---

[58] Henderson had sensed the danger that this combination of factors posed at the time of the dissolution in 1918: HC, Debates, cx.2432–4 (7 Nov. 1918).
[59] See Hinton, *The first shop stewards' movement.*
[60] On the Lloyd George coalition see Morgan, *Consensus and disunity.*
[61] K. Jeffery, *The British army and the crisis of empire, 1918–1922*, Manchester 1984.
[62] See Morgan, *Consensus and disunity*, 46–79, and R. Miliband, *Parliamentary socialism: a study in the politics of Labour*, 2nd edn, London 1972, 1–72. On government policy in India and Ireland see Jeffery, *The British army*, 75–109.

policy on Russia and the linked question of conscription. The continuation of conscription after 1918, mainly it seemed for the purpose of fighting a working-class government abroad, caused a reaction against government policy at every level of the Labour movement.[63] A general sense of disillusionment thus grew within the British working-class movement, which inevitably reduced the willingness of many Labour members to trust government policy in any area.[64] The general shift of opinion, which critics of the war required, given their weak position within the policy-making structure of the Labour party, appeared to be occurring. The release of John Maynard Keynes's *Economic consequences of the peace* at the beginning of 1920 greatly increased this sense of disillusionment.[65] There seemed to be a chance that Labour's approach to the peace could be changed. Moreover, the very fact that many in the Labour movement were more preoccupied with matters other than the exact nature of the treaty and the League of Nations created an opportunity for those primarily interested in the post-war settlement.

Events in Europe also substantially increased pressure on Labour's centrist peace policy created by the domestic situation. Indeed, the radicalisation evident in Britain was even more marked in Europe.[66] It appeared as if European socialism was at the turning-point between revolution and reformism, with the Bolsheviks determined to force a break. This was made clear when, in Berne in January 1919, a meeting of all the main socialist parties was convened for the first time since 1914. The conference was primarily intended by Henderson, Albert Thomas, a French socialist, and Emile Vandervelde, a Belgian socialist, to pressure the Versailles conference into accepting a Wilsonian peace. A united campaign by the working-class parties, it was hoped, could prevent the construction of a militarist peace and ensure the acceptance of the League of Nations. Even before the conference began, however, it was clear that unity would be a difficult enough goal to achieve. One French socialist warned, for example, that 'if Vandervelde, Henderson and Branting imagine that ... we shall limit ourselves to uttering more or less platonic wishes in favour of the Society of Nations ... they make a strange mistake'.[67]

---

[63] By the spring of 1919, the director of intelligence at the Home Office reported to the Cabinet that opposition to conscription and intervention in Russia were linked directly. 'Every section of the workers', he said, was strongly opposed to both. 'Even mild trade unionists are said to be strongly moved by these matters.' See S. White, *Britain and the Bolshevik Revolution: a study in the politics of diplomacy, 1920–1924*, New York 1980, 27–54.

[64] See Milliband, *Parliamentary socialism*, 59–92, and Ward, *Red flag*, 150.

[65] Keynes, *Economic consequences*. In fact, Keynes's approach was more moderate than that of the UDC radicals and democratic socialists (see chapter 8 below).

[66] See, for example, A. J. Ryder, *The German Revolution of 1918: a study of German socialism in war and revolt*, Cambridge 1967.

[67] A. Van der Slice, *International labour diplomacy and peace, 1914–1919*, London 1941, 315.

The foreign policy resolutions adopted by the conference reflected the change that had taken place since the last major statement of allied war aims in February 1918.[68] On every important question there was a significant shift to the left. Whereas the 1918 statement had made clear that Germany should accept its share of responsibility for the war and would be expected to pay substantial reparations to help restore the damage caused by her aggression, no mention was made of responsibility or reparations at Berne. While in 1918 it had been accepted that the idea of a League of Nations ultimately implied a collective military security pact between nations against an aggressor, in 1919 the League's power to enforce its will was restricted to the use of 'economic pressure'. The concept of a 'League of Peoples', moreover, was made more explicit. Only on the basis of international socialism, it was suggested, could any supranational body succeed. Indeed, the League proposed at Berne was a blueprint for an international socialist state. It was not just to have emergency economic powers to cope with immediate postwar shortages, but was expected 'to develop into an organ controlling the production of foodstuffs and raw materials throughout the world with a view to the raising of that production to the highest degree of efficiency'.

A Labour 'conversion'?

Pressure mounted, therefore, on Labour moderates during the early postwar period to adopt a more outspoken response to the post-war settlement, but a vital and largely neglected reason for this pressure was the general shift leftwards in Labour and socialist politics that occurred at this time. To what extent, in this more conducive environment, were critics of the war successful in altering Labour's position on the peace up to 1921?

It is clear from official Labour party statements on the peacemaking process that the successes achieved by critics of war should not be exaggerated. For the most part the efforts of Labour moderates to resist a shift in the party's policy on the peace settlement were successful. Thus conference resolutions on foreign policy drafted by the executive committee between 1919 and 1921, while strongly critical of the Versailles Treaty, all continued to place limitations on the extent of revision that was required. Significantly, there was no direct repudiation of the requirement that Germany pay reparations nor of the measures imposed to limit her armed forces. At Southport, in 1919, the foreign policy resolution called for 'the immediate revision of the harsh provisions of the Treaty, *which are inconsistent with the statements made on behalf of the Allied Governments when the armistice was made*'.[69] The 1921 resolution contained a similar statement and significantly suggested

---

[68] This statement was based substantially on Labour's MOWA: *Report* (1919).
[69] Ibid. 142 (my emphasis). See also *Report* (1920), 132.

that such a revision would facilitate 'the earliest possible reparation of the damages of war'.[70] The left did occasionally manage to get 'freelance' resolutions passed at conference.[71] However, these posed no real challenge to the generally mainstream direction of policy.

Even when critics of the war in the NEC did manage to get their views reflected in party statements, Labour moderates quickly acted to repudiate their actions. This was the case with respect to the party's official statement on the Treaty of Versailles, which was drafted first by the NEC and was clearly influenced, with regard to the causes of the war and reparations, by ILP members on the committee.[72] This was too much for the PLP, which insisted on a re-draft to reflect their more mainstream views. Thus, for example, the new statement made clear that 'Labour always insisted that Germany must make full reparation for the wanton destruction in all the Allied countries.'[73]

The biggest single success for Labour moderates occurred at the 1921 conference in a debate on the government's Reparation Bill. This had been passed in April and sought the imposition of an export tax on German products in lieu of reparations payments. In the House of Commons debate on these measures, the PLP had decided to abstain on the first two readings and both Clynes and Thomas had made strong speeches, which although critical in parts, generally supported government policy. This caused outrage on the left, which manifested itself in a conference motion condemning 'the action of the Parliamentary Labour Party'. The debate on this motion represented the best chance in the early post-war period for critics of the war to gain some kind of retrospective vindication from the rest of the Labour movement. The left certainly saw the debate in these terms. Five speakers supported the motion, including the ILP's Richard Wallhead, who demanded 'a complete reversal of the Versailles decision so far as reparations are concerned'.[74]

In response Clynes strongly defended the moderates' approach to reparations. He insisted that it was not, and never had been, Labour's policy that Germany should 'pay nothing'. 'If [Labour] said Germany was to pay nothing', he added, 'they would hear something from the Socialists of France and Belgium.'[75] On this basis, Clynes concluded, the PLP had every reason to decide that opposition to the bill would be 'contrary to the decisions of the Labour Party conference on the question of Reparations'.[76] Despite the

---

[70] Ibid. (1921), 200.
[71] See, for example, ibid. (1922), 200–3.
[72] Unlike the Berne resolutions, this statement made reference to reparations. It stated that 'the total compensation [that Germany should] be required to pay should have regard to her obligation to meet the needs of her own population': ibid. (1919), 116.
[73] Ibid. 117.
[74] Ibid. 179. See also the contributions of ILP members, Buxton and Longstaff, to this debate.
[75] Ibid. 180.
[76] Ibid. 181.

best efforts of the left, this line was accepted by the conference. The motion was defeated on a card vote by 1,959,000 votes to 571,000. The best chance that the left had had of challenging the moderates' domination of party policy on Versailles had been resoundingly defeated.

Morel himself conceded in 1921 that his attempt to convert the Labour party to his view on the treaty had failed. Writing in May to a German friend who had criticised Labour's failure to adopt a more absolutist stance on the peace treaty, Morel replied that 'I can well understand your irritation with British Labour. But I have much more cause to be irritated with it than you have.' Influencing Labour opinion, he continued, was 'bound to be slow work', but it is clear that he was beginning to lose hope of ever succeeding. 'There are times', he wrote, 'when I feel that the task is too crushing to be gone on with.'[77]

On the League of Nations too, Labour moderates were generally successful in ensuring that the party maintained a mainstream approach. The party's 1919 statement on the new League, which was to serve as the foundation for all its subsequent pronouncements during this period, reflected their constructive, but critical, line.[78] It proposed twenty-two amendments to the draft covenant of the League, the main aim of which was to reform it into a body more consistent with Labour's ideal as proposed in its 1917 and 1918 policy statements. In particular, the resolution urged the immediate inclusion of the enemy powers, the democratisation of the Body of Delegates by the inclusion of representatives from all the leading national parties and an increase in the Body of Delegates' power at the expense of the Executive Council. No substantial concessions were made to those pushing for a more leftist stance on the basis of the Berne resolutions. Thus, the limited collective security provisions of the draft covenant were accepted without major amendment. No proposal was made to increase the League's economic powers. No link was made between the League of Nations and the International. Indeed, as if to emphasise the moderate nature of the resolution, Stuart-Binning, the chairman of the PCTUC, in proposing its acceptance claimed that its major aim was 'to strengthen the hands of Robert Cecil'.[79] The left was disappointed. Snowden said that Labour should merely have reiterated the statement made at Berne.[80] Nevertheless, during the following three years no official statement was released by Labour countermanding the moderate line on the League accepted in 1919.[81] Labour accepted a reformist approach: Labour and socialist parties, it was agreed at an international Labour and socialist congress at Geneva in 1920, should 'secure entry

[77] Morel to Count Von Graf Max Monteglas, 24 May 1921, Morel papers, F8/112I.
[78] Report (1919), 23–4.
[79] Manchester Guardian, 4 Apr. 1919. See also The Times, 4 Apr. 1919.
[80] Labour Leader, 10 Apr. 1919.
[81] Indeed, the party made little comment on the League up to 1921.

of their delegates to the League *as organised at present* ... so as to change the constitution [from within]'.[82]

A missed opportunity

While Labour's official policy statements on the peace settlement continued to reflect a centrist line on the post-war settlement up to 1921, it has be recognised that remarkably few statements were made by Labour during this period. This reflected the fact that for the bulk of the party the issue was not of great interest. This was evident as early as April 1919 at the party's conference on the League of Nations where, according to one observer, delegates displayed 'indifference and lethargy' about the subject being discussed.[83] Moreover, an attempt by Henderson in the summer of 1919 to organise a campaign, with the PCTUC, to press for the reform of the League of Nations and the revision of the Treaty of Versailles, came to nothing.[84]

At the same time, critics of the war became increasingly vocal in their opposition to the Versailles treaty. Utilising their near-domination of the Labour press, UDC radicals became ever more vociferous. More significantly, given its more formal character as an institution of the Labour party, the ACIQ also became more active.[85] It produced a series of pamphlets during this period with little direction or guidance from the party leadership, NEC or PLP.[86] Reflecting the democratic socialist inclinations of most of its members, these concentrated upon developing the ideas on international government that had developed during the war. In this regard, members of the committee argued for the League of Nations to take on greater economic functions and for the continuation and extension of the bodies set up by the allies during the war to assist economic co-operation.[87] Only this, it was argued, would ensure the economic revival of the European nations, a view which contrasted with that of Keynes, who, democratic socialists argued, underestimated the degree of intervention that was required to revitalise the

[82] See 'The International Labour and Socialist Congress, Geneva, 1920', LPA, LSI/1/38/1 (my emphasis).
[83] *Labour Leader*, 10 Apr. 1919.
[84] NEC minutes, organisation subcommittee, 3 June 1919; and ibid. JIC, 11 Nov. 1919, LPA. For Clynes's criticism of Labour's failure to sufficiently support the new League of Nations see HC, Debates, cxxix.1676–81 (20 May 1920), and *The Times*, 16 Aug. 1919.
[85] On its setting up in 1918, it had been assigned the task of assisting the party's leaders 'in the formation of an instructed, co-ordinated and democratic foreign policy', but the nature of the committee's relationship with the other main institutions had not been made clear: 'Terms of reference', unnumbered ACIQ memorandum, May 1918, LPA, LSI.
[86] The advisory committee had no direct contact with the PLP before November 1920.
[87] The committee proposed that the inter-allied bodies set up to control raw materials, shipping, credit and food should be democratised, enlarged and incorporated within the League structure: 'The Assembly of the League of Nations', unnumbered ACIQ memoranda, Jan. 1919, LPA, LSI. See also Orde, *British policy*, 28–9.

post-war economy. An economic interventionist League was also regarded by ACIQ members as the only guarantee of European security: collective security was supported by many on the committee but the LNU was criticised for concentrating too much on the diplomatic symptoms, rather than the economic causes, of international tensions.

The ACIQ's pamphlets were sent to the NEC, and usually, after cursory inspection, published as a party pamphlet. They bore the author's name, presumably in order to distinguish them from official party policy. There is certainly little evidence that the committee's approach had much support within the mainstream of the Labour party.

Nevertheless, given the relative paucity of official party statements, it is not surprising that some came to regard the advisory committees' pamphlets as Labour's policy.[88] At the very least, there was considerable confusion about who spoke for Labour with respect to the post-war settlement.[89] This situation contrasted markedly with that which had developed in the last year of the war. Then, with the release of the MOWA, Labour appeared more united than at any time during the conflict and certainly more united than its Liberal opponent. Together with the setting up of the ACIQ the memorandum seemed to indicate that Labour was, at last, taking seriously issues outside its traditional areas of interest. These impressions were an important reason why the party was considered by many at that time to be the emerging force – a probable replacement for the Liberal party on the left of British politics. These efforts to engage seriously with issues outside Labour's erstwhile sphere of interest did not end entirely at the end of the war. Labour leaders and its executive bodies were vocal in criticising government policy in Ireland and India, as well, of course, as in Russia. Two official delegations were sent to Ireland and a national campaign was launched against the deployment by government of the 'Black and Tans' in late 1920 and early 1921.[90]

However, with respect to the peacemaking process, Labour proved unable between 1918 and 1921 to maintain a level of serious engagement and thus a unified stance. With the obvious exception of Russia, it seemed to lose interest in events on the European mainland. This was symptomatic of more general organisational and political problems that the Labour party encountered during this period. It was only once these problems were tackled that the party was able to establish a more coherent and co-ordinated approach to the peace. The circumstances under which this occurred and the nature of this approach are the subject of the next chapter.

---

[88] See, for example, Eglantyne Jebb to John Maynard Keynes, 4 Aug. 1920, John Maynard Keynes papers, King's College, Cambridge.
[89] See, for example, C. Masterman, 'The case for a Liberal party', *The Nation* (May 1920), 245.
[90] See Worley, *Labour inside the gate*, 68.

7

The Co-ordination of Labour's Approach to Foreign Affairs, 1921

The UDC radicals were thus only a peripheral influence on Labour's response to the Versailles peace treaty in the early post-war years. Indeed, the main characteristics of Labour's policy development were not extremism and dissent but a lack of interest among the bulk of the party and an absence of policy co-ordination. This has clear implications for any understanding of the evolution of Labour's approach to European affairs in the period up to and including the 1924 government. Most commentators have argued that, as Labour moved closer to government, so its approach to the Versailles settlement became more moderate.[1] However, given that the early post-war radicalisation of Labour's view has been exaggerated the 'taming of Labour' thesis suffers from the fact that, in reality, there was little real 'taming' to be done. While important changes did take place in Labour's approach to the post-war settlement in the early 1920s, policy was not so much altered as co-ordinated around the generally mainstream position for which Labour moderates had been arguing since 1918. This did not occur as a result of Labour's experience of government, but predated it. It was caused by the combined effects of political, economic and international developments, all of which encouraged Labour to adopt a more coherent approach to European affairs based upon practical proposals for extracting the continent from the increasingly dangerous situation that it had begun to enter by the beginning of 1921.

The politics of the post-war settlement, 1918–21

Politically, the most significant development of the early post-war period was the increasingly intense competition between the Liberal party and Labour for predominance as the main progressive force in British politics. This was important because politicians and commentators engaged in the electoral struggle at the time regarded policy development as a key factor in electoral performance, and considered foreign affairs as a matter of particular concern. They did not believe, like some later historians, that Labour's position had

---

[1] Winkler, *Emergence*, 247; Cline, *Recruits*, 84–6; Naylor, *Labour's international policy*, 6–7.

been made secure by the franchise change of 1918, which brought into the electorate a greater number of working-class voters.[2] Few regarded the subsequent general election as a breakthrough and the Liberals had certainly not been written off as an electoral force.[3] Moreover, as post-war politics developed, evidence increased of what seemed to be an even more dangerous threat to Labour than a Liberal revival: the permanent establishment of an avowedly anti-Labour coalition made up of the Conservative and centrist Liberals.[4]

Labour politicians were greatly exercised in the early post-war period by these perceived threats to the party's electoral position, notwithstanding some encouraging municipal election results in 1919.[5] The party's performance during 1920 caused particular concern. As Howard suggests, party leaders were disappointed by 1921 with the overall progress made and throughout this period 'Henderson, MacDonald, Snowden and Thomas all retained the manifold insecurities of the pre-war years'.[6]

Most agreed on the political strategy required to make Labour's position more secure. The party needed to broaden the base of its support, moving beyond the union-dominated, class conscious enclaves in which it was already strong, to attract wavering Liberal and Conservative voters, many of whose class loyalties were less clear-cut. This strategy had been in place since 1917. Broadening Labour's appeal had been an important aspect of the party's re-launch as a fully independent force at that time. It was not just

---

[2] For debates on the significance, or otherwise, of the 1918 franchise change see H. C. G. Matthew, R. I. McKibbin and J. A. Kay, 'The franchise factor in the rise of the Labour party', *EHR* xci (1976), 723–52, and D. M. Tanner, 'The parliamentary electoral system, the "fourth" reform act and the rise of Labour in England and Wales', *BIHR* lvi (1983), 205–19. For a full assessment of Labour's performance in the 1918 general election see M. Pugh, *The making of modern British politics, 1867–1939*, Oxford 1982, 200; Tanner, *Political change*, 429; and Turner, *British politics*, 405.

[3] For Henderson's concerns about the prospect of a Liberal revival see Henderson to Sidney Webb, 17 May 1919, Passfield papers, II. See also Howard, 'Henderson, MacDonald and the leadership of the Labour party', ch. viii. This view has been endorsed by subsequent scholarship: Turner, *British politics*, 435; Tanner, *Political change*, 428.

[4] Turner regards this as the broader political purpose of the Lloyd George coalition by 1918: *British politics*, 434. See also Cowling, *Impact of Labour*.

[5] In November 1919 Labour won control of many London councils, and greatly increased its representation in many provincial cities. The party also made by-election gains around this time in Bothwell, Widnes, Dartford and Spen Valley: Howard, 'Henderson, MacDonald and the leadership of the Labour party', 66; Cowling, *Impact of Labour*, 1–2.

[6] Howard, 'Henderson, MacDonald and the leadership of the Labour party', 269. Evidence of a Liberal revival grew early in 1920, with the success of Asquith at the Paisley by-election in February. Meanwhile, Labour's overall results were not particularly good: see, for example, G. Phillips, *The rise of the Labour party*, London 1992, 34–5; Howell, *MacDonald's party*, 19; and Worley, *Labour inside the gate*, 24, 29, 30.

better organisation that was regarded as important, but the adoption of a broader and more sophisticated approach to the development of policy.[7]

It is in this context that Labour's approach to foreign affairs was important. The party's more independent stance on the war had been a vital component in the development of this political strategy and played an important part in raising Labour's political credibility at this time. The 1917 MOWA had shown for the first time that the party was willing to think seriously about foreign affairs and engage knowledgeably and innovatively in a major debate outside its traditional areas of interest. The setting up of the ACIQ as an institutional mechanism through which left-leaning intellectuals could genuinely expect to influence the party's policy had also seemed to be of great value in this regard.[8]

If the party was to present itself as a credible alternative government, it was considered vital that Labour showed a continued willingness and ability to engage competently in debates on issues of foreign affairs.[9] There were three main reasons for this view. First, and most obviously, foreign affairs was throughout this period a major area of political debate, about which any party serious about taking office had to have a considered view. Second, for Labour, the political importance of having a coherent and considered policy on foreign affairs was regarded as even greater given the enduring perception that the party ultimately remained little more than one of 'wages and hours', committed primarily to advancing the economic interests of the trade union movement. Third, issues of foreign affairs were the primary interest of many of the wavering Liberal or progressive intellectuals and politicians whom Labour was hoping to attract to its banner, and who, by choosing Labour over the Liberals would, it was believed, greatly add to the credibility of the younger party.

The general consensus among historians who accept a link between policy and electoral politics is that with regard to this political purpose, Labour's approach to foreign affairs in the years after 1918 was largely successful. For the most part an entirely unproblematic relationship has been posited between the party's foreign policy and its political and electoral progress at this time. Indeed, Labour's stance on foreign affairs has been highlighted by some historians as an important reason for its gradual displacement of the Liberal party. Robert Dowse, for example, suggests that 'the Labour Party became the party *par excellence* of foreign affairs'. Largely for this reason, 'at a vital point in the rise of the Labour Party and the decline of the Liberal Party, the former gained the support of a highly intelligent and vocal group of ex-Liberals'. This, in turn, increased Labour's 'cachet of respectability' and sapped the intellectual strength of the Liberal party, thus hastening its

---

[7] See Worley, *Labour inside the gate*, 39–74.
[8] See Ward, *Red flag*, 167–72.
[9] See, for example, A. Henderson, 'The outlook for Labour', *Contemporary Review* cxiii (1918), 121–30.

collapse.[10] If some progressive Liberals were slower to make this change, it was not because they had concerns about Labour's approach to foreign policy; it was rather because they continued to believe that the Liberal party was a viable political force or had more general concerns about the Labour party, particularly its class nature and domination by the trade unions.[11] This interpretation portrays the Liberal-to-Labour process as a relatively straight-forward and self-perpetuating continuum, whereby the entry of the large group of ex-Liberal UDC-ers into the Labour party during, and shortly after, the war facilitated an almost inevitable stream in this direction.[12]

However, there are serious problems with this interpretation. The politics of foreign affairs in the early post-war period were a good deal more compli-cated. Yes, Labour did try to maintain a presence in debates on international matters, particularly those related to the empire. However, overall, the party proved incapable during the early post-war period of maintaining and devel-oping the broad embryonic coalition on European policy that it had seemed close to creating in the early months of 1918. While Labour did eventually become, during the 1920s, the main standard-bearer for most progressive critics of the post-war settlement, this was a much slower process than is often suggested. It had certainly not occurred up to 1922.

The main reason for this disappointing progress was Labour's failure to become fully involved in the campaign of support for the League of Nations and, more generally, the rapidity with which the bulk of the party lost interest in the Versailles treaty after its release. This helped again to raise all the doubts about Labour as a party of government. Once more accusa-tions that it was little more that a 'wages and hours party' became common.[13] This situation was exacerbated by the nature of the PLP in the first post-war parliament and its widely-publicised failure to pressurise more successfully the Lloyd George coalition on the post-war settlement and its consequences. In this regard, Jowett, on behalf of the NAC, wrote to Henderson in April 1920 that the committee had 'noticed with extreme regret the apathy and indifference of the parliamentary Labour Party on questions of foreign policy'. 'If the Labour Party', he continued, 'is going to justify its existence as a party with interests beyond the mere question of wages and Labour conditions, it will have to show a greater interest in International matters.'[14]

However, even the activities of those elements in the Labour party that did retain an interest in the post-war settlement were not necessarily politi-cally helpful to the party. The ACIQ, for example, had been set up with the specific aim of attracting a broad range of progressive opinion on foreign

---

[10] R. G. Dowse, 'The Independent Labour Party and foreign politics', *IRSH* vii (1962), 33–46..

[11] See also Cline, *Recruits*, 68–99, and Blaazer, *Popular front*, 105.

[12] For a recent example see Howell, *MacDonald's party*, 312.

[13] See, for example, *The Nation* (May 1920), 245–6.

[14] Fred Jowett to Henderson, 17 Apr. 1920, Johnson papers.

affairs to Labour's banner. In this regard the Webbs had believed in 1918 that the post-war world would see a greater general acceptance of the need for 'supernational' intervention in the world economy, a belief shared for different reasons by Brailsford and Roden Buxton.[15] On this basis the advisory committee demanded a more interventionist role for the League of Nations or the development and extension of wartime allied bodies. However, the domination of Labour's advisory committee by democratic socialists proved problematic politically. Leading Liberals were dismissive of their approach and regarded it as evidence that intellectually Labour was dominated by statist socialism. Led by Keynes, who remained generally supportive of the efficacy of free trade both for economic development and the harmonisation of international relations, they rejected the need for such heavy-handed supranational intervention.[16] Keynes explicitly ruled out the possibility of a united front with Labour on foreign affairs in August 1920 because of the proposals made by the party's advisory committee. 'I have seldom read anything', he commented, 'in which the remedies proposed were so disproportionate to the evils to be cured.'[17] Charles Masterman, a leading left-wing Liberal, who was repeatedly rumoured to be close to joining the Labour party, was similarly dismayed by the 'statist' and 'bureaucratic' implications of the advisory committee's proposals.[18] Moreover, by the end of 1920, the advisory committee's interest in supernationalism not only appeared to mainstream Liberals as excessively bureaucratic, it also appeared, with the winding up of the inter-allied wartime bodies, as increasingly unrealistic and out of touch.

If the socialist preoccupations of the advisory committee were a problem politically, the association of the Labour party with ex-UDC radicals, such as Morel and Ponsonby, was also damaging. Those accounts which argue that the entry of this group into the Labour party in the early post-war period was politically helpful to the party considerably underestimate the extent to which Morel, in particular, was regarded as a political pariah by mainstream Liberals by 1919.[19] Given his uncompromising defence of Germany's behaviour in 1914 and outspoken attack on Grey and the British foreign policy establishment his association with Labour was unlikely to convince wavering sympathisers that the party was capable of adopting a 'responsible' attitude to foreign affairs.

---

[15] As Trentmann has shown, the Webbs were not entirely unjustified in this belief: 'The strange death of free trade', 237–41.

[16] On Keynes and free trade see R. Skidelsky, *John Maynard Keynes: hopes betrayed, 1883–1920*, London 1983, 121–2, 227–8, and *John Maynard Keynes: the economist as saviour, 1920–1937*, London 1992, 151–2.

[17] Keynes to Jebb, 4 Aug 1920, Keynes papers, L20. Leading new liberals had always been concerned about the implications for free trade of Hobson's thought, on which the advisory committee's proposals were based: see, for example, Clarke, *Liberals*, 90–9.

[18] *The Nation*, 15 May 1920, 244–6.

[19] See, for example, Ponsonby to Gilbert Murray, 25 Nov. 1922, Gilbert Murray papers, Bodl. Lib., MS 190 (57–9).

If the pull on progressive opinion of the Labour party's approach to foreign affairs in the early post-war period can be exaggerated, so too can the push that is said to have developed because of the collapse of the Liberal party. Many Liberals continued to believe that their party would re-unite and thus represent their foreign policy interests. Alternatively, a new centrist party at times seemed a possibility.[20] Moreover, the existence, growth and relative success of the Liberal-dominated LNU in the early post-war period to a large extent masked, with respect to foreign affairs, the ineffectiveness that characterised the Liberal party's performance in other policy areas at this time.[21]

Indeed, there is little evidence to support the idea that the early post-war period saw a broad swathe of progressive opinion move from the Liberals to Labour on the basis of their respective approaches to foreign affairs. If there was a 'foreign legion' at this time, it was only the size of a platoon. Most of the Liberals who shifted their allegiance were UDC radicals and they had been semi-detached for years and, with the loss of their seats in 1918, had few other places to go.

Thus, Labour did not become the party 'par excellence of foreign affairs' up to 1922. Its approach to foreign affairs, rather than acting to counteract the growing doubts within progressive circles about the party's credibility as the main reforming party of the state, only served to reinforce them.[22] It seemed to confirm all the preconceptions held by wavering progressive politicians and intellectuals: Labour appeared politically and organisationally immature, obsessed with the interests of the trades unions and at risk of becoming ideologically dominated by socialist 'dogma'.

Labour's moderate leadership was well aware of these criticisms and concerned about them. In particular, they were worried because they helped to feed the growing representation of the party at this time as 'unfit to govern', an impression that the Conservatives were anxious to make general and Labour was desperate to counteract.[23] The Fabian lectures in April 1920 tried to address this issue directly. Entitled 'A new outlook for foreign policy', they sought to challenge 'the alleged unfitness of the Labour Party to conduct foreign policy' and the idea that 'foreign policy is in itself more difficult than domestic policy'.[24] Labour's interventions on Ireland and India were at least partially motivated by similar concerns. However, such initiatives were of limited use so long as the attention of the bulk of the party remained on other subjects and while the structure of foreign policy-making remained so haphazard. Labour would only truly appear credible on foreign

---

[20] See Cowling, *Impact of labour*, 60–9.
[21] Robert Cecil, for example, saw the League of Nations Union as the embryo out of which a new centre party might be born: ibid.
[22] *The Nation*, for example, commented on 9 July 1921 that 'The easy optimism of the early post-Armistice period is dead; and the Labour Party is now fighting for its existence.'
[23] See, for example, Milliband, *Parliamentary socialism*, 97.
[24] See Passfield papers, IX.

policy once it showed a complete commitment to the issue and spoke with one voice on the subject. Fortunately for Labour, broader economic and international changes in 1920/21 made this more likely. A growth in unemployment and a worsening in the international situation put foreign affairs firmly back on Labour's agenda. At the same time, the political purchase of a more moderate international stance rose as the constraints on – and limitations of – the government's military-based approach became clear, not least to government ministers and officials.[25] These events, in turn, increased the party's need for a more co-ordinated and practically-minded approach to the issues raised by the post-war settlement.

Unemployment, reparations and Labour's approach to foreign affairs, 1920–1

In the first two years after the war there had seemed little material reason for trade unionists to concern themselves with events in the west of Europe.[26] However great the outrage expressed by some about the Versailles settlement, there seemed little chance that hostilities would be resumed in the foreseeable future. Moreover, given the post-war boom, the treaty appeared to be having a minimal effect on the economic situation.

Matters changed rapidly after the late summer of 1920. Important developments in the economic and international situation, and the interpretation of these events by Labour leaders, dramatically altered the policy priorities of the Labour movement. As a result, the issues raised by events in Germany and France once again moved near the top of Labour's political agenda, with the consequence that the need for the party to develop a more co-ordinated and coherent approach to them was reinforced.

Of these changes, the transformation in the economic situation was the most dramatic and important. The post-war economic boom proved to be extremely short-lived. It began to break in the middle of 1920. By the following year, industrial production in Britain had fallen by 18.6 per cent. Unemployment rocketed. In 1920 on average 2.4 per cent of trade union members were unemployed; during 1921 this figure reached 14.8 per cent.[27]

The causes of this slump remain an area of controversy.[28] However, for the purposes of this study, what is most important is Labour's response, and the effect this had on its approach to the post-war settlement. As a party committed to full employment, and electorally reliant to a significant extent

[25] See Jeffery, British army.
[26] See Thorpe, British Labour party, 48–9.
[27] Orde, British policy, 146.
[28] For details of this debate see D, Winch, Economics and policy, London 1969; S. Pollard, The gold standard and employment policy between the wars, London 1970; and D. Moggridge, British monetary policy, Cambridge 1972.

on a working-class constituency that was likely to be badly affected by an economic downturn, it was vital that Labour have credible proposals for dealing with the new situation. This need was made greater by the fact that rising unemployment was an issue that the newly-emerging British Communist party could seize upon to gain new adherents. There were a number of possible responses realistically open to Labour.[29] It could, for example, have taken an explicitly socialist line and argued that unemployment was an inevitable feature of capitalism, which could only be addressed by taking into common ownership the means of production.[30] This response was certainly favoured on the left of the party. However, such an approach would be of little benefit to unemployed workers in the short-term. Even if Labour came to power, its plans for the socialisation of the means of production were long-term ones, which – assuming that they were effective – were unlikely to have any immediate effect on the level of unemployment. Thus, while the party did make clear in most of its statements on unemployment that ultimately the only long-term solution was the introduction of socialism, Labour also needed a policy response to cover the period before this goal was achieved.

Labour had also been committed, since Beatrice Webb's minority report to the Poor Law Commission in 1909, to public works as a solution to unemployment.[31] However, as Evan Durbin suggests, the attitude of the party to public works was 'ambivalent', particularly among the trade unions that were sceptical about them 'because of their connotations of relief work and the dreaded Poor Law'.[32] This was evident in 1921, when little mention was made of public works.

For these reasons, Labour leaders sought to explain the economic downturn of 1921 very much in relation to events in Europe. What was required to reduce unemployment was the revitalisation of trade on the continent. Such an approach fitted in well with the beliefs of most leading Labour members and trade unionists, such as Henderson, Thomas and Clynes, who as committed international free traders were used to making connections between foreign affairs and domestic policy. From being a peripheral issue in Labour politics for most of the two years after the Treaty of Versailles, therefore, the post-war settlement was swiftly transformed at the beginning of 1921 into a matter at the forefront of its concerns.

This development was reinforced by the fact that, due to continued wranglings between the wartime allies and Germany over reparations, the

[29] Of these realistic responses, a less stringent approach to budgetary policy was not one. Keynes's General theory remained fifteen years down the line and Labour remained very conservative with respect to budgetary matters: E. Durbin, New Jerusalems: the Labour party and the economics of democratic socialism, London 1985, 52–61.
[30] See ibid. 52–6, and N. Thompson, Political economy and the Labour party: the economics of democratic socialism, 1884–1995, London 1996, 64–5.
[31] Durbin, New Jerusalems, 55.
[32] Ibid. 57.

international situation was becoming more volatile, a situation which was confirmed in January 1921 by France's decision to occupy a number of Ruhr towns. After twenty-four months, during which the relationship between the wartime allies and Germany had remained strained but unthreatening, suddenly in 1921, a renewal of hostilities seemed possible. For those in the Labour party whose attention had been elsewhere, these events were a timely reminder that, while the war was over, the potential for conflict between the wartime foes remained substantial.

Given this transformation in the economic and international situation at the beginning of 1921, foreign policy enthusiasts within the Labour party suddenly encountered a more receptive response. The reaction of the NEC in February 1921 to an advisory committee memorandum on unemployment and the international situation by Brailsford was particularly significant. This document, 'Unemployment, the peace and the indemnity', made a detailed and systematic link between the economic problems being experienced in Britain and the demands made on Germany as a consequence of the post-war settlement.[33] At Henderson's prompting, it was hastily agreed that the memorandum would be the subject of a joint meeting of the PLP, NEC and PCTUC. This was an unprecedented response to an advisory committee memorandum.[34] At the meeting it was decided that the memorandum should be published immediately and undersigned by the three committees.[35]

However, in many ways this was an *ad hoc* and opportunistic response to a growing crisis. Henderson had seized the opportunity raised by Brailsford's memorandum to ensure that Labour had an adequate policy on the unemployment crisis, consistent with its political and ideological aims. However, it was not clear that adopting the line proposed by Brailsford represented the best approach. There was much in his memorandum that was controversial.[36] Indeed, in its comments on the post-war settlement it was considerably more outspoken than the more careful line that Labour moderates had been seeking to maintain since 1914. Thus, for example, it was equivocal with respect to the role of German militarism in the coming of war in 1914, and claimed that the conflict had been 'unduly prolonged'.[37] Both these claims carried echoes of the wartime position of the UDC and were in contrast to Labour's wartime stance. Moreover, the memorandum continued to reflect, in parts, Brailsford's support for international economic government and, in

[33] ACIQ memoranda, Feb. 1921, LPA; Labour party, *Unemployment, the peace and the indemnity*, London 1921.

[34] Advisory committee memoranda had previously been passed over by the national executive with very little comment.

[35] NEC minutes, 16 Feb. 1921, LPA. See also meetings between the NEC, PLP and PCTUC, 14, 17 Feb. 1921.

[36] Labour party, *Unemployment*.

[37] Ibid. 6, 5 respectively. On the issue of war responsibility, the memorandum implied that the conflict was the result of an accident rather than a definite policy decision; that Germany's leaders 'stumbled' and 'staggered' into the war.

tone, adopted a noticeably more critical line towards France than previous Labour party statements.[38] There was little evidence that the step away from free international trade that Brailsford's memorandum seemed to imply, would mobilise general support, especially given the collapse of the inter-allied bodies and Keynes's criticisms. A more critical line towards France, on the other hand, conflicted with the PLP's approach to the reparations issue. If these difficulties were not ironed out, Labour's renewed interest in the post-war settlement threatened simply to expose its divisions and organisational deficiencies, with negative consequences for its electoral standing.

The greatly increased salience for Labour of the issues raised by the post-war settlement thus had the effect of reinforcing the party's need for a more co-ordinated, coherent and detailed approach to the questions of European reconstruction and security than had been the case since 1919. For this to occur, what was required was a thorough reorganisation of the party's foreign policy-making procedures to remove the many ambiguities between the various party institutions with respect to questions of responsibility and accountability. In fact, for other reasons, the momentum for just such a step had already begun to grow.

Labour party reorganisation and foreign policy-making

The reorganisation process in which Labour engaged between 1920 and 1921 has generally been regarded as resulting from Henderson's desire to unify the industrial and political wings of the Labour movement, and there is little doubt that this provides an important part of the explanation.[39] However, as Howard has argued, the reorganisation must also be placed in the context of political developments at this time, and be seen as a response by Labour leaders, particularly Henderson, to the party's continuing electoral vulnerability.[40] Howard focuses on administrative and institutional reforms to Labour's electoral apparatus. However, the 1920/21 reorganisation also involved important changes to the party's policy-making structure, most of which were designed to co-ordinate policy development and presentation. Labour's approach to foreign affairs was a major priority. The reorganisation of 1920/21 thus provides an important and largely ignored explanation for the important changes that took place in Labour's approach to foreign policy in the early 1920s. What occurred in 1921 was that greater co-ordination was established between the PLP and the other institutions of the party, the

---

[38] Ibid. 11–12. Nevertheless, the document did emphasise the 'cruel devastation' that France had suffered and proposed that she should receive priority in the distribution of reparations: see chapter 9 below.

[39] See McKibbin, *Evolution of the Labour party*, 210–11, and Minkin, *Contentious alliance*, 18–19.

[40] Howard, 'Henderson, MacDonald and the leadership of the Labour party', ch. viii.

ACIQ was brought more firmly under the control of the party leadership and the party's presentation of policy was revamped.

The process was initially sparked by the TUC's decision to reconsider its own organisational arrangements in light of co-ordination problems that had occurred between the three members of the Triple Alliance during the September 1919 rail strike.[41] As a result, in November 1919, a Trade Union Co-ordination Committee was set up and assigned the task of increasing the powers of the PCTUC. Henderson was a member of this committee, but his agenda was considerably more ambitious. He had long been obsessed by the organisational unity of the German labour movement around the SPD, and saw the committee as an opportunity to emulate this model, by linking more formally the industrial and political wings of the Labour party.[42] As V. L. Allen suggests, Henderson's proposals for reform were 'based on the premise that there should be the maximum co-operation between the trade unions and the Labour Party to devise a common policy and effect joint action'.[43]

Henderson's plan was not just based on a desire to bring together the administrative and policy-making processes of the TUC and the Labour party, however. It was also a response to repeated problems of administration and policy co-ordination that had occurred within the Labour party since 1918.[44] Henderson's aim was to make less ambiguous the relationships between the NEC and the PLP, the advisory committees and the PLP, and the advisory committees and the NEC. In all these relationships, clear lines of communication and co-ordination were notably absent. Henderson frankly admitted that the existing situation was chaotic. He argued that 'Hitherto it must be acknowledged the relationships between the various departments have been too haphazard and each department has generally pursued its own particular work without much attention to relations with other departments.' There was thus a need for 'closer co-operation all around'. The establishment of 'closer working' between the advisory committees, the PLP and the party's press and publicity department was highlighted as a particular priority.[45]

The difficulties caused by lack of policy co-ordination had often manifested themselves in Labour's presentation of its policy on the post-war settlement. The ACIQ's pamphlets on that subject, for example, which few in the

---

[41] V. L. Allen, 'The reorganisation of the Trades Union Congress, 1918–1927', *British Journal of Sociology* xi (1960), 26–7. The failure of the National Union of Railwaymen even to consult its partners about the strike emphasised the *ad hoc* arrangements that existed for communication and co-ordination in the Alliance and, more generally, within the Labour movement. See also McKibbin, *Evolution of the Labour party*, 210.

[42] McKibbin, *Evolution of the Labour party*, 246.

[43] Allen, 'Reorganisation', 26. As Howell shows, however, the reorganisation that took place on this basis was to be short-lived: *MacDonald's party*. See also Worley, *Labour inside the gate*, 37–8.

[44] See Henderson's memorandum on co-ordination, section B: NEC minutes, 19 Oct. 1920, LPA.

[45] Ibid.

party had seen, let alone endorsed, and which conflicted with comments made by others in the party, emphasised the organisational failings of the party and its divisions.

It was to prevent a recurrence of these problems that important changes were made to the foreign policy-making apparatus of the Labour party as part of the 1920/21 reorganisation. These included the setting up of a joint department of the TUC and the Labour party on international affairs – including representatives of the NEC and PCTUC – which would oversee the work of the ACIQ. The involvement of the trade unions in the development of Labour's approach to the post-war settlement was thus increased. At the same time, the role of the advisory committee was made less ambiguous and more focused as part of a general review of the party's advisory committee structure. In contrast to the relatively free role that they had enjoyed since 1918, the advisory committees were assigned more specific tasks, namely to work out a general policy for the Labour party executive to consider; to assist the parliamentary party; to advise the Labour party executive on current questions; and to assist Labour representatives on local bodies.[46] They were effectively to become 'the day-to-day service departments of the party'.[47] Important changes were made to the personnel and structure of the committees to emphasise this new role. William Gillies, secretary of the International Department, was appointed secretary of the ACIQ.[48] He would be the 'international officer of the party' and be directly accountable to Henderson. At the same time, the non-MP membership of the committees was overhauled and the publication of party material brought under greater central co-ordination. The link between the advisory committee and the PLP was also made stronger. Henceforth, Tom Shaw, one of the leading spokespersons on foreign affairs in the PLP, was to chair the committee and its meetings were to be held in the House of Commons. Moreover, they would be open to all Labour MPs.

The 1920/21 reorganisation process thus included a concerted attempt by Labour's leadership to gain a firmer hold on the development and presentation of policy on foreign affairs to ensure that all party statements and memoranda reflected the mainstream views held by the majority of the movement. The views of the UDC radicals were further marginalised. Even when, in 1922, Morel, Ponsonby and Trevelyan were returned to parliament as Labour MPs for the first time, and gained an automatic right to attend advisory committee meetings, the new organisational arrangements, together with the continued involvement with the advisory committee of

[46] Ibid.
[47] McKibbin, *Evolution*, 218.
[48] Gillies had joined Labour's research staff in 1912. He was later described by Denis Healy as 'a cantankerous Scot, who distrusted foreigners and hated all Germans': Collette, *The international faith*, 49.

individuals with whom they disagreed, ensured that they were unable to exert any great influence over policy development.

However, there was a further problem which had to be resolved, if the party was to present a more organised and united face. This was Ramsay MacDonald, his position in the party and relationship with the party leadership. The former party leader had been defeated at the 1918 election and, other than his membership of the NEC, appeared to be facing a future in the political wilderness. However, he remained a potent focus for dissent, particularly for those who opposed the centrists' line on the war. Moreover, to a large extent, MacDonald also remained Labour's biggest electoral asset, despite his wartime role.[49] For these reasons, considerable effort was expended, by Henderson in particular, from mid-1920 on reincorporating MacDonald into the party's mainstream.[50]

Given MacDonald's moderate line on most policy areas, it might be thought that his approach to foreign affairs would have caused the most difficulty. After all, MacDonald's semi-detached relationship with the party leadership since 1914 had been due mainly to differences on the war and Labour's policy on the peace. However, MacDonald's views on the war were considerably less clear-cut than many of his supporters appreciated. With Labour's adoption of the MOWA in 1917, there was very little between him and the party leadership. Moreover, while his condemnation of the post-war settlement had been every bit as outspoken as Morel's, his view on how the settlement should be revised was different. The way forward, he believed was to adopt 'a "European" attitude about the peace terms, rather than a pro-German one, protesting against the Treaty on the grounds that it does not rebuild the economic life of the world and provide for industrial reconstruction'.[51] On this basis, as was quickly to become clear once MacDonald regained the leadership of the party, his views on reparations, the treatment of Germany and the reconstruction of Europe were close to those of Henderson, Clynes and Thomas. His reincorporation into the party mainstream therefore proved relatively straightforward. In November 1920 he was persuaded to act as secretary of the Berne International. This tied him much more closely to the party mainstream, a situation which was ultimately cemented when he was re-elected Labour's leader after the general election of December 1922.

To summarise, Labour's political difficulties in the early post-war period,

---

[49] In this regard Marquand argues that 'by temperament and conviction, MacDonald was better fitted than any of his potential rivals to become the focal point around which [a progressive] coalition could take shape': *Ramsay MacDonald*, 245–6.

[50] In June 1920 an attempt was made to involve him in an advisory capacity with the PLP, an initiative which collapsed due to opposition from within the PLP: Beatrice Webb diary, Passfield papers, I, unpublished entry for 18–25 June 1920.

[51] Sidney Webb to Beatrice Webb, 23 June 1919, ibid. II3. His views on the League of Nations remained different from Labour moderates. However this did not become an issue until 1924.

together with the requirement to respond positively to the changed economic and political context, made urgent a rationalisation of party organisation and procedures. This not only involved improvements in the party's electoral machinery, but also focused on Labour's policy-making apparatus. As part of this process, and because of the growing political and economic importance of international affairs, the co-ordination of the party's approach to foreign affairs was a central task. What this meant with respect to Labour's approach to the substantive issues raised by the post-war settlement was that the party's position became more consistent than previously. It also become more practically-minded, focusing less on the underlying causes of international conflict and more on the ways in which immediate problems might be solved. Ideologically, Labour became more definitely Keynesian on reparations and further entrenched its Gladstonian liberal line on the League of Nations. However, there was another significant development, Labour's developing relationship with its sister parties in Europe, which greatly reinforced these trends.

The Labour and socialist Internationals and the post-war settlement, 1919–21

The changing situation within the International socialist movement in 1921 and, in particular, the renewal of direct contacts between British Labour and the French Socialist party as part of the gradual reunification of the non-Bolshevik parties, has largely been ignored by historians as an influence on the policy Labour adopted on the post-war settlement up to 1924.[52] As David Marquand has suggested, '[t]o a generation for whom the whole concept of international socialism is at most a memory', developments in the relationship between the various European socialist and Labour parties at this time might appear 'remote and irrelevant'.[53] This is consistent with the prevalent belief that the British Labour party was 'parochial, that it had few contacts with international socialists from other countries, and that it was not particularly interested in European socialism'.[54]

Yet such a view is inconsistent with developments in 1917 and 1918, when Labour's adoption of a more independent line on the war took place in the context of negotiations with allied socialists and was based, at least in part, on a desire to re-open contact with German and Italian socialists. Ultimately, these developments led to the Berne conference in January 1919, in the management and organisation of which Labour played an extremely large part.

However, Berne did not mark the end of Labour's negotiations with her sister socialist parties over the shape of the post-war world. Labour remained

---

[52] For a recent exception see Vickers, *Labour party and the world.*
[53] Marquand, *Ramsay MacDonald,* 252.
[54] Berger, *British Labour party,* 207.

committed to this process in the early post-war period. Indeed, for some, such as MacDonald, it was regarded as Labour's central and most important task with respect to the avoidance of another war.[55] Henderson also had a long-standing commitment to the International movement, although his interest was also by this stage based on more prosaic considerations, particularly the role he envisaged for a moderate reformist international socialist and Labour movement in providing a bulwark against Bolshevism. Nevertheless, whatever the exact reasons, Labour maintained extremely close contact with its sister parties in the early post-war period.[56]

With regard to the changes in Labour's approach to foreign affairs after 1921, what is most important about this association is that the nature of the party's international contacts changed from the beginning of this year. Two changes are particularly important. The first relates to the divisions in the International movement that had developed after the Berne conference and attempts from 1921 to pull together the non-Bolshevik socialist forces. The second concerns negotiations on the international situation, which also began at this time, at least partially explaining the increased desire for socialist unity, and which continued simultaneously with the reunification process.

With regard to the first development, the eighteen months since Berne had seen the splits evident at the conference – mainly the result of differing attitudes towards Bolshevism – become institutionalised in the form of three separate 'Internationals'. Thus, while the Berne International continued and was dominated by anti-revolutionary parties, such as the British Labour party and the German SPD, the early post-war period also saw the creation, by the Bolsheviks, of the Third International. In the meantime, the independents, including the USPD, the French Socialist party and the British ILP, who were more sympathetic to the revolutionary ideal but critical of Bolshevik methods, together formed the Vienna Union in February 1921.[57]

Given these divisions, for most of the eighteen months after Berne, Labour's contact with the International movement was overwhelmingly dominated by attempts to minimise their extent. Little attention was thus given, within the International movement, to the international situation. The construction of a common working-class policy was a non-starter. Moreover, the conversations that the British Labour party did have with international socialist opinion on the post-war settlement were limited by the divided nature of the International movement. The party with which Labour had most contact in the early post-war period was the German SPD

55 Marquand, *Ramsay MacDonald*, 252.

56 Berger, *British Labour party*; J. F. P. Wrynn, *The socialist International and the politics of European reconstruction*, Amsterdam 1976.

57 The Vienna Union was not an alternative International, but aimed to work for the creation of a unified international movement. On developments in the International movement during this period see Wrynn, *Socialist International*.

while direct contact with the French Socialist party (SFIO), on the other hand, was lost.

There are good grounds for believing that this situation had a distorting effect on Labour's view of developments on the European mainland. Many in the German SPD had backed the war and, although this support had retrospectively been disavowed, there was evidence that similar attitudes persisted in the early post-war period.[58] As Wrynn suggests, for example, there remained a good deal of ambiguity about the German SPD's acceptance of an obligation to reconstruct the war-damaged areas in France and Belgium.[59] Moreover, for the entire period up to the summer of 1920, the German SPD was in government, mainly with coalition partners from the centre. Given the political situation in Germany and the intense unpopularity of the Versailles Treaty, the party could not afford to become too closely associated with a pro-reparations position; such a stance would have been electorally disastrous. Thus, while the German SPD never adopted a purely nationalistic policy on the post-war settlement, neither was it, in contacts with the British Labour party, likely to argue strongly against a fundamental revision of the Versailles Treaty.

At the same time, Labour lost direct contact with important elements of international working-class opinion whose views on the post-war settlement were more positive, particularly with respect to reparations. Most important was the loss of contact with the French Socialist party. This might seem surprising. After all, the reason for the French socialists' split from the Berne International was the fact that the anti-war group associated with Jean Longuet managed to gain control in 1919.[60] For this reason, one might have expected this anti-war group to have been unequivocally hostile to the post-war settlement. However, while this was certainly true of some in the party, there remained a significant number, particularly among the SFIO's National Assembly deputies, who strongly supported the reparations clauses of the Versailles Treaty, particularly as they related to the devastated areas in northern France. As Wrynn suggests, while '[f]rom the very beginning, French socialism advocated a policy of revision with regard to the work of

---

[58] On the German SPD's attitude towards the post-war settlement see S. Miller and H. Potthof, A history of German social democracy from 1848 to the present, Leamington Spa, 1986, 78–95, and R. N. Hunt, German social democracy, 1918–1933, Chicago 1964, 26–38.

[59] Wrynn, Socialist International, 52.

[60] For developments in French socialism at this time see N. Nugent and D. Lowe, The left in France, London 1982, 29–37; M. Adereth, The French Communist party: a critical history (1920–84): from Comintern to the 'colours of France' (1920–84), Manchester 1984; and T. Judt, Marxism and the French left: studies in labour and politics in France, 1830–1981, Oxford 1986.

the Paris Conference ... it always took the obligation of reparations quite seriously'.[61]

The effect of these developments on Labour's approach to the post-war settlement should not be overstated. The party's attitude towards European developments in the early post-war period was certainly not pro-German, notwithstanding its greater contact with the German SPD than with the French Socialist party. Nevertheless, there is a strong case for arguing that Labour's loss of direct contact with the SFIO had reduced its appreciation of the continued strength of feeling about reparations at all levels of French society. There was certainly a concern within the SFIO by 1921 that this was the case. In a meeting with Labour's ACIQ in June, Jean Longuet expressed concerns about developments in Labour's policy, and urged greater contacts between British and French socialists. The minutes of the meeting record his comments: 'While explaining that he was not necessarily expressing his personal opinion, he dwelt on the need of understanding French views on reparations and other questions. Even French Socialists thought some of the British criticisms of French policy were made from a narrowly British point of view.'[62]

Longuet's meeting with the advisory committee was part of a renewal of contact between international socialists, which had begun with a meeting of the Berne International in Amsterdam at the end of March 1921. This was called, in the face of the worsening international situation, to allow European socialists 'to try to arrive at some practical solution of the problem of reparations upon which Socialist Parties could make their stand in all the countries concerned'.[63] So began a series of international contacts and meetings on the international situation over the next two-and-a-half-years, in which MacDonald, Henderson, Thomas and Shaw were full and active participants.[64] These meetings did not always involve direct contact between all of the various socialist parties, given the continued divisions of the Internationals, but gradually, during 1921, relations between the Berne International and Vienna Union began to improve, such that by 1922 all the parties affiliated to the organisations were usually involved. At the same time, similar attempts were made to revitalise and reunite international trade unionism. Most important for Labour's approach to the reparations and reconstruction debate and the security question, this process involved a renewal of regular and repeated contact between party officials and leading trade unionists, and representatives of the French labour and socialist movement. Indeed, special efforts were made by the two sides during this period to consult and compare

[61] Wrynn, *Socialist International*, 52. See also Trachtenberg, *Reparation in world politics*, 45, 105, 116–18, 139–41, 219.

[62] ACIQ minutes, 22 June 1921, LPA, LSI.

[63] Camille Huysmans to MacDonald, 12 Mar. 1921, ibid. LSI 10/7/1.

[64] See, for example, ibid. LSI 11/1/21, LSI 11/4/4, LSI 10/10. See also MacDonald diary, MacDonald papers, PRO 30/69/1753, entry for 3 Apr. 1921.

viewpoints.[65] In the early summer of 1922, for example, a series of discussions on the European situation took place between leading figures in both parties, including MacDonald, Henderson, Thomas Tillett and Shaw.[66]

By the time that Labour entered these discussions it was finally in a position to develop a coherent and informed approach to the post-war settlement. Renewed contacts between the Labour party and the SFIO further assisted this process. On this basis, over the next two years the party began to concentrate on the details of the post-war settlement and ways of mitigating international tensions in Europe. It began indeed to develop the policies on European reconstruction and security with which it entered government in 1924.

[65] NEC minutes, 19 Oct. 1921, LPA.
[66] See *Report* (1923), 31–6.

8

Labour and European Reconstruction, 1921–1924

Up to 1921 Labour had no detailed policy on reparations and European economic reconstruction. The general party line was to criticise the Versailles Treaty, insofar as it was inconsistent with the stipulations of the 1918 armistice, but insist that some reparations must be paid. No attempt was made to construct a detailed critique of the treaty. The party did not engage fully with the government in its handling of the post-Versailles negotiations. Keynes's attack on the post-war settlement was debated by some in the advisory committee, but not by the party as a whole. Labour instead relied, in official statements, on almost ritualised calls for a 'revision of the Treaty'. Exactly what was meant by this phrase was not made clear. It was only as a result of economic, political and international developments of the early post-war years that Labour finally began to think seriously about what precisely it wanted to 'revise'. As a result, between 1921 and the end of 1923, and in contrast with the earlier period, Labour's leadership engaged fully in debates on the financial and economic situation in Europe, such that by the time that they entered government they had a firm idea of the approach that they wished to pursue.

In making its views on the post-war settlement more clear and coherent, Labour had to clarify where it stood with respect to the difficult and complex issues that were reaching their climax between 1921 and 1923. By the beginning of 1921 reparations negotiations and the wider question of economic reconstruction had begun to reach crisis point as the approaches of the two main disputants, France and Britain, began to diverge.[1] French impatience over Germany's attitude towards reparations was growing and, in particular what she regarded as the tardy approach to the payment of the 20 milliard gold Mark interim reparations figure, set at Versailles in anticipation of agreement on the final German liability.[2] Germany consistently failed to make the coal quota of this payment, even after it had been revised downwards and the cost of its shipment subsidised. The French pressed the British to agree to the application of sanctions, such as an occupation of the Ruhr, to force

---

[1] For most of this period, Germany was the subject of this dispute, rather than a participant in it. The second half of the 1924 London Conference was the first time since the war that she had been treated as an equal partner in negotiations.

[2] The exchange rate was four gold marks to the dollar and twenty to the pound: Marks, *Illusion*, 38.

German compliance. The British resisted. However, when at the beginning of 1921 negotiations on Germany's final liability also reached deadlock, the French lost patience and took matters into their own hands. French troops were sent to occupy Dusseldorf, Duisberg and Ruhrort, much to the chagrin of the British.[3]

At the heart of this conflict over tactics lay fundamental differences of interest between Britain and France, which grew steadily more obvious in the years after 1919. The reparations dispute was the main issue, but there were also questions of inter-allied debts and broader economic matters. The traditional view of French policy – and one that was shared by many contemporary critics of the Versailles treaty, particularly the UDC radicals – was that it was largely motivated by vindictiveness and a desire to crush Germany. Thus the imposition of a massive debt on the Germans was seen as designed permanently to inhibit her recovery from the war. Reparations were also used, it was suggested, to justify a continuing French presence in the Rhineland: by setting a high figure that Germany could not pay the French had an excuse for maintaining the occupation of German territory well beyond the time set by the Treaty of Versailles, the ultimate aim being to separate the Rhineland from the rest of Germany.

As Marc Trachtenberg has shown, however, this is a simplistic interpretation of French policy. Certainly, France was almost obsessively concerned about her own security and for this reason was anxious to maintain a presence (preferably with the other allied countries) in the Rhineland. There were undoubtedly some French politicians and officials who wanted to use the opportunity presented by Germany's defeat to substantially alter the relative power of the two nations.[4] But '[c]rushing Germany was out of the question – a powerful nation could not be destroyed, and ultimately France and Germany had to live together'.[5] It was not France that had pressed for a crushing indemnity at Versailles, but the British. French reparations policy was generally moderate in comparison. Her main priority was the mobilisation of a loan for the reconstruction of the devastated areas and guarantees of her future economic security.[6] Debate continues about Germany's capacity to pay and the 'transfer problem' involved in the payment of reparations,[7] but there is no doubt that as the uncertainty over reparations continued and

---

3 As Michael Dockrill and J. Douglas Goold suggest, 'The French had every reason to be irritated by Britain's behaviour. At Paris Britain had led the way in insisting on a very high level of reparations. Later, however, she gave little or no support to French efforts to extract them': *Peace without promise: Britain and the peace conferences, 1919–1923*, London 1981, 85.

4 See Fischer, *Ruhr crisis*, 9.

5 Trachtenberg, *Reparation*, 100

6 Ibid. 56. See also E. Glaser, ' The making of the economic peace', in Boemeke, Feldman and Glaser, *Treaty of Versailles*, 371–400, and Fischer, *Ruhr crisis*, 5–28.

7 For the most recent contributions to this debate see Beomeke, Feldman and Glaser, *Treaty of Versailles*. On the transfer problem see Trachtenberg, *Reparation*, 338–42.

tensions rose, Germany's chance of recovery diminished and the stability of the new republic was threatened.[8]

However, most commentators agree that France's attitude to these problems would have been more conciliatory with unambiguous evidence of good faith on the part of the Germans.[9] This was largely lacking from the very start of the post-war peace negotiations.[10] As Conan Fischer, generally quite sympathetic to Germany's position, concedes, 'German negotiators seemed unable to decide whether they represented an unbowed great power, a repentant liberalized Germany or quite simply a destitute, starving country'.[11] Perhaps understandably, given their experience of the war, French officials responded to any evidence of assertive attitudes on the part of the Germans with exasperation. The perception grew that Germany was not taking her obligations seriously, notwithstanding her quite determined attempts up to 1923 to pay some of her reparations bill.[12] Thus, greater sanctions were required.

In contrast, Britain's willingness to take action to enforce compliance with the reparations clauses of the post-war treaty declined rapidly after it had been signed. The harsh line taken at Versailles had been justified on the basis that, having met much of the cost of the war through loans to her wartime allies, and having borrowed heavily from the United States, Britain should receive some compensation from the post-war settlement: reparation should not be limited to the devastated areas. However, British policy quickly began to change as concern grew about instability in Germany. A more indulgent line was further encouraged in 1920 by the economic downturn, which was blamed primarily on the inhibiting effects on the German economy of the post-war settlement.[13] By the end of 1920, therefore, Britain's overriding aim was for a settlement of the reparations question, as part of a general stabilisation of the European situation.

---

[8] See Fischer, *Ruhr crisis*, 6–28.
[9] This would have strengthened the hand of those in France who argued for a more co-operative approach to the reparations and reconstruction issue. It is also likely that the attitude of French policy-makers would have been more liberal if the security aspects of the treaty had succeeded: D. Stevenson, 'French war aims and peace planning', in Boemeke, Feldman and Glaser, *Treaty of Versailles*, 87–109.
[10] See, for example, K. Schwabe, 'Germany's peace aims and the domestic and international constraints', and A. Sharp, 'A comment', ibid. 37–67, 131–44.
[11] Fischer, *Ruhr crisis*, 6
[12] Ibid. 173–4, 205–6. As Ferguson has shown, Germany contributed between 4% and 7% of national income to reparations up to the Dawes Plan: 'Balance of payments', 424–5.
[13] As Marks suggests, 'Germany was, in fact, a competitor in such sickly British industries as steel, shipbuilding, and coal export, and German distress redounded to British benefit. But the British held fast to Lloyd George's nostalgic belief that a healthy Germany in a healthy Europe would alleviate Britain's deep-seated economic problems': *Illusion*, 47. On Keynes and the importance of an economically healthy Germany see Skidelsky, *Keynes: hopes*, 385.

This did not involve, however (up to the end of 1923) a renunciation of financial benefit from the post-war settlement on Britain's part. The debt to the USA remained a major concern for British policy-makers.[14] If it had to be paid then Britain remained determined to meet some of the cost from the post-war settlement. However, given that Britain was increasingly reluctant to enforce the reparations clauses of the Versailles Treaty, this inevitably focused attention on the question of allied debts, particularly those owed by France. This link was made explicit in the Balfour Note, despatched to her allies by Britain in July 1922, the main message of which was that Britain 'would not in any circumstances ask more from her debtors than was necessary to pay her creditors, but … could hardly be content with less'.[15] In France, however, such a policy reinforced the growing determination to exact payment from Germany: the money for debt repayment had to come from somewhere and reparations seemed the ideal source.

It was into this debate that Labour entered to a greater extent after 1921. In seeking to clarify its position on treaty revision, the party had thus to make clear its view on a number of questions. Were reparations wrong in principle or was it only certain elements of the reparations clauses that were unjust? Should Britain renounce all reparations even though she still owed a large debt to the USA? How should Britain treat the question of the debts owed to her by France? How would revision be negotiated given that it was not favoured by all the signatories to the treaty? Should Britain be prepared to make bilateral agreements with some countries and exclude those that did not favour 'revision'? On the progressive side of the political divide two distinct approaches competed for influence in providing answers to these questions, the Keynesian and that of the UDC radicals.

Keynes, the UDC radicals and treaty revision

There were various ways of approaching the debate over reparations and reconstruction between 1921 and 1923, all of which were consistent with a general commitment to the 'revision' of the Versailles treaty. Of these, it is particularly important to examine the Keynesian approach and that of the UDC radicals. The former was the best elaborated and most widely respected critique of the treaty constructed by a progressive commentator at this time. Keynes had close links with the Liberal party and his general approach to foreign affairs had much in common with the Gladstonian liberal perspective.[16] The UDC's approach on the other hand is said to have exercised an overwhelming influence on the approach to revision of the Labour party.

[14] See Orde, *British policy*, 208–26.
[15] Ibid. 215.
[16] See chapter 7 above.

In 1920 Keynes had launched a scathing attack on the Versailles treaty in his *Economic consequences of the peace*,[17] and continued to be a leading critic, commenting regularly in the main progressive newspapers and journals on post-Versailles inter-governmental negotiations. At the beginning of 1921, he summarised these comments in *The revision of the treaty*, which proposed a six–part revision plan,[18] the main purpose of which was to stabilise the economic situation in Europe by substantially reducing Germany's liability, while at the same time ensuring that France and Belgium had sufficient funds to re-build their devastated areas. It proposed that the claim on Germany for the payment of war pensions should be dropped; that Britain should renounce the bulk of her claim to reparations;[19] that France and Belgium should thus receive priority in the payment of reparations; that the USA and Britain would guarantee 'all reasonable assistance short of warfare' to France and Belgium to secure their claims; that the debts owed by the continental allies to Britain and the USA would be cancelled;[20] and that all German territory would be evacuated and the Rhineland demilitarised. The hope was that Britain and the USA, by renouncing their share of debts (and reparations in the case of the former), would convince France to reduce her claim to reparations.[21] This would create a more stable, and ultimately vibrant, economic situation in Europe, which, Keynes argued, would benefit everyone. Indeed, even France would be better off.[22]

There was much in Keynes's plan with which UDC radicals agreed. His books and other writings on the treaty were regularly quoted in *Foreign Affairs* and other UDC publications. Nevertheless, for most UDC radicals, he did not go far enough. They remained far more uncompromising with respect to the Versailles treaty and insisted that, because Germany had been no more responsible for the war than any other of the belligerents, there was no reason why she should pay reparations to her erstwhile enemies. This had been the general line adopted by Morel and his supporters during the peacemaking process, and it was one he maintained in 1922. Thus he insisted that 'The Treaty of Versailles is vitiated by an historical falsehood and an economic fallacy. The historical falsehood is that Germany was solely

---

[17] See Skidelsky, *Keynes: hopes*, 384–400.
[18] J. M. Keynes, *A revision of the treaty, the collected works of John Maynard Keynes*, iii, London 1971.
[19] Keynes suggested that she should receive only 1 milliard gold marks: ibid. 120.
[20] Keynes made clear that he was not including Britain's debt to the USA in this proposal: ibid. 125.
[21] Ibid. 124–5.
[22] See ibid. 121–2. Keynes estimated that, under existing arrangements, the most that France could hope to receive was a net annual sum (i.e. excluding debt repayments) of 0.91 milliard gold marks. Under his plan, she would receive 1.08 milliard gold marks. However, the French argued that the premise of this plan, that German reparations (payable because of her aggression) could be equated with France's debts (liable because of her efforts in fighting off German aggression), was offensive.

responsible for the war … [T]o attribute sole responsibility to her is not only untrue, it is grotesque … The economic fallacy [is that] it seeks to make Germany pay … and at the same time make Germany into paupers.' On the assumption that he spoke for his new party, he added: 'We of the Labour Party repudiate the whole thing from beginning to end.'[23]

Although few of the detailed arguments made by Keynes and the UDC radicals were addressed by Labour in any detail up to 1921, the official statements that were made on the post-war settlement had been closer to the position of mainstream Keynesian opinion than that of the UDC radicals. Party leaders, such as Henderson, Clynes, Thomas and Shaw, had made clear that, because Germany was overwhelmingly responsible for the war, she had an obligation to make reparation payments to all the allied countries. This position was supported by the PCTUC through its membership of the joint international committee established with Labour's executive committee in 1917.[24] Thus, it was only with respect to 'certain of its clauses' that the Treaty of Versailles was deficient. The UDC radicals' more trenchant and absolutist policy on the post-war settlement had been resisted. This was to remain the case during Labour's construction of a more detailed 'revision' policy.

The Labour party and 'revision' of the Treaty of Versailles

Labour's renewed interest in the European situation initially manifested itself in the form of two conferences on unemployment in 1921 – which linked closely the economic and international situation – and a far greater engagement in parliament with the government's handling of foreign affairs. With regard to the latter, a series of party statements on reparations and the inter-allied negotiations were released.[25] These had gradually developed by the middle of 1922 into a clear and coherent policy on reparations and reconstruction. This had emerged on the basis of a process that involved, first, the more concerted coordination and control of policy by party leaders, second, the input of the advisory committee, and third, negotiations with European socialists and trade unionists undertaken by leading Labour party and union figures.

Since the 1921/22 reorganisation, the advisory committee had been a body that was less concerned with democratic socialist ideas about inter-

[23] Undated speech, 1922 election meeting in Dundee, Morel papers, F2/2/5I. See also letter to Dundee constituency, 12 May 1920, ibid. F2/1/7, and to bishop of Winchester, 29 Aug. 1921, F8/139. For similar views expressed by Ponsonby see *The Times*, 20 Oct. 1920.

[24] See peace treaty revisions, Trades Union Congress, MRC, MS 292/940/3–5.

[25] See, for example, NEC minutes, joint meeting with PLP and PCTUC, 14 Feb. 1921, and joint meeting with TUC general council, 23 Nov. 1921, LPA.

national economic government and more firmly under the direction of the party executive and leadership. Increasingly, in fact, the committee became the transmission belt by means of which Keynes's detailed ideas on revision were taken up by the Labour party. [26] The change of ideological direction was not mainly the result of a dramatic change in the personnel of the advisory committee, although increasingly after 1922 the PLP was more involved in its proceedings.[27] Nor was it due to an ideological conversion: Labour's democratic socialist intellectuals had always sympathised with Keynes's approach to reparations but their belief in the need for greater economic government and the continuing existence of the wartime allied bodies had led them to concentrate on this issue, rather than revision of financial aspects of the treaty. However, with the collapse of wartime bodies and Labour's political need for an immediate, practical and plausible policy on European trade, it was to Keynes that they turned.

Labour's moderate leadership strongly encouraged the advisory committee in this task; for them Keynes's approach seemed to offer a pragmatic way forward, acceptable to a broad cross-section of domestic and international opinion. Thus, under their direction, the advisory committee gradually developed, from the middle of 1921, a detailed and coherent policy on European reconstruction which reproduced almost exactly Keynes's revision plans.

However, it is important not to neglect the role of Labour's negotiations with the international movement in this process. Many of the memoranda which helped to develop policy were drafted as part of the developing efforts of the International movement to influence the debate on reparations and reconstruction. As part of this process, a detailed policy on revision was produced jointly at Frankfurt in February 1922 by the Berne International and Vienna Union.[28] This incorporated elements of Keynes's ideas but, under the influence of proposals drawn up by the French Socialist party during 1921, was more interventionist than he was.[29] British Labour signed up to this, but the importance of its international contacts was less in the detailed policy prescriptions that were negotiated than the general effect that they had on the party's approach to reparations.[30] Party leaders and leading trade unionists gained a fuller appreciation of – and sympathy for – the policy positions and concerns of the main European powers, particularly

[26] See, for example, NEC minutes, 22 Apr. 1921, LPA; 'Memorandum on threatened reparation crisis', ACIQ memorandum, no. 251a, May 1922; and 'Draft report for the international socialist conference: reparations', July 1922, LPA, LSI.

[27] Brailsford was also a less frequent attender after 1922.

[28] See Wrynn, *Socialist International*, 53–4, 186–7.

[29] It recommended, for example, an internationalisation of the reconstruction effort by the establishment of an international office, which would oversee the organisation and implementation of the work, and the raising of an international loan with the German debt to the allies as collateral.

[30] Wrynn, *Socialist International*, 64.

the French.[31] The main features of the policy that Labour developed on this basis were clear: the Versailles treaty required revision rather than replacement; Germany should and could pay reparations; France and Belgium had valid claims to reparations for the reconstruction of the devastated areas and these should receive priority; Britain should renounce the majority of her claims to reparations; inter-allied debts should be dealt with as part of an overall settlement; an independent committee should arbitrate on any outstanding issues; and the occupation of all German territory should be ended. If the main features of this approach and the reasons for their adoption are considered in more detail, a clear impression is gained of the nature of Labour's policy on the reparations crisis during this period, and of the debt owed to Keynes and the difference between Labour's approach and that of the UDC radicals.

On Versailles itself, Labour's policy remained consistent with the line that had been taken up to 1921: the treaty required limited amendment, not replacement. Tom Shaw, for example, told the 1922 conference that Labour was 'asking for a *readjustment* of the Treaty of Versailles'.[32] In the meantime, attempts by absolutist opponents of the treaty to convert the party to a more uncompromising line were resisted. Thus, an attempt by UDC radical elements on the advisory committee to have an unequivocal 'repudiation' of the treaty inserted into the 1922 party conference resolution was blocked.[33]

On reparations, the party's approach was significantly different from that adopted in the immediate post-war period. At the party's second 1921 conference on unemployment, in December, Labour announced for the first time an explicit commitment to renounce most of the British share of reparations. Britain should only claim the relatively insignificant amount required for 'damage done to civilians and their property'.[34] Such a commitment had been implied by previous resolutions during the immediate post-war period, but had not been stated explicitly.[35]

However, this move did not indicate an acceptance of the UDC radical position. Labour continued to insist firmly that Germany should and could pay reparations. The December 1921 resolution, for example, stated categor-

---

[31]   See, for example, draft memorandum on Labour's foreign policy, ACIQ memorandum, no. 228a, Feb. 1922, LPA, LSI. For trade unions involvement in these negotiations see Trades Union Congress, International Federation of Trade Unions, MRC, MS 292/915/2 (my italics).

[32]   *Report* (1922), 189.

[33]   ACIQ minutes, 24 May 1922, LPA.

[34]   The resolution is quoted in an advisory committee memorandum on reparations by C. R. Buxton: 'Draft report for the international socialist conference. reparations', ACIQ memorandum, no. 252, July 1922, ibid. LSI

[35]   The resolutions at the 1919–21 conferences which called for a revision of the reparation clauses of the treaty in line with the armistice could be read as referring to the decision made at the Versailles conference to include payment by Germany of pensions and allowances, upon which Britain's claim to reparations was largely based.

ically that, with regard to the remaining liabilities, 'full reparation' should be made by Germany. Moreover, it continued, 'we are satisfied that it is within the capacity of Germany to make good [the] damage [to civilian life and property]'.[36] Attempts, by UDC radicals, to challenge this position were resisted. A resolution drafted for the 1922 Labour conference by Morel (or his sympathisers[37]), which sought to re-open the question of Germany responsibility for the war, on which the reparation clauses were ultimately based, was rejected.[38] Rather, Labour's renunciation of most of the British share of reparations was consistent with developments by 1921 in main-stream Liberal thinking, particularly that of Keynes, on the post-war settle-ment.

The corollary of Labour's commitment to renounce most of Britain's share of reparations was that more money would be available to France and Belgium for the restoration of the devastated areas. The party's commit-ment to the validity of the French and Belgian claims remained total and was strengthened by regular and close contacts by Labour leaders and trade unionist with French opinion in the early and mid-1920s. This can be gauged from Roden Buxton's speech on reparations at the 1922 party confer-ence. Buxton was not a natural ally of France and was a strong critic of the Versailles treaty. However, he told the conference that '[A]nyone who had stood amongst the ruins of Verdun and other towns must have felt that what-ever may be blameworthy in the methods of reconstruction that had been adopted, nevertheless there the ruins were and there the ruins would remain, and the people living amongst those ruins could not but be expected to place first the reconstruction of those ruins.'[39] On the question of France's debts to Britain, Labour was more reserved. In official party statements up to the end of 1923, no clear-cut commitment to cancellation was ever made.[40] The most that was said was that Britain 'should adopt a generous attitude in the matter of inter-allied debts, as part of a general settlement of the reparation problem'.[41] Labour, like the government, was not prepared to forego payment from France while Britain still owed money to the USA.

---

[36] See 'Draft report for the international socialist conference: reparations', ACIQ memorandum, no. 252, July 1922, LPA, LSI. See also Henderson's speech in the House of Commons in February 1923: HC, Debates, clx.710 (19 Feb. 1923).

[37] It is not clear which.

[38] See 'Draft resolutions for annual conference', ACIQ memorandum, no. 245, 13 May 1922, LPA, LSI.

[39] Report (1922), 190. See also Shaw's speech at the same conferences (p. 191). See also Peace treaty revision, Trade Unions Congress, MRC, MS 292/940/4; Trade Unions Congress, International Federation of Trade Unions, MS 292/915/2 .

[40] Labour leaders agreed to such an undertaking at international level, but did not back this up in domestic statements, despite pressure from the advisory committee to do so.

[41] Report (1923), 221. See also joint declaration by the general council and national executive committee, NEC minutes, 5 Oct. 1923, LPA.

The Labour party and the 1923 invasion of the Ruhr

By the end of 1922, therefore, a clear and consistent Labour policy on repa-rations and reconstruction had begun to emerge, closely based on Keynesian ideas, but also influenced in important respects by the negotiations that had taken place among leading European socialists since the early months of 1921. The formation of this policy had involved all the leading figures of the party – MacDonald, Henderson, Thomas and Shaw, together with a signifi-cant input from leading trade unionists. A newly-revitalised MacDonald was seamlessly reincorporated into the Labour leadership and, despite his differ-ences with the party during the war, he adopted the moderate, mainstream leadership line on the revision debate. UDC radicals were unable to make much impact, notwithstanding their slightly improved position in the party: all their efforts to alter Labour policy in line with their views were repulsed.

Labour moderates' policy on the peace soon faced its sternest test, however. On 11 January 1923 French and Belgian troops marched into the Ruhr, with the ostensible purpose of helping to procure coal deliveries. France's patience – with Britain as much as with Germany – had finally run out. In a last frantic initiative to maintain their predominant post-war position, French leaders sought to enforce the stipulations of the Versailles Treaty, which it seemed that Germany had long since begun to discount.[42]

However, to critics of post-war French policy and the Versailles treaty, such as the UDC radicals, France's action was confirmation of the argu-ments that they had been making since 1918. On this reading, militarists, such as Poincaré, the new French prime minister, were now indisputably in the ascendant in Europe. They were finally in a position to impose the settlement that they had always wanted, one that secured the dismember-ment and long-term weakening of Germany. To Morel, the implications of France's action were clear. They exposed the 'great flaw in our policy for the last five years'. What now had to be removed was 'the belief that … a great nation could be treated, five years after the end of a desolating war as if every man, woman and child in that nation were a criminal'.[43] UDC radical allies of Morel joined him in calling for a complete reversal of policy. Trevelyan, for example, suggested that 'the whole course of western policy has got to change, drastically, dramatically, completely and of set purpose … [T]he world should know that there is a great and growing force in Britain which will whenever it obtains power cut adrift from the Versailles policy, by an open avowal of its wickedness and by reversal in action wherever we are

---

[42] See Fischer, *Ruhr crisis*, and also S. A. Schuker, *The end of French predominance in Europe: the financial crisis of 1924 and the adoption of the Dawes Plan*, Chapel Hill 1976, 49–51.

[43] See *Report* (1923), 223. See also *Foreign Affairs* (Aug., Sept., Oct. 1923).

responsible as a nation and can act independently of France'.[44] As a symbol of the general change of approach for which they argued, the UDC radicals called for Britain's involvement in the occupation of the Rhineland, which had been established as part of the Versailles settlement, to be ended immediately.[45] Considerable pressure was put on the Labour leadership to accept this policy, with repeated resolutions to this end presented to the various party bodies.[46]

None the less, a change of policy was resisted. In the party's first statement on the new situation on 15 January 1923, the actions of France were condemned unequivocally, but no attempt was made to pressurise the government into using the Ruhr invasion as a turning-point in its relationship with its former ally. The party continued to maintain that France and Belgium had 'valid claims … for the reconstruction of the devastated regions'.[47] It continued to call for some form of independent arbitration as a means of resolving the reparations dispute.

As to the immediate withdrawal of British troops from the Rhineland, Labour's statements made clear that any move in this direction should only take place as part of a general agreement.[48] MacDonald wrote in the *New Leader* in February that 'a simple resolution demanding withdrawal of our troops from the Rhine' would not be helpful as it 'merely dealt with the Ruhr occupation as an isolated problem' and not as a symptom of a much larger one.[49] These positions were maintained throughout 1923. Certainly, patience with France was beginning to wear thin, but no dramatic change in policy was made, and in September 1923 this moderate approach was confirmed by a joint meeting of the Executive Committee and General Council.[50]

However, Labour did not just respond to events; it also tried to shape them. Thus, Labour's leaders sought to take advantage of the Ruhr crisis to

---

[44] *New Leader*, 26 Jan. 1923. In the same publication Seymour Cocks, another UDC radical stalwart, and a longstanding ally of Morel from Congo Reform Association days, called for the Treaty of Versailles to be scrapped.

[45] In making this proposal, they received support from left-wing trade unionists, such as Robert Smillie, and elements of the Clydeside left, such as John Wheatley: *New Leader*, 2 Mar. 1923.

[46] See, for example, NEC minutes, 27 Aug., 27 Sept. 1923, LPA.

[47] See national joint council meeting, NEC minutes, 15 Jan. 1923, and joint meeting of the general council of the TUC and the NEC, 25 Jan. 1923, ibid. See also HC, Debates clx.710–11 (19 Feb. 1923).

[48] NJC statement, NEC minutes, 15 Jan. 1923. The closest Labour came to acceding to the demands of UDC radicals was in a PLP statement in May 1923. This stated that Britain should 'consider' withdrawing her troops if agreement was not forthcoming: NEC minutes, LPA.

[49] *New Leader*, 23 Feb. 1923.

[50] NEC minutes, 27 Sept. 1923, LPA. In a speech to the House of Commons, soon after the rejection by France of a German statement on the crisis, MacDonald betrayed his impatience, with probably his most critical speech on France of the period: HC, Debates, clxvii.1772–83 (2 Aug. 1923).

put pressure on the government, gain recognition for their own policy and thus increase Labour's credibility as a party of government.[51] So MacDonald emphasised the moderate, 'responsible' nature of Labour's response to the crisis, based, it was suggested, on 'practical' proposals for extracting Europe from the dangerous situation that it had now entered. An open letter was sent by MacDonald to Bonar Law in February 1923 to emphasise this respon- sible, statesmanlike approach. MacDonald wrote that 'We know the deli- cacy of the situation, but feel that a discussion under the conditions which, whilst imposing responsibility, nevertheless allow a frank statement of … various well-considered proposals as to how Great Britain could become an active agent for peace and sanity.'[52] He criticised the government's diplo- matic inactivity and, to emphasise this point, proposed the development of an alternative and inclusive 'peoples' diplomacy with the aim of mapping a way out of the crisis.[53] This would involve meetings and the maintenance of contact between parliamentary representatives of any party from the major European countries which wanted to be involved, but in the first instance Britain, France and Belgium. If successful, it would show that a peaceful solu- tion to the problem was possible given the existence of an internationalist spirit and thus place concerted pressure on the 'nationalist' and 'militarist' governments of Europe to move towards a negotiated settlement.[54] With regard to domestic politics, it would also emphasise the freshness and energy of Labour's approach in comparison with the inactivity of the government, and the unique attributes that Labour could bring to negotiations on the future of Europe.[55]

Ultimately, only the socialist and Labour deputies of the various parlia- ments appear to have become involved in this exercise and only two meet- ings seem to have occurred, albeit that regular contact was maintained thereafter between the British, French and Belgium parties.[56] Nevertheless,

---

[51] These efforts did not involve any change in the substantive content of Labour's policy on the post-war settlement, which remained consistent with the policy established since early 1921.

[52] See NEC minutes, LPA. The letter is placed after the minutes of the meeting of the JIC, 31 Jan. 1923. MacDonald later explained to Labour's 1923 conference that the party 'must remember it was not a demonstration, or a general resolution that was required, but proposals and propositions that had a precise bearing upon the problem as it was at that moment': Report (1923), 223.

[53] HC, Debates, clxi.320–1 (6 Mar. 1923). See also NEC minutes, JIC, 22 Jan. 1923, LPA.

[54] See NEC minutes, JIC, 31 Jan. 1923, LPA.

[55] Executive committee and PLP meeting, 27 Feb. 1923, ibid. On the government's inactivity see Orde, British policy, 237.

[56] Records for only two meetings of this inter-parliamentary conference were found. Both took place at the French Chamber of Deputies, the first on 20 March and the second on 28/29 March 1923. With regard to the first meeting see MacDonald papers, PRO 30/69/1753 pt 4. On the second see LPA, LSI4/4/5. See also NEC minutes, JIC, 22 Jan. 1923, LPA.

at these meetings, detailed negotiations took place on how the Ruhr crisis might be ended and agreement was reached on a firm set of proposals. Both MacDonald and Henderson played a central role and it is therefore fair to regard the proposals as an extremely important indication of Labour's thinking on reparations and reconstruction in the year before the party entered government. The inter-parliamentary conference emphasised the need for a de-politicisation of the reparations dispute as a means to stabilise the international situation, on the basis of negotiations between all interested parties about a final agreement. Concretely it proposed an end to the system of annual payments set over a long future time period; a final reparations value of 30 milliard Marks; a loan from an international financial consortium to provide immediate resources for reparations; and a three-year moratorium on reparation payments.

These proposals were the culmination of a period since 1921 in which Labour had engaged fully with the debate on reparations and reconstruction. They show that, as a result, by the middle of 1923 Labour had constructed a moderate and reasonably sophisticated policy on the issue that owed little to the recommendations of the more absolutist elements in the party. However, to what extent did this policy inform Labour's actions once it entered government?

Labour in government: the Dawes Plan and the London conference

Accounts of the first Labour government's policy on reparations and reconstruction tend to emphasise the extent to which it differed from the party's policies during the previous five years. Cline's commentary on Labour's approach to foreign affairs is typical in presenting the period of government as a series of 'setbacks' for 'the foreign policy views generally accepted by the Labour Party during the immediate post-war years'. '[T]he policies which had constituted Labour's views in 1923' were changed 'during the party's first term of office'.[57]

Various reasons have been posited for this 'betrayal' of the party's previous commitments. Cline suggests that Labour came face-to-face with 'the hard facts of the international situation', a view with which Marquand and Winkler largely concur.[58] Others have suggested more political explanations for the change of approach in government which emphasise the extent to which MacDonald, in particular, saw the period of government as a opportunity to prove the essential 'respectability' of the Labour party and its 'fitness

---

[57] Cline, *Recruits*, 85. See also, for example, Marquand, *Ramsay MacDonald*, 333, 342; Keohane, 'Labour's international policy', 363–82; and Vickers, *Labour party and the world*, 85.

[58] Cline, *Recruits*, 6; Marquand, *Ramsay MacDonald*, 333. See also Winkler 'Emergence', 255. The latter moderated his view slightly in his later work: *Paths*, 124–54.

to govern'. To this end he chose to pursue a moderate approach in foreign affairs which emphasised 'continuities' with previous governments rather than differences.[59]

In terms of substantive issues, what these accounts concentrate on is the Labour government's acceptance of the Dawes Plan and its efforts during the 1924 London conference to negotiate a deal based upon it between the various interested nations. It is suggested that Labour in government thus adopted a less hard-line approach on the need for a revision of the Treaty of Versailles, was more accommodating to the concerns of France and was prepared to accept reparations totals from Germany that it had previously condemned as unjust.[60] In short, Labour to a large extent maintained the policies of its predecessors on the post-war settlement.[61]

However, most accounts misinterpret, or are based on misinterpretations of, the development of Labour's approach after 1919, in that they exaggerate the extent to which it was influenced by UDC radicals such as Morel, Ponsonby and Trevelyan, and underestimate the sophistication of its policy on reparations and reconstruction by the end of 1923.

As a result, the comparisons that are made between the 1924 Labour government's reparations policy and its attitude in the previous five years are false. It is hardly surprising that Labour's policy in government appears conservative in comparison to a policy in opposition, the radicalism of which has been exaggerated. Labour's approach to reparations and reconstruction in 1924 did not in fact represent a 'betrayal' of previous commitments: although compromises were undoubtedly made, the policy pursued was, for the most part, consistent with that which had emerged within the Labour party since 1919, and especially since 1921. Labour's acceptance of Dawes was largely congruent with the approach negotiated in 1923 by the international socialist and labour movement. Indeed, for this reason the plan was generally welcomed by this group.[62] Existing accounts tend to underestimate the degree to which the Dawes Plan and the London conference did, in fact, amount to a significant revision of the Treaty of Versailles, albeit an implicit one.[63]

The Dawes Plan was produced by a committee, established by the Reparation Commission in November 1923, which was charged with considering Germany's capacity to pay reparations and the steps necessary for her

[59] This was something that MacDonald himself came close to arguing once he left office in 1925. Explanations at the time by supporters of Morel tended to focus more on the 'personal failings' of MacDonald: Miller, *Socialism and foreign policy*, 137–40.
[60] On the Labour government and German reparations see Cline, *Recruits*, 86.
[61] Marks, for example, states that the shift in British policy under Labour was 'barely perceptible': *Illusions*, 54.
[62] See Wrynn, *Socialist International*, 160–2.
[63] See Schuker, *End of French predominance*. See also Marks, *Illusion*, 53–4, and Orde, *British policy*, 245–65.

to balance her budget and stabilise the Mark.[64] It was designed to bring about an immediate stabilisation of the European financial situation and, on French insistence, was intended to propose a long-term reparations settlement.[65] When the plan was eventually issued in April 1924 it recommended the payment by Germany of a rising scale of reparations starting with 1 billion gold Marks in 1924/5 and increasing up to 2.5 billion by 1928/9; reparations to cover all Germany's liabilities, including occupation costs; the use of mortgage bonds issued on the assets of Germany industry and the railways to pay half the annual reparations bill; a foreign loan to Germany of 800 million gold Marks; and a complete reorganisation of German finances with some foreign supervision of the banking system.

What these proposals left unstated or unclear was how reparations would be divided up; the future, if any, of the Reparation Commission; and what would happen if Germany failed to meet the new schedule of payments. The relationship of the proposals to the question of French withdrawal from the Ruhr and the other occupied territories was also unspecified. It was assumed that the fiscal and economic unity of Germany would be restored, but a purely military occupation of the Ruhr was not (and could not be, given the committee's remit) explicitly excluded as part of the proposals.

By the time that the Dawes Committee reported, Labour was in government. During its first three months in power, it had stalled with respect to reparations and reconstruction, asserting that it was awaiting the findings of the Dawes Committee. Nevertheless, some historians have suggested that indications of a change of policy were already clear, pointing to the prime minister's early conduct towards France as evidence. For example, in his diary on 3 February, MacDonald wrote that 'France must have another chance. I offer co-operation but she must be reasonable and cease her policy of selfish vanity.'[66] What this entry was referring to was an exchange of notes which MacDonald had had with Poincaré, and in which the British prime minister had taken a generally conciliatory line.[67] These have been regarded by some commentators as evidence of an immediate change of approach by Labour once in government. 'Far from attacking "the wrecker of European civilization"', MacDonald was extending 'the warm hand of friendship.'[68]

In fact MacDonald's actions were entirely consistent with the approach that Labour had adopted towards France since 1921. That France had genuine grievances which had to be addressed if a settlement were to be reached was

---

[64] For accounts of the circumstances under which the Dawes Committee was established see Schuker, *The end of French predominance*, 171–80, and Orde, *British policy*, 237–45.

[65] Orde, *British policy*, 250–1. See also Marks, *Illusion*, 52–3.

[66] MacDonald diary, MacDonald papers, PRO 30/69/1753, entry for 3 Feb. 1924.

[67] See cabinet conclusions 8(24), 28 Jan. 1924, CAB 23/47, and Marquand, *Ramsay MacDonald*, 336–7.

[68] Lyman, *First Labour government*, 160–2. Poincaré was referred to as the 'wrecker of European civilization' by the *New Statesman* on 22 December 1923. For a similar interpretation of MacDonald's actions see Marquand, *Ramsay MacDonald*, 333.

a commonplace within the Labour party by the beginning of 1924. It was a view that had been reflected in the 1922 and 1923 conference resolutions and, despite the French invasion of the Ruhr, had remained a key element in the 1923 international socialist diplomacy in which leading Labour figures had played such a major part. It is certainly true that MacDonald and some of his colleagues had grown increasingly impatient with France, and with Poincaré's refusal to compromise as the Ruhr invasion continued, but they had never proposed a break with France. The 'chance' that MacDonald was offering to the French government in January 1924 was to take part in the type of detailed negotiations on the reparations crisis in which he had engaged with French socialists a year earlier, and which were meant as a model for inter-governmental diplomacy.

Historians have also highlighted a speech made by Henderson at a by-election meeting in Burnley in February,[69] in which he took a strong stand on the need for a revision of the Treaty of Versailles, which he suggested was 'very much overdue'. 'All of us who value world-peace', he said, 'and desire to see the inauguration of a new era of international co-operation and goodwill must insist as an absolute essential upon the revision of the Treaty of Versailles with all expedition possible.' This was no more than a statement of Labour party policy, albeit (perhaps understandably given the context) an extremely imprecise one. However, at a time when the administration, of which Henderson was a member, was engaged in delicate negotiations on the European situation with the French government, for whom any mention of the word 'revision' was unwelcome, it caused the government considerable embarrassment.[70] When challenged in the House of Commons, MacDonald distanced himself from the statement.[71] Catherine Cline regards this action as 'an alteration in the party's stand': Labour had been 'forced … to set aside one of the party's chief foreign policy objectives … Party orators … had long demanded the calling of a conference which would *completely* revise the settlement'.[72]

However Labour's call since 1919 for a revision of the Versailles treaty had never called for a complete revision, but had placed limitations on the changes that were required. Increasingly since 1921 the party had specified in detail with respect to the reparations clauses what it meant by 'revision'. Labour and MacDonald remained firmly committed to this form of 'revision', notwithstanding the prime minister's equivocation about Hender-

---

[69] Henderson had been defeated at the 1924 general election.

[70] Henderson's statement received considerable attention in the French press. It is likely that he was not aware of the delicacy of the negotiations with France. MacDonald was later criticised by colleagues for his failure to consult on the conduct of foreign policy: *Beatrice Webb's diaries, 1924–1932*, ed. M. Cole, London 1956, 43. See also S. Webb, 'The first Labour government', *Political Quarterly* xxxii (1961), 20.

[71] HC, Debates, clxx.605–12 (17 Feb.1924).

[72] Cline, *Recruits*, 85–6 (my italics). See also Marquand, *Ramsay MacDonald*, 334.

son's statement. Indeed, MacDonald reiterated this policy in his House of Commons speech. All MacDonald was seeking to do was to ensure that Henderson's imprecision on this question, in the heat of an election meeting, was not misunderstood by the French at a time when more detailed negotiations on the future of the Versailles settlement were taking place.[73]

Surely, however, the 1924 government's full acceptance of the Dawes Plan, which was agreed in Cabinet on 10 April 1924, represented a major change in policy in comparison with Labour's commitments when in opposition?[74] This was certainly the view at the time of some leading UDC radicals, such as Morel. He launched a concerted attack on the government's decision through the pages of *Foreign Affairs* and also tried to instigate opposition to Dawes on the Labour backbenches. He claimed that by supporting the plan the party was 'being re-committed to support ... a general policy which is a repetition, under another name, of the policy embodied in the Versailles Treaty'.[75] He criticised the amount of reparations that Germany would have to pay from 1928/9 and claimed that France would again use any default as an opportunity to occupy German territory.[76] What Morel objected to most of all was the Dawes Plan's failure to commit Britain to a renunciation of German reparations. Given that Labour was committed to a renunciation and that the plan's authors had insisted that it be taken as a whole or rejected, Morel argued that Labour could not accept it.[77]

To what extent was Labour's acceptance of the Dawes Plan inconsistent with the approach to reparations and reconstruction that it had adopted since 1921? Labour had repeatedly called for the reparations dispute to be solved by some form of independent arbitration and detailed negotiations between the interested powers. Indeed by 1923 the facilitation of all-inclusive negotiations had become the primary aim of Labour's policy. The Dawes Committee might not have been exactly what Labour had in mind, but the central involvement of the Americans, as independent arbiters, made it an important development away from the Anglo-French-dominated Reparation Commission. Moreover, it was clear that, if nothing else, the committee's report would provide a basis upon which negotiations could start. It did

---

[73] Indeed, MacDonald was quite specific about this in his speech. He told MPs that the word 'revision' was 'a very imperfect word', which was extremely 'prejudicial to fears abroad': HC, Debates, clxx.610 (27 Feb. 1924).

[74] Cabinet conclusions, 26(24), CAB 23/48. MacDonald told the House of Commons that 'The Reports constitute, in our opinion, an unbiased and carefully thought-out endeavour to aid the Governments concerned in their task of reaching a settlement of this vital and longstanding problem ... [T]here will be a universal desire to use the opportunity which such authoritative documents give to end the existing unsettlement': HC, Debates, clxii.1333–4 (15 Apr. 1924).

[75] Speech delivered to ILP in House of Commons in August 1924, but written on 31 July 1924, Morel papers, F2/3/ii.

[76] Ibid.

[77] Ibid.

finally seem as though an inclusive settlement was within reach. Labour's decision to accept the Dawes should not therefore be seen as surprising or inconsistent with its previous commitments.

When the details of the plan are compared with the proposals agreed by the inter-parliamentary conference in March of the previous year, any sense of surprise should be dissipated even further. Both plans had as their immediate goal the creation of a period of stability and calm during which the reparations dispute could be de-politicised to the greatest extent possible. The socialist plan hoped that a final agreement on reparations could be reached, which would concentrate on providing immediate resources and end the demand for annual payments stretching into the distant future. It fixed the final value of reparations at 30 milliard gold Marks. However, the French government, in agreeing to the establishment of the Dawes Committee, was not prepared to contemplate a final agreement at a time when the weakness (temporary, as they saw it) of the German economy was likely substantially to reduce estimates of Germany's capacity to pay. Nevertheless, the Dawes Plan, like the socialist plan, concentrated on the short-term and only set a definite reparation total for the following five years. Moreover, while in theory it was harsher on Germany with respect to reparations during this period than the socialist plan, in practice it was little different. As Simon Schuker suggests, the reparations set out in Dawes had a real capital value of far less than 40 milliard Marks.[78]

The two plans were similar in other areas too. The centrepiece of both was a loan that was to be provided by an international financial consortium, the only difference being that the socialist plan regarded the loan as a means of providing immediate resources for reparations, whereas for Dawes its main purpose was to help to stabilise the Germany financial system. With regard to a moratorium, the socialist plan called for a three-year break in reparations; Dawes was less specific, but according to Schuker, its proposals amounted to a 'partial moratorium lasting four years'.[79] On the German financial structure, the proposals of the two plans were also very similar, with both envisaging some measure of external control over Germany's banking system.

What of Britain's claim to German reparations? Labour's acceptance of a plan that did not explicitly involve the renunciation of Britain's share of German reparations clearly represents a change of approach in comparison with its policy in opposition. However, what this decision did not indicate was a renewed belief in the idea that Germany must pay on the basis of a Versailles-type settlement. MacDonald remained committed to minimising Germany's obligations. His government's continued insistence that Britain should receive some reparations was, as Orde has shown, a bargaining tool

[78] Schuker, *End of French predominance*, 183. Indeed, some British Treasury officials believed that because of the transfer problem, the capital worth of Germany's reparations liability, set by the Dawes, was unlikely to be more than 16 milliard gold marks (p. 248).
[79] Ibid. 185. See also Marks, *Illusion*, 53.

in negotiations with the French over their debts.[80] The government was not prepared to concede to France all the proceeds of reparations until an agreement was reached on this question. It also wished to maintain a say in any final settlement on reparations between France and Germany. In this regard, Labour's policy in office was not substantially inconsistent with its policy on these matters in opposition. The party had always been fairly coy about the question of inter-allied debts. No official commitment had ever been made to unilaterally cancel French debts; rather, Labour only ever committed itself to 'look generously' at this matter or attempt to resolve it 'as part of a general settlement'. If, in government, Labour adopted a slightly harder line, and maintained a nominal claim to German reparations, this was merely the product of an ongoing process of negotiations, the goals of which remained, in all important respects, the same as those for which it had aimed in opposition.

This position was understood by some of the less hot-headed elements in Labour's advisory committee. Thus Angell argued in a letter to Morel that the question of renunciation was mainly 'a question of strategy in handling France'.[81] He later added that 'By formally surrendering our claims now, all that happens, it seems to me, is that we have much less say in the negotiations about the Reparations question. I would maintain our claims, not for the purpose necessarily of recovering them from Germany, but for the purpose of keeping down the amount France and Belgium will attempt to recover.'[82]

Dawes's proposals for the immediate stabilisation of the European financial situation were accepted at the London conference, which was convened by the allied governments in June 1924, and was mainly designed to deal with those matters left open by the plan: the future of the Reparations Commission and the timescale for France's withdrawal from the Ruhr. Some elements within MacDonald's government wanted to take advantage of France's weak negotiating position, caused by a financial crisis, to force the maximum number of concessions.[83] Snowden, the chancellor of the exchequer, for example, remained close to the UDC radicals on foreign affairs and was almost as implacably anti-French as Morel.[84]

However, MacDonald maintained a conciliatory attitude which recognised the non-negotiable interests of the French, while facilitating a general

---

[80] See Orde, *British policy*, 233.
[81] Norman Angell to Morel, n.d. *c.* June 1924, Morel papers, F7/3.
[82] Angell to Morel, 3 July 1924, ibid. F7/3I.
[83] On French policy at London see Schuker, *End of French predominance*, 298–300, and Orde, *British policy*, 255.
[84] Even Stresseman, the German foreign minister, commented that the Labour minister let slip 'no opportunity to deal the French a blow': Schuker, *End of French predominance*, 349. In adopting this stance, he had the support of many Treasury officials (pp.174, 193–4).

negotiated settlement.[85] He sponsored a compromise on the Reparations Commission which maintained it in being, but strengthened the role of its independent members, limited its powers to declare a default and assigned a role to the World Court at the Hague to arbitrate on outstanding matters of dispute. With regard to the evacuation of the Ruhr, MacDonald agreed a staged pull-out over a year with the French. Snowden and the Treasury's line were resisted.[86]

Largely as a result of compromises such as these, agreement was finally reached and on 16 August the conference protocol was signed. In his farewell speech at the London conference, MacDonald declared that 'We are now offering the first really negotiated agreement since the war ... This agreement may be regarded as the first Peace Treaty, because we have signed it with a feeling that we have turned our back on the terrible years of war and war mentality.'[87] However, in agreeing to the London settlement, Labour had not turned its back on the approach to the peace that it had taken since 1919. The agreement was, rather, the culmination of the moderate and practical approach to reparations and reconstruction that it had always proposed during this period. Labour had never repudiated its support for the war during this time. It had retained its belief that Germany had been responsible for the conflict and, on this basis, should pay reparations, particularly to France. Calls from the UDC radicals for a more absolutist stance on the Versailles treaty had been repeatedly resisted, even after the French invaded the Ruhr.

Thus, while the 1924 Labour government's policy on reparations and reconstruction is undoubtedly open to criticism, it is not open to reproach on the grounds that UDC radicals used to attack it at the time, and which have subsequently dominated accounts of the Labour party's foreign policy development.[88] It was not merely dictated to the party by permanent officials – official opinion had moved more since 1919 than had the Labour party – nor foreign governments. It did not represent a betrayal of past commitments.

[85] MacDonald's diplomatic skill were strongly praised by Hankey: Maurice Hankey diary, Maurice Hankey papers, Churchill College, Cambridge, entry for 11 Oct. 1924, and Hankey to Richard Haldane, 20 Aug. 1924, Richard Haldane papers, NLS. Hankey wrote in the latter: '[M]ake no mistake it was Ramsay MacDonald's conference. He ran it in his own way from first to last.'

[86] On MacDonald's disputes with Snowden during the conference see MacDonald to Phillip Snowden, 14 Aug. 1924, MacDonald papers, PRO 30/69/1753, pt 4; Hankey diary, Hankey papers, entry for 11 Oct. 1924; and MacDonald to Lord Parmoor, 13 Aug. 1924, MacDonald papers, PRO 30/69/200. See also Schuker, *End of French predominance*, 349.

[87] Quoted in Marquand, *Ramsay MacDonald*, 351.

[88] Some historians, for example, have suggested that the London settlement was based on a fundamental misunderstanding of the weakness of the French position in Europe: Marks, *Illusion*, 54.

9

Labour and European Security, 1921–1924

Labour had committed itself in 1917/18 to a moderate internationalist approach to foreign affairs. It envisaged an international future where in a more open, interdependent world, countries would trade freely with each other and the salience of national boundaries would gradually diminish. In such a world, security would not be a concern; nations would be able to disarm with confidence and disputes that did arise would be capable of solution by arbitration.

If this was the vision of the future, Labour remained much more divided over its approach to the world with which it was faced. International rivalries were intense, protectionist sentiment was high and armaments abounded; the security question loomed large. What should the response of internationalists be? Should they merely blame militarists and protectionists and argue that the emergence of a more democratic and internationalist spirit would gradually dissolve such problems? Should they press for immediate progress on disarmament? Or should they accept that security concerns were currently understandable and seek to alleviate them by some form of pact or guarantee? If the latter, should intervention be organised collectively, through the League of Nations, or on a bilateral basis? How important was the military component of such an arrangement?

In 1917/18 the approach of the Labour leadership to these issues was based firmly on a Gladstonian liberal approach, which suggested that current security concerns were genuine and had to be addressed. Some form of security apparatus, it was agreed, was essential in the immediate aftermath of the war, which had been blamed on German militarism. However, given Labour's resistance to the alliance system and hope for a more internationalist future, a League of Nations-based collective security arrangement was supported for this purpose. This would also allow progress towards national disarmament.

Nevertheless, the decline in the party's interest in security issues after 1918/19 raises questions about the strength of Labour's early post-war attitude to collective security. Was the party really fully committed to this idea by the early 1920s? Had it seriously thought through the implications of such a commitment, most particularly the use of armed force involving British service personnel? Was the commitment maintained during the early post-war period, when the Treaty of Versailles fundamentally altered the balance of forces in Europe and changes in the economic and political situation dramatically altered the way in which European affairs were regarded?

The context within which the security issue presented itself had certainly changed in important respects by 1921. Labour's concerns about security in 1918 had to a large extent been based on continuing anxieties about German militarism, but after Versailles and the reduction of Germany's military capabilities the situation became a lot less clear-cut. From a British perspective the threat posed by Germany to European security, particularly that of Britain, had been substantially reduced. For the French it had not; they remained obsessively worried, less about the short-term situation than the future, especially given the declining French population and Germany's continued economic potential.[1] This concern was increased by the collapse of the Anglo-American security guarantee, under which the two nations had pledged as part of the 1919 treaty to assist France if she was the victim of German aggression.[2] France thus had to be satisfied, so far as allied agreements were concerned, with the reductions in Germany's armed strength, the demilitarisation of the Rhineland and its occupation for fifteen years.

France did not regard the League of Nations as an adequate substitute for the guarantee. She was not prepared to trust her fate to an international 'experiment', a view that was strengthened by a lack of enthusiasm on the part of British policy-makers for the new body and the idea of collective security.[3] Thus, while a League structure was put in place which provided an embryonic form of collective security, the British and French governments largely ignored it in early post-war debates about European security. In all other respects, however, the two governments' approaches began to diverge. France continued to equate her security with the maintenance of some form of allied control of the Rhineland. She also strengthened her links, in the 'Little Entente', with the newly-created states on Germany's eastern border, the integrity and independence of which the French regarded as a vital counterbalance to German power.[4]

Meanwhile, British policy-makers, as with reparations and reconstruction, quickly came to regard a revitalisation in European trade, not security, as the main priority.[5] Increasingly, French concerns were seen as, at best, paranoid and unjustified; at worst, they were regarded as an attempt by France to secure her domination of the continent.[6] Nevertheless, by 1921/2

---

[1] See Fischer, *Ruhr crisis*, 5–14.

[2] The guarantee lapsed when the American senate refused to ratify the treaty: Dockrill and Douglas Goold, *Peace without promise*, 34–8. This increased, in turn, French determination to ensure German compliance with the financial clauses of the treaty: Stevenson, 'French war aims'.

[3] Britain feared that she would be committed to military, especially naval, action in defence of interests that were not her own, and attempted to minimise the security functions of the League.

[4] Marks, *Illusion*, 87–9.

[5] See Skidelsky, *Keynes: hopes*, 384.

[6] The Admiralty and Foreign Office, in particular, increasingly regarded France as the major threat to the balance of power in Europe: Schuker, *End of French predominance*.

British policy-makers recognised that, as with the reparations dispute, no progress was likely unless French interests were addressed. Consideration was given to ways in which France could be convinced that Germany's economic recovery did not pose her a threat. At the Cannes conference in January 1922, the security guarantee idea – bilateral now rather than trilateral, given America's withdrawal into isolationism – was revived. Lloyd George proposed to Aristide Briand, the then French prime minister, a formal treaty of guarantee as part of an all-encompassing package of measures aimed at securing a final European settlement.[7] These negotiations failed, due largely to Britain's unwillingness to extend the guarantee to France's eastern allies; and, with the collapse of the Briand government, were not revived again before 1924.

It was left to the League of Nations to investigate security options, notwithstanding the unenthusiastic attitude of many of its member governments. It did this as part of its attempts to draw up a general plan on disarmament, a task that the League had been assigned when it was set up.[8] This soon involved the new organisation in the security debate because the League secretariat concluded that disarmament would only occur if states felt confident about their own security.[9] In 1923, therefore, the Draft Treaty of Mutual Assistance (DTMA) was recommended as a means of firming up the collective security functions of the League. It proposed that if any signatory suffered an act of aggression it would be assured of immediate support from all other signatories on the same continent if it had previously reduced its armaments in line with an agreed plan.[10] It would be left to the League's council to determine what constituted an act of aggression, the application of economic sanctions and what military forces each signatory should provide to support the wronged state. On the insistence of the French (who with Robert Cecil were the main forces behind the draft treaty) it was also proposed that signatories be permitted, with the approval of the council, to conclude special security agreements among themselves.

The Labour party, internationalism and the European security question

Labour largely ignored these debates up to 1921 at which point security issues re-emerged strongly on the party's agenda. This was for two reasons. First, by 1921 it was becoming difficult to separate the issues of reconstruction and security. They had become inextricably linked in British policy, as

---

[7] See Trachtenberg, *Reparations*, 232–4. In return, France would have to limit her submarine construction and co-operate with Britain in Greece and Turkey.
[8] This power was granted under article 8 of the League covenant: Walters, *League of Nations*, 218.
[9] For details of this involvement see ibid. 220–1.
[10] Ibid. 223.

Lloyd George attempted to convince France to compromise with respect to German reparations by offering a security guarantee and some form of alliance. Labour, through its increased interest in the reparations dispute and full involvement in the search for a settlement up to 1924, thus also found itself having to address the security question. Its continuing importance for a general European settlement also became more obvious once Labour leaders re-established regular contact with their socialist comrades in France and Belgium in 1921. The second reason why security issues re-emerged on Labour's agenda was political. As Keith Robbins suggests, 'the League of Nations came to have major significance in the context of a Liberal and Labour competition for the votes of the high-minded who liked to think that it might be possible to vote for a foreign policy which was in the interests of humanity'.[11] It was thus important politically for the party to engage fully in the debate about the European security situation and the role of the League.

In doing this the party was confronted with some difficult questions given the changes in the international and economic situation after Versailles. Were French concerns genuine and understandable, or were they purely the creation of French militarists? If the former, what should be Labour's response?

UDC radicals and their supporters in the Labour party had no doubt. Their attitude towards France was uncompromisingly and consistently hostile. Even as early as December 1919 a *Labour Leader* editorial, probably written by Snowden, complained that 'for four hundred years France has kept Europe, through her insane passion for military glory and imperial ambition, in a state of war or under the menace of war ... [A]re the [the British people] going to continue to be dragged to slaughter at the bidding of French militarists?'[12] As the reparations dispute continued, hostility grew. French security concerns were dismissed. *Foreign Affairs*, the UDC newspaper, made clear that 'with the attitude of the rulers of France from the armistice to the present day we have no sympathy whatever: nor with the claim that their acts are justified by their fear of Germany.'[13] The Ruhr invasions confirmed this view for UDC radicals. How could France feel insecure Morel asked on the eve of Labour entering government. She had 'provided for her own security in masterly fashion'. Germany had been territorially, economically and militarily enfeebled. France dominated the Rhine frontier and was persistently seeking to destabilise the Rhineland. France's security concerns were merely a fiction, designed by French capitalists and militarists to justify her attempt to dominate and permanently weaken Germany. Indeed, Morel concluded, it was France, not Germany, that had become the main threat to European security: 'The problem of French security is

---

[11] Robbins, *Politicians*, 257.
[12] *Labour Leader*, 11 Dec. 1919. For similar views expressed by Trevelyan see *The UDC* (Feb. 1919).
[13] *Foreign Affairs* (July 1922).

not the pivot upon which the European problem turns. The problem is how to obtain protection for the peoples of Europe ... from the far-reaching and stupendous plans of French nationalistic imperialism.'[14]

Not all UDC radicals were as outspoken as Morel, but there was general agreement that French fears were distorting the entire debate about European security and the League of Nations. The focus was on military guarantees and collective security when it should be on disarmament and arbitration. In a memorandum written for Labour's advisory committee, Lowes Dickinson joined Morel in arguing that 'The correct angle from which to approach the problem of security is ... that the condition of States and peoples today is one of perpetual and growing insecurity, as the result of ever increasing perfection in the art of human-slaughter and material and wealth-producing destruction.'[15] The way out of this cycle of militarism was through the encouragement, by the League of Nations, of international arbitration, to which all nations should compulsorily submit their differences. This would open the way for a comprehensive scheme of disarmament. The League should operate as a pacific organisation, leading nations away from a reliance on armed force, rather than merely making the use of force collective.

Indeed, for Morel and Ponsonby in particular, too much store could be put in the League of Nations. It was not the priority, Ponsonby told the LNU's Gilbert Murray in November 1922. He would concentrate on 'the Peace Treaties and the myth of German sole responsibility' on his return to parliament.[16]

Some commentators suggest that the Labour party as a whole took a similarly trenchant line. David Marquard, for example, observed that 'Suggestions that the French might have genuine grievances and legitimate interests and that concessions might have to be made to them if the problem were to be solved, provoked uneasy apprehension.'[17] Certainly there is no doubt that Labour's initial reaction to the re-emergence of the security question was generally supportive of the UDC's approach. When news leaked out in June 1921 of Lloyd George's plans to offer France some form of security alliance, an emergency resolution was prepared for the 1921 conference, which warned that[18] 'Such an Alliance, while professedly aiming at defence against aggression, would in fact be based on the concession by each Government to the other of a free hand for Imperialist expansion in certain spheres. It would

[14] 'French policy and the problem of European security and peace', Jan. 1924, unnumbered ACIQ memorandum, Morel papers, F2/3/1. On Morel and the security threat posed by France see his speech to the 1923 Labour party conference: *Report* (1923), 223.
[15] 'An alternative policy for a British Labour government to the policy embodied in the draft treaty of mutual assistance', ACIQ memorandum, no. 318, Feb. 1924, LPA, LSI.
[16] Ponsonby to Murray, 25 Nov. 1922, Murray papers. On Morel's cool attitude towards the League see Parmoor to Morel, 4 Mar. 1924, Morel papers, F7/3; speech on Anglo-American relations, n.d., F2/2/5ii; and *Foreign Affairs* (Nov. 1923).
[17] Marquand, *Ramsay MacDonald*, 333. See also Winkler, *Paths*, 1.
[18] NEC minutes, 18 June 1921, LPA.

be wholly opposed to the spirit of the League of Nations, whose object is to render such partial alliances unnecessary.'[19] Little else was said. No details were offered of how the League of Nations would take the place of bilateral alliances, nor was any reference made to the party's previous commitment to collective security. However, in the one speech that accompanied the resolution, the speaker, John Bromley of the ASLE, adopted an outspokenly UDC radical line: 'He was of the opinion that France was now the truculent military bully of Europe.'[20]

The Labour leadership's underestimate of French security concerns, however, did not last long. Lloyd George's persistence with his alliance policy, and Labour's increased engagement with debates over the post-war settlement, convinced party leaders that a general European settlement was unlikely unless they were addressed. Moreover, Labour leaders' appreciation of the strength of feeling about this issue in France was substantially increased by the renewed contacts made with French socialists from July 1921. Detailed discussions on security issues, involving leading Labour figures and trade unionists,[21] including Henderson, MacDonald, Shaw, Thomas, Tillett, Gillies and Jowett, took place during the early part of 1922 and at the beginning of 1923 after the Ruhr invasion. During these Labour leaders were left in no doubt that concerns about the future security of France were not merely confined to the militarist right but were felt throughout French society. The minutes of a meeting held between French and Belgian socialists and Henderson, MacDonald, Shaw and Gillies in May 1922, for example, record that 'The French delegates explained how the French mind was dominated by the fear of the rapid economic recovery of Germany, and as a consequence, the revival of her military strength and the possibility of revenge.'[22]

There is little doubt that this exchange of views had an impact on the thinking of Labour's leaders. The results are evident in the approach that they took to the question of French security in the two years up to 1924. In contrast to the line proposed by the UDC radicals, Labour's leaders repeatedly emphasised their acknowledgement that France's fears were genuine, an attitude that was maintained even after the invasion of the Ruhr. Shaw explained these fears to the 1922 Labour conference. After informing delegates of the detailed conversations that had taken place with the French socialists, he continued: 'In France there was a deep-seated fear of Germany. People feared that secret preparations were going to be made, and there was no doubt that in France the overwhelming mass of opinion, including

---

[19] *Report* (1921), 201.
[20] Ibid.
[21] Ben Tillettt represented the PCTUC at a meeting with French trade unions on the proposed Anglo-French security pact on 29 Mar. 1922. For the TUC's involvement in these negotiations see MRC, MS 292/940/4.
[22] *Report* (1922), 189.

socialist opinion, was in favour of agreement with this country so that they might have some guarantee of security.'[23] In February 1923 Henderson spoke in the House of Commons of France's 'well-founded' fears of attack.[24]

However, while Labour's contacts with French socialists undoubtedly raised awareness of the centrality of the security question to the achievement of a general settlement, it did not lead the party to abandon its opposition to a security alliance with France. Such a change would have signalled a return to the old balance of power policy to which Labour remained united in objection. Rather, what the contacts did was revive debate in the party about the merits of a League of Nations collective security policy.

Continuing support for such a policy at the top of the Labour party was indicated as early as February 1922 in a manifesto released by the National Joint Council of the Labour executive committee and the PCTUC to coincide with the Genoa Conference. This conference was once again due to discuss an Anglo-French guarantee. Labour released statements reiterating its opposition[25] but, in contrast to its 1921 conference resolution on this issue, the party was much more forthcoming in proposing an alternative. It called upon France 'to join with Great Britain in an effort to create a real League of Nations … [that] will *guarantee* France equally with other nations'. It continued: 'The Council believes that the only safe policy is that of a League of Nations in which all countries would *reciprocally guarantee one another against unprovoked aggression.*'[26] This was close to being a clear commitment to collective military security through the League of Nations. However, the statement was ambiguous. In particular, it was not clear what military component, if any, Labour envisaged as part of this 'guarantee'.[27]

Henderson, who had already emerged by this time as the firmest supporter of collective security in the party, provided more details in a 1922 pamphlet on foreign affairs. In this, he explicitly condemned the existing League for not 'guarantee[ing] its members against aggression'. He continued: 'It ought clearly to undertake that if any member of the League is subjected to any act of aggression by another State which has not submitted or refuses to submit a dispute to peaceful settlement, all other members of the League will

[23] Ibid. Just prior to his return to Britain after a visit to France in July 1922, Shaw told a meeting of the French socialist party that 'he brought back from his visit to France the impression of a country essentially pacific and not at all chauvinist': *The Times*, 18 July 1922.

[24] HC, Debates, clxii.714 (10 Feb. 1923). For similar views expressed by Clynes see *The Times*, 20 May 1922; 8 May 1923.

[25] For more on the Genoa Conference see Orde, *British policy*, 183–208.

[26] *Report* (1921), 31 (my emphasis).

[27] Such a component was implied, but no unequivocal commitment was made. The statement also insisted on reform of the League of Nations to allow the inclusion of Russia and Germany: ibid. See also *Report* (1922), 123.

come to the assistance of the member against which a warlike act has been committed.'[28]

These views are perhaps unsurprising when expressed by those who had supported the war and thus had greater sympathy for the plight of France. However, a willingness to accept that France had genuine security concerns was not confined to Labour's pro-war moderate leadership. In the advisory committee, opinion was also moving in this direction. One reason was that, increasingly from 1921, mainstream supporters of the League, such as Shaw and Gillies, played a greater role in the committee's activities as a result of the reorganisation. However, democratic socialists, who had previously dominated the committee, also came to view collective security more positively. They had always argued that, in a competitive world system, nation-states would have fears about their economic security, that the existence of armaments was thus a systemic problem of capitalism. In the early post-war period they had pressed for the supranational distribution of essential raw materials as a way of mitigating the security fears that resulted. However, just as the gradual dismantling of the wartime inter-allied bodies had shifted their views on economic reconstruction, so too did it shift their view on security. How in the short term were the security concerns of the nation states to be addressed, given that supra-nationalism appeared increasingly unrealistic? Disarmament was dismissed as a solution: 'talk of limiting armaments without touching their cause is to delude ourselves', insisted Brailsford.[29] The concerns of France had to be taken seriously by the British left. 'The [French] People are moved', he wrote in *Labour Leader*, 'by a fear of the unknown German mass, with its industry, its discipline and its high birth rate.'[30] These arguments were reflected in a series of memoranda, written as part of a 1923 advisory committee debate on the DTMA.[31] In the first of these, for example, it was argued that:

the disarmament problem cannot be solved by the summary procedure of voting against armament credits ... Parallel with any scheme of disarmament must proceed the development of some instrument for ... maintaining those securities heretofore made or maintained by armaments ... [T]he Labour Party

[28] A. Henderson, *Labour and foreign affairs*, London 1923, 9.
[29] 'Disarmament', ACIQ memorandum, no. 198, Apr. 1921, LPA, LSI. Leonard Woolf was more optimistic about the prospects for immediate progress on disarmament, but nevertheless increasingly accepted that progress was not possible until the security issue was addressed.
[30] *New Leader*, 9 Feb. 1923. See also Roden Buxton's speech to the 1922 Labour party conference: *Report* (1922), 190. Initially, Brailsford believed that, given their lack of confidence in the League of Nations, only a bilateral agreement with France would reassure the French. However, by the end of 1924, and with evidence that the French were adopting a more positive attitude to the League, he was prepared to accept the Geneva Protocol.
[31] See ACIQ minutes, 2 Apr. 1923, LPA, LSI, and James Middleton papers, LPA, JSM/ADV/157.

will only be able to reduce the army and navy effectively in proportion as it provides other protection or reduces the danger of and damage from war.[32]

The choice had become one between 'a joint guarantee or mutual defence against an aggressor' and a return to the balance of power. The memorandum favoured the former, but only if any collective security arrangement was open to all nations, definitely including all the major European powers, and was linked to a process of national disarmament.[33] Morel, Ponsonby and their supporters tried hard to resist this approach, but gradually those in favour of collective security began to gain the upper hand and, after lengthy consideration, the advisory committee came down in April 1924 in favour of the DTMA. Despite the 'very grave' problems with the treaty, supporters of collective security argued that Labour should adopt a pragmatic and constructive approach.[34]

Opinion in the Labour party was thus clearly moving towards the acceptance of a League of Nations collective security policy, including a military component, in the final two years before it entered office. The party's policy owed very little by the end of 1923 to the approach recommended by the UDC radicals. The security concerns of France, dismissed by Morel, had been accepted as genuine by Labour. A firm commitment had been made to a form of collective security through the League of Nations. Disarmament, most Labour leaders agreed, would only be possible after the security question had been addressed. One thing complicated this picture, however: Ramsay MacDonald's return to the leadership in December 1922.

MacDonald and collective security, 1922–3

MacDonald's return to the leadership had little effect on the party's attitude towards the debate on reparations and reconstruction: his views on this issue were much closer to those of the existing Labour leadership than those of the UDC radicals and thus continuity of policy was maintained.

On security questions, on the other hand, the situation was different. MacDonald's views on the League of Nations, collective security and disarmament had always been significantly different from those of Henderson, Clynes and Thomas and this did not change in 1922. So, while MacDonald became slightly more positive about the League after 1919 and was prepared to support it as a general force for good on the international scene, he

[32] 'Principles of a disarmament policy', ACIQ memorandum, no. 278a, 3 May 1923, LPA, LSI.
[33] 'Disarmament policy', ACIQ memorandum, no. 284a, June 1923, ibid.
[34] 'The draft treaty of mutual assistance', ACIQ memorandum no. 327, May 1924, ibid. Even within the UDC voices were beginning to be raised in opposition to Morel's policy: W. Arnold-Forster, France, ourselves and the future (UDC pamphlet xlva, 1922).

remained extremely sceptical about whether the organisation should be placed as firmly at the centre of Labour's approach to international affairs as Henderson and others in the party proposed.[35]

MacDonald's scepticism on the League of Nations' policy on collective security was in part personal, but mainly ideological.[36] Hence it was entirely consistent with the general approach that he had taken to foreign affairs since the pre-war period. MacDonald was essentially a liberal radical, who, while sympathetic to Gladstonian moralism, had never been associated with ideas about a permanent international body. Rather, he believed that the growth of democracy, as represented by the progressive forces throughout Europe, would inevitably result in a more reasoned approach to diplomacy and disarmament. To the extent that the League of Nations had a role in MacDonald's approach, it was as a potential facilitator of arbitration and improved international contacts.

However, while these were MacDonald's core beliefs, he was prepared to compromise. He was realistic about the situation in Europe, recognising that insecurity and armaments were dominant.[37] However, he questioned whether a definite commitment to a collective security policy through the League of Nations was the appropriate response, for it constituted a major concession to the view that ultimately security could only be ensured by armed force.[38] Moreover, it would place the power to use this force in the hands of an organisation about which he still had severe reservations due to its domination by the governments of the great powers. Rather, the best approach was to address the issue that was at the root of the European insecurity – the reparations dispute, which he believed substantially reduced trust and confidence on all sides. If this dispute could be settled, or even eased, then the security questions could be approached in an environment more conducive to the type of approach MacDonald favoured. MacDonald acknowledged French security concerns but, to a greater extent than his colleagues, argued that France by her own actions was exacerbating the situation. He was strongly critical of the reliance she continued to place in 'military ideas … of force and so on'. '[W]ill you tell us', he asked, 'when an army ever made you secure?'[39] Before Labour conceded that military means – even if they were collective – were required to maintain security, it should at least try to improve the international atmosphere, in the hope that this would

[35] See, for example, MacDonald to Cecil, Feb. 1923, Cecil of Chelwood papers, BL, MS 51081.
[36] See Robbins, *Politicians*, 251.
[37] See *The Times*, 12 Nov. 1923.
[38] This was consistent with MacDonald's general argument in *National defence: a study in militarism*.
[39] HC, Debates, clxvii.1775/6 (2 Aug. 1923). See also clx.547 (16 Feb. 1923). On the latter occasion, MacDonald told the House of Commons that, while it was important to understand France's concerns, any 'sympathy' should be 'of a practical kind [rather] than merely to understand France from the sentimental point of view'.

make elaborate security arrangements seem less necessary. Thus, he told the 1923 Labour party conference that 'the practical policy of peace consisted in getting the peoples of the countries into such sympathetic touch with each other that they would realise that security lay in the moral character and not in the air, on the sea, or the land'.[40] This did not mean that security issues could be ignored. MacDonald recognised that, given the level of French concerns, a settlement of the reparations dispute was unlikely to occur if the security question was not also addressed. However, his aim, both in opposition and government, was to ensure that the security question did not take precedence over the reparations issue. Security could be discussed and ideas investigated, but no commitments should be made until substantial progress occurred in negotiations on reparations.[41]

Labour in government: the DTMA and the Geneva Protocol

It is clear that significant support existed in the Labour party in the period 1919–23 for the idea of collective security. In power in 1924, the debate about the efficacy of such a policy continued on the basis of the DTMA. This culminated in an intense dispute within government about Labour's attitude to the Geneva Protocol, a document drafted at the Fifth Assembly of the League which built on the DTMA and strengthened the collective security elements of the international body's original covenant.[42] Labour's consideration did not therefore represent a new departure, as has often been suggested, but a continuation of a debate that had begun in the party in 1918/19. Labour was not forced to consider the scheme because of a 'diplomatic quid pro quo' with the French, as Cline suggests.[43] It did not represent 'a revolution in Labour thinking on the security question', as Lyman, argues.[44] Rather, the party's consideration of the Protocol was an entirely predictable consequence of the development of Labour's policy on European security since 1918. This does not mean that in negotiations on the Protocol there were not areas where Labour had to compromise on positions adopted

---

[40] *Report* (1923), 222. See also *Report* (1922), 190.
[41] See, for example, MacDonald to Cecil, 1923, Cecil papers, MS 51081.
[42] See F. P. Walters, *A history of the League of Nations*, London 1952, 273–4. If passed the Geneva Protocol would have bound all signatories to the League Covenant to submit all disputes to compulsory arbitration. Any state that refused would be judged an aggressor and the other signatories would have a duty to support the covenant and assist (economically, financially and militarily) the attacked state. The protocol's ratification was dependent on the establishment of, and agreement to, a general plan for disarmament. On the fall of the Labour government, the protocol lapsed. A copy of it is in Wrynn, *Socialist international*.
[43] Cline, *Recruits*, 90.
[44] Lyman, *The first Labour government*, 179.

in the pre-government years, but these compromises concerned tactics and details, not fundamentals.[45]

Such a reinterpretation of the pre-government development of Labour's policy on European security throws a different light on its approach when in government. The main question becomes not 'why did Labour consider a League of Nations-based collective security in Government?' but 'why in its consideration of this policy wasn't the administration more positive and successful?' To answer this question it is necessary to concentrate on the resistance placed in the way of such a policy by MacDonald. He was not the only person involved with the 1924 government who was opposed to a League-based policy of collective security. Entrenched opposition existed within the Foreign Office and the service departments, such that, even without MacDonald, there is no guarantee that Labour could have pressed successfully for a policy based on collective security. However, what MacDonald's efforts ensured was that this was a battle that never really took place. His decisions about the formation of his Cabinet and its committees as they related to foreign affairs, his handling of the government's debate on the DTMA and his treatment of the delegation that negotiated the Geneva Protocol at the Fifth Assembly of the League of Nations all show a concern to block a policy of collective security.

With regard to the 1924 Cabinet, MacDonald's decisions on foreign affairs constituted a deliberate attempt to ensure that his view of the security issue and the League of Nations prevailed once Labour was in government.[46] Of those figures who had played a leading part in the development of pre-government policy – Arthur Henderson, J. H. Thomas; J. R. Clynes and Tom Shaw – only Thomas, as Colonial Secretary, was given a brief that involved him in any way in negotiations on issues of European security. The other three could only exercise influence on foreign affairs through the Cabinet. With respect to Foreign Office appointments, both MacDonald himself and his assistant secretary, Arthur Ponsonby, were League sceptics and outspoken opponents of collective security. They were joined in the Foreign Office by Lord Parmoor, who was given special responsibility for League affairs. The creation of such a position represented a clear break with the past. The League, it seemed, was finally to have an advocate at the heart of British foreign policy-making. However, Parmoor was not the man League supporters would have chosen.[47] An ex-Conservative, he was a pacifist, who

---

[45] In any case, as Labour ministers realised on assuming office, Germany's tardy entry into the League was due as much to her own delaying tactics as to opposition from elsewhere: see, for example, MacDonald to Lord D'Abernon, 19 Sept. 1924, TNA, FO 411/1.

[46] On MacDonald's general approach to Cabinet appointments see Worley, *Labour inside the gate*, 77–8.

[47] They would have preferred Robert Cecil, but, according to MacDonald, 'certain troublesome difficulties' prevented this: MacDonald to Cecil, 24 Jan. 1924, Cecil papers, MS 51081. On Parmoor's background see Howell, *MacDonald's party*, 319.

had a very limited conception of the League's likely role. He was a staunch opponent of collective military security, an idea, he later told the Cabinet, which was 'alien to the principle of the League of Nations [and] would tend to reproduce the old principle of the balance of power under a different name'.[48]

MacDonald's appointments to the Committee of Imperial Defence (CID) were also sceptical about the League. This committee performed a vital role in foreign policy-making by, for example, commenting on any proposal that was likely to affect British security and deployment of arms. It was the main means by which the views of the armed forces were represented at Whitehall. As such, it lay at the heart of the traditional balance-of-power approach to foreign affairs and was, thus, the body from which the greatest opposition to a change of approach might be expected. Labour would need to challenge, or at least neutralise, the CID's arguments if a more League-based policy was to be adopted. MacDonald, however, had no intention of doing this. Instead, his attitude is summed up in a conversation that Hankey, the Cabinet secretary, was later to record in his diary:

I passed (with some trepidation) to the Committee of Imperial Defence. Rather to my surprise he displayed a good deal of interest ... He promised me every support at the CID. He then went on to discuss frankly his difficulties in finding Labour ministers suited to take charge of the three service departments, and in particular pressed me for details as to how far as Prime Minister he could expect to control their policy. I told him that, through the medium of the CID he could do a good deal.[49]

Eventually, MacDonald appointed Lord Haldane, an old Liberal imperialist and League sceptic as the chair of the committee.[50] Thus, MacDonald surrounded himself in the Foreign Office and associated departments with colleagues who shared, albeit sometimes for different reasons, his deep scepticism of the potential role of the League of Nations in British foreign policy.[51] His closest intimate on security questions was to be Hankey, also a strong critic of the League.

[48] 'Draft treaty of mutual assistance', cabinet memorandum 34(4), 27 May 1924, CAB 23/48. See also Parmoor to MacDonald, 1 June 1924, MacDonald papers, PRO 30/69/21, and Parmoor minute, 1 Mar. 1924, PRO 30/69/207.

[49] Hankey diary, Hankey papers, entry for 11 Oct., 1924. Hankey writes that the entry is a description of his first meeting with MacDonald, which occurred just prior to Labour taking office.

[50] For details of Haldane's appointment see MacDonald to Haldane, 19, 23 Dec. 1923, Haldane papers, MS 5916; and Haldane to his sister, n.d. MS 20060. Hankey was delighted at Haldane's appointment and told him in August that '[P]rovided you remain at the helm throughout the first term of office at the least, we shall have nothing to fear': Hankey to Haldane, 20 Aug. 1924, Hankey papers.

[51] For details of Haldane's involvement in foreign affairs in 1924 see Haldane to his mother, 5, 21 Feb., 24 Mar., 20 May, 18 July 1924, Haldane papers, MS 6007.

MacDonald's appointments in 1924 thus strongly suggest a determination to prevent the development of a policy on security issues of which he disapproved. His plan, which was very much in accord with the Foreign Office line, was to keep the whole issue of security off the political and diplomatic agenda for as long as possible, in the hope that, in the meantime, an agreement could be reached on reparations.[52] 'The problem of security would [then] be very much different', he believed, and the prospects for considering a less militaristic approach would increase.[53]

The biggest challenge for MacDonald and his officials in this was the DTMA. Although the government did not officially have to make its views clear to the League of Nations until July 1924, it inevitably came under pressure from supporters of the League to give an indication of its thinking earlier. They saw it as a major test of the government's attitude.[54] Given MacDonald's opposition to the idea of collective security, there is no doubt that he was opposed to the draft treaty. However, in the development of the government's response to it, he showed himself willing not just to reject it, but also to use this rejection to undermine the whole case for a League-based policy of collective security. The first draft of his response was written by the CID, despite pressure from League supporters for the issue to be considered by a Special Cabinet Committee rather than sceptical government officials who, they feared, would dismiss the treaty out of hand. This fear proved well-founded.[55] The draft response amounted to a virtual line-by-line dismantling of the treaty: it would not fulfil its own aims: the guarantees it provided were 'so precarious that no responsible government will feel justified in consenting to any material reduction in its armaments in return', and the obligations it imposed were so onerous that nations could not with any conscience commit themselves to carrying them out.[56] The final paragraph of the draft, appended to Hankey's paper for the CID, was utterly dismissive of the League of Nations. It questioned the right of the League even to involve itself in this area of policy. The League of Nations, Hankey made clear, should confine itself to 'the elimination of causes of friction between nations, the settlement on equitable lines of longstanding differences, and the prompt consideration and public ventilation of disputes which had reached an acute stage. The development of material force, for which international organisations are but ill adapted, should be contemplated only in

[52] See Nicolson minute, 27 Aug. 1924, FO 371/9819, and Lampson minute, 16 Apr. 1924, MacDonald papers, PRO 30/69/207. For the Foreign Office's opposition to collective security see Crewe minutes, 6 Nov. 1923, 21 Feb. 1924, FO 371/10568.
[53] MacDonald to Robert, Lord Crewe, 24 Mar. 1924, MacDonald papers, PRO 30/69/101.
[54] See, for example, C. Delisle Burns memorandum to Labour's advisory committee, 22 Feb. 1924, Philip Noel-Baker papers, Churchill College, Cambridge, NB 4X/57
[55] Parmoor minute, 3 Mar. 1924, FO 371/10568. See also HC, Debates, clxx.973 (3 Mar. 1924).
[56] PRO, CAB 24/167, C(24)309, 21 May 1924. For the CID's consideration of the DTMA see MacDonald papers, PRO 30/69/21.

the last resort'.[57] The adoption of such a view by the British government in an official letter to the League would have been a major blow to the organisation. Was MacDonald prepared to let this happen? His comments on, and amendments to, the draft paragraph suggest not only that he was, but also that he wished to reinforce Hankey's points. The prime minister removed all reference to the use of material force on behalf of the League and added that the organisation 'had been created essentially to provide for forms of security against war other than military'.[58]

Supporters of the League were not prepared to accept such a negative attitude towards its endeavours and the limited view of its functions proposed by MacDonald. The prime minister's approach faced concerted opposition in Cabinet and he had to give way. After 'considerable discussion', it was agreed that the whole of the last paragraph should be redrafted, with the particular aim of giving 'greater prominence to the constructive side of the Government's attitude towards the Treat[y] of Mutual Assistance'. Thus the final draft that was sent to the League of Nations secretariat stated that the DTMA should not be discarded, but merited 'full exploration and examination', together with 'other lines of enquiry' (such as demilitarisation and the internationalisation of frontiers) by an international disarmament conference.[59]

Labour and the Geneva Protocol

The Cabinet dispute over the government's response to the DTMA marks the beginning of a fight-back by supporters of the League against the policy pursued by MacDonald and his advisers. Pressure mounted inside and outside the government for MacDonald to take a greater interest in the security issue and a more positive attitude towards the League of Nations. With respect to the former, the French pressed strongly, as the London conference on reparations drew to an end, for more definite security commitments from Britain. MacDonald had successfully fobbed off Herriot, the new French premier, during negotiations on the Dawes Report, with vague promises that the security question would be dealt with after the conference.[60] By August it was becoming clear that he would have to make good on this promise.[61]

---

[57] Hankey showed this draft to Tyrrell before sending it to MacDonald: Hankey to Sir William Tyrrell, 28 Apr. 1924, FO 371/10568.

[58] The draft reply containing MacDonald's comments and amendments can be found ibid.

[59] See MacDonald to secretary-general of the League of Nations, July 1924, FO 411/1.

[60] He agreed with Herriot in July 'to cooperate in devising through the League of Nations or otherwise, as opportunity presents itself, means of securing … complete pacification … and to continue the consideration of the question until the problem of general security can be finally solved': Edouard Herriot to MacDonald, 11 Aug. 1924, MacDonald papers, PRO 30/69/101

[61] See Sir Eric Phipps to MacDonald, 30 Aug. 1924, ibid. PRO 30/69/183.

The French pinned their hopes, in particular, on the forthcoming Fifth Assembly of the League of Nations, which was to be held in Geneva. MacDonald had committed himself to attend with Herriot, as part of his deal on security. The meeting was also important for League supporters. It represented the ideal opportunity for the Labour government to show its full support for the new organisation and its difference from its predecessors. Considerable pressure was put on MacDonald to adopt a more constructive and ambitious attitude towards the League. An all-party petition was sent by MPs to the prime minister in August, which called on him to be more positive towards the League in its approach to the security question.[62] Within government, supporters of the League used this external pressure to their own benefit. This was reflected in the make-up of the British delegation to Geneva, agreed in Cabinet on 5 August 1924. The main delegation was to include Henderson, the League's biggest supporter in the government, and Gilbert Murray, a leading light in the LNU, as a substitute delegate.[63]

Nevertheless, MacDonald remained firmly resistant to the line proposed by League supporters. In his reply to the MPs' petition, he reiterated his belief that the DTMA was 'quite wrong in its psychology' and that his aim was to improve the 'orientation of international policy' so that other approaches to the security question might be considered.[64] He was ambivalent about the forthcoming League assembly and seriously considered pulling out.[65] He had no new policy initiatives to announce and his effect on the other British delegates, on his arrival in Geneva, was to deflate their expectations. Murray told Cecil that 'He came strange to the atmosphere, and was inclined to think that not much could be done, except to have a talk and arrange a [disarmament] conference.'[66] In response to pressure from his delegation, MacDonald decided that, in his speech to the assembly, a more positive tone towards the League's efforts was required. However, he had no intention of committing himself on the concept of collective security. He thus warned the assembly:

> The danger of supreme importance which is facing us now is that national security should be regarded merely as a military problem and based solely on the predominance of force … If, after all the appalling evidence in history that military force cannot give security, we to-day go back and repeat the follies of our ancestors, then the security we give for the day is only a betrayal of the nation that we lull to sleep under it.[67]

[62] Ellis Hume-Williams to MacDonald, n.d. ibid.
[63] Cabinet conclusions 47(24), 5 Aug. 1924, CAB 23/48.
[64] MacDonald to Hume-Williams, 11 Aug. 1924, MacDonald papers, PRO 30/69/183. In this regard, he argued that the success of the London conference was a major step forward.
[65] See MacDonald to Parmoor, 11 Aug. 1924, ibid. PRO 30/69/200.
[66] MacDonald diary, ibid. PRO 30/69/1753, entry for 21 Sept. 1924, and Murray to Cecil, 4 Sept. 1924, Cecil papers, MS 51081.
[67] 'Verbatim record of the fifth assembly of the League of Nations, Sixth plenary meeting', 4 Sept. 1924, FO 411/1.

This was no less true, he added, of collective military measures organ-ised through the League of Nations than of national or bilateral arrange-ments. The League's role, MacDonald insisted, should merely be pacific. 'A machinery of defence is easy to create', he cautioned, 'but beware lest in creating it you destroy the chances of peace. The League of Nations has to advance the interest of peace … [It should be] looked up to, not because its arm is great, but because its mind is calm and its nature just.'[68]

MacDonald's positive proposals were thus limited to a promise that Britain would fully support improvements in the League's apparatus and procedures for arbitration, and an extension of the League's membership.[69] This was a major disappointment to the French. They were not looking for improve-ments in the arbitration arrangements, but for firm military guarantees.[70] They came close to walking out of the conference, only being prevented from doing so by MacDonald's agreement to a hastily drafted resolution which stressed his support for the League's continued efforts to investigate the provisions for security outlined in the DTMA.[71]

MacDonald then left it to the British delegation to find a compromise between Britain's extreme reluctance to consider any form of continental military commitment, collective or otherwise, and the French delegation's determination to strengthen and make more precise the military guarantees offered by the League of Nations. He gave instructions to the delegation about how much they could concede: they were to ensure that any agree-ment on collective guarantees be made dependent on the successful outcome of a disarmament conference; they were not to allow any external agency to stipulate how Britain should use her forces, especially the navy, in the event that sanctions were required; and, moreover, any agreement reached would still have to be considered by the governments of League members.[72]

In helping to draft what came to be known as the Geneva Protocol the British delegation was largely successful in carrying out his instructions. On the operation of military sanctions, the powers of the council were reduced and individual countries retained control over their own forces. They were bound to assist only insofar as their geographical position allowed them to do so. In addition, the entire Protocol would only come into effect once a disarmament conference, arranged for 15 June 1925, had met and accepted a general plan for arms reduction. One official described the delegation's

[68] Ibid.

[69] Ibid.

[70] 'Verbatim record of the fifth assembly of the League of Nations, eighth plenary meeting', 5 Sept. 1924, ibid.

[71] Parmoor's speech to the Assembly, which was later described by Murray as a 'pure pacifism', did not help the situation: Murray to Cecil, 5 Sept. 1924, FO 411/1; Cecil papers, MS 51081. See also 'Reduction of armaments: continuation of the discussion. resolution', FO 411/1.

[72] See Parmoor to MacDonald, 29 Aug. 1924, MacDonald papers, PRO 30/69/200, and MacDonald to Parmoor, 25 Sept. 1924, FO 411/1.

success in this regard as 'a substantial victory for Mr Henderson', who had negotiated the deal.[73]

Despite the British delegation's efforts to remain within the guidelines laid down by the prime minister and thus minimise commitment to collective security, it is clear that MacDonald began backing away from the concessions that he had made in Geneva soon after his return home. In a note to officials just days after the assembly resolution was adopted he reiterated his determination to resist collective security. He stated firmly that 'By turning down the Draft Treaty of [Mutual Assistance] we have saved this country from a serious danger, but the battle has still to be fought. I anticipated some reaction in France against us but we must not buy it off by handing ourselves to French views.'[74] As negotiations continued, and concern began to grow in Whitehall that Labour might after all commit Britain to some form of collective security, albeit in a watered-down form, MacDonald began to distance himself from the Geneva delegation. In the final week of negotiations, the delegation received almost daily telegrams from the prime minister reminding them of the limited nature of their remit.[75] In private, MacDonald told officials that 'if they [the delegation] could avoid signing any draft protocol it would be best'.[76] For their part it is clear that Foreign Office officials did not feel bound in any way by decisions made by the delegation. They reassured the service departments that they would have 'ample opportunity to state their views' once a completed agreement had emerged.[77] Thus, as the delegation moved closer to a final agreement, preparations were already being made in Whitehall for the campaign against it. In these MacDonald was a leading player.

The Geneva delegation was pleased with the Protocol. As Parmoor wrote to MacDonald, with the explicit approval of Henderson and Murray, '[We are] more than satisfied with the terms … My view is that on every vital point we have fully maintained your instructions. [The French] have not pressed us to abandon points which we regarded as of essential importance.'[78] However, on its return to Britain, the delegation received a less than enthusiastic reception, with MacDonald, in the face of concerted official opposition, showing no intention of fighting for the Protocol that they had negotiated. Cabinet consideration of the document was delayed and was ultimately never to take place before the government's resignation, which was caused by a separate issue. While MacDonald indicated support for the Protocol in opposition, when there was no chance that it would be implemented, there

73 C. W. Orde minute, 23 Sept. 1924, FO 371/10570.
74 MacDonald minute, 10 Sept. 1924, FO 371/9813.
75 MacDonald to Parmoor, 25, 26, 29 Sept. 1924, FO 411/1. See also cabinet conclusions 51(24), 29 Sept. 1924, CAB 23/48.
76 MacDonald note on R. H. Campbell minute, 24 Sept. 1924, FO 411/1.
77 Tyrrell note on Orde minute, 22 Sept. 1924, ibid.
78 Parmoor to MacDonald, 1 Oct. 1924, MacDonald papers, PRO 30/69/200.

can be little doubt that he would not have done so had he remained prime minister after October 1924.

Despite MacDonald's efforts, the first Labour government had shown itself prepared to press strongly for a League-based policy. Labour had not meekly accepted a balance of power policy; it had pushed hard in what it believed was a more progressive direction. Even MacDonald's approach was based, not on a craven retreat in the face of official opposition, but on the ideological difficulties that he had repeatedly expressed with the League idea. The commitment of other party leaders to collective security was based on the belief, formed after the experience of 1914, that permanent international mechanisms had to be put in place to preserve peace. Germany's willingness to go to war reduced faith among moderate internationalists, such as Henderson, Clynes, Thomas and Shaw, in free trade as a pacifying force, by itself. Non-intervention and domestic democratic control, as the radicals proposed, were not sufficient because it was not the British Foreign Office that had been to blame for the war. Nor was the instability in the international system that had led to the conflict an inherent part of capitalism. Rather, it was caused by the existence of an anti-democratic, militarist pariah state. The existence of such a state in the recent past meant that, while most international disagreements in the post-war world could be resolved by conciliation, the international community nevertheless had to secure itself, collectively, against those forces determined upon war.

Conclusion

This study has involved a detailed investigation of the development of the Labour party's foreign policy between its formation and the end of its first period in government. It has explored the development and interaction of progressive ideas on foreign policy in this period and shown how these ideas fared in the Labour party. It has not been assumed that Labour was doctrinally united, nor that policy proposals were the result of a straightforward translation of ideas, be they socialist, radical or liberal, into a programme. Rather, the ideological divisions that existed within the Labour party have been delineated, and policy development has been regarded as a process that takes place in – and is informed by – a political and institutional context. Thus policy, as well as serving a programmatic function, can also play a part in maintaining or building up a party's coalition of support. For this reason, analysing policy development must involve consideration of the distribution of power in the party's policy-making process.

Politics and ideology in the development of a Labour party foreign policy, 1900–24

Past misinterpretations of developments in Labour's foreign policy have occurred for two main reasons. First, the richness of the ideological debate on foreign affairs has been underestimated. Only on the basis of a detailed elucidation of the ideas and policy proposals of the most influential groups and individuals associated with the strands of progressive thought identified in this work is it possible to make a proper assessment of the ideological influences on the Labour party at this time. Second, this diversity of view on international affairs did not match organisational developments. Genuine co-operation between individuals whose basic ideological approach differed was possible in some areas, because there were some general issues on which some, or all, progressives could unite. Such co-operation was sensible politics: coalitions were formed with the aim of attracting support or forcing a change of party or government policy, with areas of difference down-played until after the general campaign goal had been secured. The UDC was the classic example of this phenomenon. It brought together many of those critical of Britain's involvement in a European war, but ideologically included a heterogeneous mix of individuals. Similarly, strong support for the League of Nations movement came from individuals whose basic assumptions about international affairs were very different. This political opportunism, while understandable, has created difficulties for analysts who have tended to assess ideological influences on the Labour party on an organisational basis.

This study has argued that the strand of thought most consistently influential on the development of Labour foreign policy up to 1924 was the Gladstonian liberal, not either of those most closely associated with the UDC. It was this type of approach that dominated the 1917 MOWA – the first major statement by the party on foreign affairs and the most complete outline of Labour's general approach throughout the period – and various associated statements. Thus, on the war, the party as a whole agreed for the first time in 1917 that the conflict was being fought in defence of certain limited principles: democracy and anti-militarism. German militarism, it was accepted, had been the main cause of the conflict and had to be defeated: a negotiated settlement would thus not be welcome unless it was based on the destruction of the German military machine and fair compensation for the damage caused. On the peace settlement in 1917, Labour committed itself firmly to the establishment of a League of Nations as the overwhelming priority. The League it envisaged would be a governmental body with a definite commitment to collective security.

It was on the basis of this type of approach that a significant body of opinion in the Labour movement had always supported the conflict, and on which Henderson and MacDonald had sought to construct a compromise policy on the outbreak of the war. In the chaotic and traumatic circumstances of late 1914 and early 1915, compromise had proved impossible – knee-jerk patriotism had prevailed. In the changed domestic and international situation of 1917, however, the patriotic wing of the party was unable to block the establishment by moderate internationalists throughout the movement of a more critical approach to the conflict.

The decisions made by Labour on foreign affairs in 1917 and early 1918 were the basis for its approach for the next seven years. The Gladstonian liberal line on the peace was repeatedly reiterated in statements and resolutions emanating from the party's most important institutions. Thus, the Versailles treaty was constructively criticised rather than unequivocally condemned. It required amendment not re-negotiation. Similarly, the League of Nations, while clearly flawed, was broadly welcomed and considered capable of reform. Despite strong pressure from critics of Labour's centrist approach, calls for a more absolutist policy were rejected, even when, as a result of the worsening economic and financial situation from 1921, international tensions began again to rise.

Certainly, the views and policy proposals of the other ideological strands sometimes appeared in Labour party statements or were articulated through Labour party bodies and organs. However, the importance of these, particularly those associated with the UDC, has been overstated because of a failure fully to allow for the role of political and institutional factors in the development of policy.

As far as political factors are concerned, because of the ideological diversity that existed in foreign affairs at this time, policy development played a major role in the construction and maintenance of the Labour party's coalition of support. It is this that explains the limited inclusion of policy proposals associated with the UDC radicals and democratic socialist ideological strands in some Labour statements and the involvement of individuals associated with these approaches in the party's advisory bodies. This was particularly true of the 1917 MOWA. This should be seen as part of a process aimed at reuniting the labour alliance after its division on the war in 1914, and extending the party's coalition of support in preparation for the next general election, which the Lloyd George coalition was preparing to fight on the basis of an anti-Labour manifesto. It was part of the same process that led to the 1918 'socialist' constitution. Thus, while it was dominated by a Gladstonian liberal approach, it also included ideas associated with the UDC radical and democratic socialist strands.

The inclusion of these concessions to different viewpoints has created a serious misunderstanding of the document, which has, in turn, had a considerable influence on the way in which Labour's post-war foreign policy development has been interpreted. The publication of the MOWA did not mean that Labour had been converted to the foreign policy views of critics of the war.[1] It had not – and was not throughout the whole period up to 1924.

Indeed, from 1921, the party increasingly began to distance itself from the views of the UDC radicals in particular. After the relative political disappointments of the early post-war years, and in the face of an economic and diplomatic crisis, the party acted to reorganise its structures, including those involved in policy-making. With regard to foreign policy, the resultant increase in control over policy development of the party's main institutions entrenched the Gladstonian liberal approach. Labour's political need for a practical and coherent policy relevant to the current domestic and European crisis, reinforced the overwhelming ideological support that, in any event, existed throughout the party for this approach. The party's renewed contact with the French socialist party emphasised just how unreliable the UDC radicals' view of French policy had become.

The coalition-forming role of policy means that close attention needs to be given to the distribution of power within the policy-making processes of the party. The only way to determine which ideological faction, if any, holds sway is by considering which was the most consistently dominant in those party bodies where executive decision-making power lay. It is on this basis, that the Gladstonian liberal strand can be identified as the most influential. Thus, while there is no doubt that democratic socialism dominated the advisory committee in its early days, that the UDC radical approach was supported by most of the left-wing press, and that ILP pacifism continued

---

[1]   This misinterpretation is also the result of the credit mistakenly given by some to UDC radicals for the development of the league idea: see chapter 4 above.

to maintain a presence in the ILP, none of these bodies ultimately decided the policy of the Labour party. In those bodies that did – the NEC, the PLP, the party conference, the leadership – the Gladstonian liberal approach remained dominant.

It was with this attitude towards foreign policy that the Labour party entered government. In January 1924 the party therefore had a clear, well-established agenda, which it tried to implement during the following nine months.[2] Its policy in government was not dominated by the views of permanent officials, nor did the party compromise all its principles in negotiations with the other European states. That the policy ultimately pursued was not that much different, on reparations and reconstruction at least, from the one that permanent officials would have anyway proposed, said more about the development of official policy since 1918 than the efforts of the Labour government.

The influence of Gladstonian liberalism was apparent in Labour's attitude both to reparations and reconstruction, and to the League of Nations. With regard to the former, Labour adopted a pragmatic, moderate approach. The aim was never to re-negotiate the post-war settlement, but rather to remove by inclusive diplomacy the obstacles to trade that the Treaty of Versailles was perceived to have created. This approach did not reflect a belief that the treaty was fundamentally unjust, nor did it amount to a retrospective acceptance that Versailles was the product of a war that should not have been fought. Rather the genuine concerns of France were accepted and the responsibility of Germany for the 1914–18 conflict upheld.

More broadly, Labour's approach also revealed the party as firmly committed, with respect to the international economy, to the benefits of free trade. Like Keynes, Labour's analysis of the post-war economic slump was one that emphasised the difficulties created by the allied governments at Versailles, rather than any inherent structural problems with international capitalism. If management of the international economy was needed at all, it should be inter-governmental and limited.

On this matter the government was generally ideologically united behind a Gladstonian liberal line. Despite MacDonald's past associations with the UDC, his approach to the war and the post-war settlement had always been different from that of the more outspoken UDC radicals. He had always favoured an inclusive 'European' solution to the reparations question rather than a 'pro-German' one. In government he resisted demands, both from

---

[2]   The Labour government's decision to 'inaugurate a new practice of laying all treaties with other nations on the table of the House of Commons for a period of twenty-one days' was not, as Vickers implies, evidence of the continuing influence of the UDC; rather such an approach was consistent with the views on the proper conduct of international diplomacy of most progressives. Indeed, the government refused to grant parliamentary time to Morel's more broad-ranging 'Motion on the parliamentary control of foreign relations': Vickers, *Labour and the world*, 7- 86; Howell, *MacDonald's party*, 32.

Snowden and permanent officials, for a harder line to be taken with the French.

With regard to European security the government was more divided, but nevertheless its policy was again generally consistent with Gladstonian liberalism. Labour showed itself unwilling to accept uncritically an approach based on preserving the balance of power, but believed that limited supranational intervention in international affairs was necessary to prevent future wars. Its more serious engagement with the League of Nations, exemplified by MacDonald's speech at the assembly, the appointment of a League minister in the Foreign Office and serious consideration of a strengthened element of collective security through the Geneva Protocol, were all attempts to challenge Britain's traditional policy. All were policies that the Gladstonian liberal LNU could welcome unequivocally. It was only MacDonald's continued, ideologically-based, scepticism about the League that prevented Labour pushing this line harder in government.[3]

Like most governments, the Labour government did not get things all its own way on foreign policy. Compromises had to be made. Labour's policy involved negotiation with other governments whose interests and ideology in some areas differed fundamentally from those of the British government. Within government also, the basic assumptions of many permanent officials in the Foreign Office and other departments involved in international affairs were at odds with Gladstonian liberalism, particularly with respect to the League of Nations. The pursuit of a traditional foreign policy, based primarily on the preservation of Britain's role and the maintenance of the balance of power in Europe, was deeply embedded in the mindset of permanent officials, and this undoubtedly affected the policy pursued. It strongly reinforced MacDonald's already considerable scepticism about a League-based collective security policy, for example.

In some areas, moreover, Labour's pre-government approach was shown in office to be inadequately thought through. Like many governments in any area of policy, the first Labour administration entered office with a broad framework of ideas on foreign policy rather than a detailed plan. On the whole, this broad framework proved sufficiently coherent to provide a reasonably robust guide to the party's actions in office. Some detailed policy development, such as the Geneva Protocol, was undertaken 'on the hoof' and in negotiation with other parties, but the principles upon which the final proposal was based were broadly consistent with the policy proposed in opposition.

That Labour attempted to pursue a policy consistent with a Gladstonian liberal approach does not mean that that ideology was the only determinant of policy. With regard to reparations and reconstruction, in particular, Labour leaders regarded their approach as closely congruent with the inter-

---

[3] It would still have faced sizeable opposition from within Whitehall.

ests of the trade unions and their wider working-class constituency. In this regard Labour's diplomatic policy was also an important policy instrument in the fight against unemployment. Labourism and Gladstonian liberalism went hand-in-hand and were regarded as mutually compatible.[4] However, the material interests of the trade unions do not in themselves explain why Labour pursued the policy it did.

Politically too, a Gladstonian liberal approach made sense. If Labour could show that in office it would pursue a foreign policy little different from that proposed by leading Liberal intellectuals and politicians, this was bound to assist the party in its electoral competition with the older progressive party. The left, of course, was unhappy, but the ILP's influence had greatly declined by 1924.[5]

The foreign policy developed by Labour in the years before 1924 was not then primarily influenced by the ideas of those associated with the UDC. Rather, the party's policy most closely reflected ideological developments since 1914 in Gladstonian liberal thought and was developed further in negotiations with the International movement. On this basis, by the time that it entered government the party had constructed a relatively sophisticated policy both on European reconstruction and security, which it then attempted to implement in office.

Despite the general consistency of Labour's policy in government with that in opposition, the policy pursued in 1924 was vigorously attacked by some in the party in the months after MacDonald resigned. Some of this criticism was the legacy of Morel's attacks on the government during the previous summer.[6] Thus George Young, a former diplomat and previously an ally of Morel, campaigned in the advisory committee for Labour to adopt a policy of root-and-branch reform of the Foreign Office 'in light' of its experience in government.[7] At the TUC's conference in the following September, moreover, left-wing trade unionists, taking advantage of concerns that the Dawes Plan might make British coal uncompetitive, succeeded with a resolution strongly critical of Labour's acceptance of the plan.[8]

However, opposition from the left to the moderate internationalist line adopted by Labour had been a constant feature of its foreign policy development since 1917. It remained so throughout the 1920s. The ideological groupings that had emerged during the war continued to compete for influence. Brailsford continued to push, through the ILP, for the acceptance of

---

4   Some in the TUC were less convinced. They believed that the London agreement on reparations, particularly with respect to coal, disadvantaged British miners: Miller, *Socialism and foreign policy*, 154–6.
5   See McKibbin, *Evolution of the Labour party*, 244–5.
6   Morel himself had died in November 1924.
7   See ACIQ minutes, 21 Jan. 1921, LPA, LSI. MacDonald firmly resisted this proposal: 20 May 1925, ibid.
8   See Miller, *Socialism and foreign policy*, 154–5.

his proposals for greater international economic intervention.[9] The UDC, while considerably weakened by the death of Morel, and pacifists in the ILP remained consistent critics.[10] On occasions, one or other of these groups achieved some successes.[11]

However, overall, these approaches were resisted. Criticisms of Labour's policy in 1924 were generally brushed aside and the official policy position remained remarkably consistent with the approach developed after 1917. Thus on German reparations Labour remained insistent that payments should be kept up. In government in 1929 the Young Plan, which set a fifty-nine-year plan for payment and reduced the total by 20 per cent, was accepted, and the following year Henderson, now Foreign Secretary, firmly resisted German pleas for a moratorium.[12] On the broader issue of international economic co-operation, Labour remained circumspect.[13] Greater co-operation was encouraged, but only of a very limited sort. The party's commitment to international free trade remained total and Briand's 1930 plans for greater European economic co-operation were treated with caution.[14]

On the security issue, too, Labour's policy in the later 1920s was consistent with that of the earlier period. The unresolved debate on collective security, which had marred the 1924 government's League policy, was on-going. Thus, while Labour, in its opposition to the foreign policy of the Baldwin government, repeatedly harked back to the Geneva Protocol as a missed opportunity, party policy on the military aspects of this commitment remained ambiguous.[15] MacDonald and Snowden remained fundamentally opposed to a League policy of this sort, and continued to regard its role as to facilitate disarmament. However Henderson, backed by a new generation of Labour politicians, such as Hugh Dalton and Phillip Noel-Baker, insisted that military sanctions had to be accepted if collective security was to have any real credibility and disarmament made a realistic proposition.[16] Given this fundamental division, as David Carlton has suggested, Labour in opposition decided 'in the interests of party unity … to concentrate attention on the

---

[9] See Trentmann, 'The strange death of free trade', 242.

[10] See Miller, *Socialism and foreign policy*, 161–3.

[11] The 1926 Labour conference, for example, approved a pacifist resolution, which called upon 'workers' to resist any future wars by refusing to bear arms. However at the same conference a resolution condemning the Locarno pact was defeated: *Report* (1926), 256. See also Miller, *Socialism and foreign policy*, 163, and Naylor, *Labour's international policy*, 9.

[12] Indeed, the original draft of the plan was amended to increase the amount of reparations due to Britain. On the Young Plan see Marks, *Illusion*, 102–4. On Henderson and German reparations in 1930 see Carlton, *MacDonald versus Henderson*, 68–9.

[13] See Labour party, *Labour and the nation*, London 1928, 37, 42.

[14] See Miller, *Socialism and foreign policy*, 227–9, and Carlton, *MacDonald versus Henderson*, 83–7.

[15] See Miller, *Socialism and foreign policy*, 194–5, and Wrigley, *Arthur Henderson*, 164.

[16] See *Report* (1929), 185; H. Dalton, *Towards the peace of nations: a study in international politics*, London 1928, 211–12; and Wrigley, *Arthur Henderson*, 163–7.

less contentious issues of arbitration and disarmament'.[17] However, failure to resolve this debate meant that it inevitably recurred during Labour's second period in government. Efforts to persuade France to disarm foundered due to her continued concerns about security, which Henderson, despite his best efforts, was unable to address because of opposition from MacDonald and Snowden in the Cabinet.[18] The problem that had marred Labour's League policy in 1924 did so again in 1929–31.

The Labour party's ideology and policy up to 1931: a reassessment

How does this reinterpretation of Labour's foreign policy development between 1900 and 1924 relate to the broader debate on the early Labour party's ideological and policy development? How does it contribute to a broader understanding of the Labour party during this period?

The contribution of the Labour party to the development of progressive ideas and policy has generally been regarded as limited or non-existent. If Labour had any properly elaborated policies by the mid-1920s, these were not based on a coherent ideological approach. Labour was, rather, ideologically unsophisticated, particularly in relation to European socialist parties. Its policies were based on the narrow concerns of the trade unions and/or nineteenth-century liberal ideas.[19]

Increasingly, however, as part of a broader reassessment of the history of the early Labour party the dismissal of the party's ideological and policy development has been questioned.[20] Historians have investigated in more detail Labour's approach in a broad range of policy areas and concluded that the characterisation of party policy as merely reliant on nineteenth-century liberalism, or representative of trade union interests, is mistaken. In fact, they argue, ideological and policy debates were considerably more sophisticated than has previously been suggested. They generally entailed the consideration of new and innovative ideas, often of socialist inspiration. They involved attempts to construct reformist programmes appropriate to the problems faced and capable of mobilising electoral support. They did not occur in domestic isolation, but were similar to developments occurring in European socialist and labour parties.

The result of these ideological and policy debates, it has been suggested, was not the carte blanche acceptance of either old or new ideas, but the interaction of liberal, radical and socialist approaches, in which it was not just the socialist ideas that were new: older traditions of progressive thought were also adapted to respond to the new problems of the early twentieth

---

[17] Carlton, *MacDonald versus Henderson*, 74. See also Labour party, *Labour and the nation*.
[18] Carlton, *MacDonald versus Henderson*, 129–33.
[19] See chapter 1 above.
[20] For details of this broader reassessment see chapter 1 above.

century.[21] Moreover, these debates did not only involve party leaders and intellectuals. Trade unionists' ideas too were more sophisticated than is generally appreciated, even when they involved a rejection of socialism.[22]

In this reassessment, some historians have stressed the continuity of Labour's thought and policy with advanced liberalism and a renewed popular radical tradition. Others have emphasised the role of socialist ideas, influenced by Marxist and Revisionist approaches. With regard to the former, Pat Thane has shown, for example, that both in Labour's approach to local politics, particularly in London, and in MacDonald's political thought, updated popular radical ideas were to the fore.[23] Thus, the main targets for reform were privilege and vested interests and the main 'route to change' was democratic political reform.[24] Duncan Tanner, too, has noted the continuity between Labour's approach and the popular radical tradition, but he stresses to a greater extent that the intention of Labour leaders was to develop versions of 'democratic socialisms'.[25] None of these more recent accounts has looked specifically at the development of Labour's foreign policy, although Trentmann has investigated views on the left about the broader area of free trade, which showed how some ILP figures were beginning to question the domestic implications of this policy.

This reassessment of Labour's ideological and policy development in its early years has opened up the possibility that the history of the Labour party might be judged more 'against its own aims and values, and against what might reasonably have been expected', than against the 'absolute standards [and] agendas of others'.[26] However, while these new accounts have all shown that Labour was involved and brought something new to progressive debates of this time, not all of them have investigated how these ideas fared within the policy-making process of the Labour party and once the party entered office.[27]

While previous accounts of the development of Labour's foreign policy up to 1924 have not been concerned to locate their work within broader debates about the early history of the party, they have none the less tended to reinforce the predominant view of the party as unsophisticated ideologically. They have strengthened the view that Labour's rise brought nothing new to ideological and policy debates on the left of British politics up to 1924. They have given the impression that, if a socialist foreign policy existed at all in the Labour party, it bore little relation to any Marxist, or even Revisionist, understandings of the term, but remained tied to nineteenth-century liberal

---

21 See Howe, 'Hungry forties',
22 Reid, 'Old Unionism reconsidered'.
23 Thane, 'Labour and local politics'.
24 Ibid. 269.
25 Tanner, 'The development of British socialism'.
26 Tanner, Thane and Tiratsoo, *Labour's first century*, 2.
27 An exception is Thompson, *Political economy*, 3–86.

ideology;[28] and, by emphasising the role played by former Liberals in policy development, they have reinforced the labourist notion that the Labour movement was not interested in issues outside the immediate concerns of the trade unions.[29]

By challenging this view, this book clearly has implications for the broader debate about the ideology and policy of the Labour party. Indeed, overall, its findings strongly support the argument that previous neglect of ideas and policy development by labour and social historians has distorted understanding of the party at this time. Labour was more sophisticated ideologically and with respect to policy development than has generally been suggested. The party was not merely the new cipher for Victorian liberal ideas. It cannot simply be dismissed as 'labourist'. Its ideological approach did not evolve in isolation from developments in Europe.

With regard to the sophistication of Labour's approach to foreign policy, the party's development in this area did not merely involve the uncritical adoption of a Victorian liberal-dominated approach brought into the party by ex-members of the Liberal party at the end of the war. Nor were foreign affairs an area left to the party's intellectuals for most of the period, only for their ideas to be over-ruled by the leadership's pragmatism once in government, or the nationalistic patriotism of the rest of the trade union-dominated party, at moments of crisis.

Ideologically, in fact, the Labour party was involved in an intense and heated debate on international affairs that was taking place on the centre and left of British politics. This debate, similar to ones taking place in other policy areas, involved the re-evaluation of many of the basic assumptions, derived from nineteenth-century progressive thought, about Britain's relationship with the rest of the world. Liberal internationalism, the almost unchallenged progressive creed of the previous hundred years, was systematically updated, to a degree, indeed, that was unacceptable to the more radical proponents of this approach. Thus, by the end of the war, the liberal approach to foreign affairs, while remaining true to the free trade nostrums of the previous century, envisaged a level of intervention (British and supranational) in international relations that would have been unthinkable twenty years earlier, even among Gladstonians. Foreign policy radicalism, by comparison, remained relatively static. Non-intervention and domestic democratic reform remained during this period its overriding principles.

Democratic socialists were also deeply involved in this debate. Their input, like that identified in other areas of policy, built on the liberal and radical traditions, but also involved a critique of these approaches that utilised aspects of Marxist thought.[30] A concerted attempt was made to understand

---

[28] Gordon, *Conflict and consensus*; Miller, *Socialism and foreign policy*.
[29] For example, Taylor, *Troublemakers*, and Cline, *Recruits*.
[30] See, for example, Trentmann 'The strange death of free trade', and Tanner, 'The development of British socialism'.

the forces of international capitalism within the political economy that
were responsible for the war and to develop a democratic socialist strategy
to control them. The proposals that emerged envisaged a move towards a
supranational system of managed trade – an idea that also had enthusiastic
proponents in France – and were clear precursors of Briand's 1930 proposal
for European federal union, and ultimately the post-Second World War
European Economic Community.[31]

Debate on international affairs was not confined to the party's intellectuals. The broader Labour movement was also consistently represented, most
obviously by a number of leading figures such as Henderson, Thomas and
Shaw, whose backgrounds were in the trade unions, but who nevertheless
had strong and well-developed interests in international affairs, and also
by a significant body of opinion within the wider movement. What they
brought to this debate was not merely a concern with the material interests
of the trade unions, as labourists would suggest, but a moderate internationalist ideological commitment. Support for such an approach was a product
of the political apprenticeship that many Labour and trade union leaders
had served in the Gladstonian Liberal party and/or their international trade
union activities. Members of Labour's non-intellectual leadership were not,
therefore, empty vessels open to conversion by foreign policy intellectuals,
but strong-minded, independent politicians with well-established views of
their own, who were in a powerful position, given their domination of the
party's main institutions, to dictate Labour's approach.

Moreover, while the labourist view is undoubtedly correct in arguing that
international affairs was not a primary concern for many within the Labour
movement for most of the time, it was not the case that when, during crucial
debates, the mass of the party did become involved, it insisted unequivocally
on a nationalistic approach. Labour's initial equivocation over the war in
1914, agreement to the MOWA in 1917 and increasing disillusionment with
the post-war settlement are all testament to the persistence of a moderate
internationalist consciousness in the mainstream party. Nationalistic patriotism was undoubtedly always a force in the broader Labour movement, but
it never went unchallenged and, as the period progressed, gradually became
a minority viewpoint.

This study has also confirmed the view that the early Labour party was
very much in contact with ideological and policy debates that were taking
place in Europe. Indeed, at crucial times in Labour's foreign policy development – i.e. 1917 and 1921–3 – negotiations with some or all of the main
European parties had a major influence on the policy adopted. In 1917 one
of the central objectives of the MOWA was to unite the allied parties in
the adoption of a centrist policy on the war and, once the document was

---

[31] For thinking on European union among continental socialists see Wrynn, *Socialist
international*.

published, it was further developed in negotiations with allied socialists.[32] After 1921 Labour's approach to the European economic and diplomatic crisis was purposely developed in negotiations with the European parties.

Moreover, negotiations between British Labour and European socialists did not involve discussions between a patriotic British party and more sophisticated socialist internationalist Europeans. Labour cannot simply be characterised as patriotic, but nor were the main European parties principled upholders of socialist internationalism.[33] All had been involved to some extent in their national war effort and after the war the approach of both the German SPD and the French SFIO continued to reflect national, as well as international, concerns. After 1917 they, together with Labour, began the process of developing a reformist internationalist approach, which, while based on the unique contacts developed by working-class organisations during the previous half-century, nevertheless involved a recognition that each party's approach had also to represent their own national interests, given their reliance for support on a domestic electorate.[34]

Thus, with respect to the sophistication of the early Labour party's policy debate on foreign affairs and its engagement with similar debates taking place in Europe, this study has argued that some of the features of Labour's early ideological and policy development, evident in other recent studies, are also evident with respect to foreign policy.

While the continuation in the Labour party of the popular radical tradition and the emergence of distinctive democratic socialist approaches, evident in other policy areas, were also noteworthy features of Labour's debate about international affairs, ultimately they were not the most important influence on the foreign policy that the party actually adopted. Rather, it was liberal ideas that were the most influential. They were liberal ideas certainly that had been substantially adapted to the international situation of the early twentieth century; and Labour's adoption of them was not because other types of approach were not considered. Nevertheless, while a type of foreign policy radicalism survived as an influential force in the party, particularly in the person of MacDonald, the pure 'no foreign politics' radicalism of Morel, Ponsonby and Trevelyan was firmly rejected. Similarly, although a coherent and sophisticated democratic socialist approach was developed and became influential in the party's advisory committee in the early post-war period, it too was ultimately rejected after 1921.[35]

There are a number of reasons why this was the case. One was simply that the Gladstonian liberal approach had the strongest backing within the higher reaches of the Labour party. However, there are also strong grounds for arguing that the adoption of this policy was not just based on 'unex-

---

[32] See Van der Slice, *International Labour diplomacy*.
[33] See Ward, *Red flag*, 103–4.
[34] See also Horne, *Labour at war*, 333–49.
[35] See Trentmann, 'Wealth and welfare', 91–2.

amined habits and loyalties' but was rather 'a conscious intellectual and political choice', particularly after 1921.[36] It was regarded as the policy that had most to commend it in terms of its appropriateness to the international and political problems that Labour faced: it was the most practical progressive policy on offer; it was one that might feasibly be acceptable to the other European nations; and it was the policy that had the best chance of mobilising electoral support for the party.

On the question of practicality, the context within which Labour had to construct a co-ordinated policy on international affairs in 1921 was one of economic and international crisis. The greatest immediate requirement in these circumstances was to stabilise the situation. Proposing the root-and-branch renegotiation of the Treaty of Versailles, as the UDC radicals suggested, would merely have made matters worse, for it would have alienated France. Abstract demands for greater democratic control were merely a distraction. Similarly, proposing a major extension of the economic powers of the League of Nations, as the democratic socialists had suggested, was not what was required in the circumstances. This had seemed like an idea that might catch on in the later stages of the war and there was much that ultimately proved prescient in the democratic socialists' approach. However, the collapse of the wartime inter-allied economic bodies showed that there was simply insufficient support for this level of supranationalism at this particular time.[37]

The adaptation of policy to the international context was not merely opportunism, however, nor did it involve the abandonment of principle in the face of international realities. At the heart of Labour's policy was a firm progressive core. Its main aim was to get the continent trading again by reducing the perceived barriers to Germany's participation in the European economy. Its approach to security was one that emphasised nations' shared interest in peace and rejected the traditional notion of a European balance of power.

It was a policy that could also attract significant mainstream Liberal support. Politically as well, therefore, the policy adopted by Labour in 1921 was appropriate. The electoral experience since 1918 had shown, or was perceived to have shown, that Labour needed to reassure centrist opinion if it was finally to overtake the Liberals as the main progressive party of the left. On foreign affairs it had failed to do this up to 1924, for reasons that were entirely understandable in a new and growing party. Its adoption in 1924 of a strongly Gladstonian line helped to ease concerns among mainstream Liberals.

There undoubtedly remained problems and weaknesses with the approach to international affairs that Labour constructed in opposition and attempted

---

[36] See Biagini and Reid, *Currents of radicalism*, 17.
[37] This was also true of European socialists' attitudes towards these ideas: Wrynn, *Socialist International*, 184.

to pursue in government. It underestimated the depth of the problem in European affairs caused by the imbalance, economic and demographic, between Germany and France.[38] It underestimated the continuing power of nationalism and militarism in Germany and misjudged the extent to which these forces could be mollified by anything significantly short of a reversal of the outcome of the war. It was based on too naïve a belief in the willingness of nations to commit their economic and military power to a problem in which they had no immediate national interest.[39] Moreover, Labour's attempted implementation in office of a collective security policy was fatally undermined by continuing indecision on this issue at the top of the party.

However, many of these weaknesses and problems are only identifiable with hindsight. In 1924 Labour was not alone among progressive opinion in Britain and Europe in underestimating both the nature of the European problem and the continuing power of German nationalism.[40] Another world war would have to take place before these problems were addressed. Moreover, while the problems of a League-based collective security are now well-established, in 1924 it represented the only feasible progressive alternative to a return to the balance of power.

It is not on this basis, therefore, that Labour should be judged. Rather, it should be remembered that in 1924 Labour was still a very new party. Less than ten years previously it had been little more than a pressure group for the trade unions. Many continued to believe in the early 1920s that it was incapable of forming a government and properly conducting the affairs of state. Labour's conduct of foreign affairs in 1924 showed that the party was perfectly able to manage the government's business even in those areas of policy with which it was not generally associated.

Even more important, given its claims to be a party of reform, it also showed that, when in government, Labour would not merely manage the diplomatic affairs of state, but also attempt to push policy in a progressive direction. The direction chosen was not the one in which those most closely associated with the UDC wanted Labour to go. It was not the direction that most previous accounts of Labour's foreign policy have erroneously suggested that the party had proposed to head when in opposition. However, it was nevertheless a direction that was eminently sensible given the international situation with which the party was faced, and the clear limitations of the alternative progressive approaches. As a result, on foreign affairs at least, Labour's first period of government helped firmly to establish it as the leading progressive party on the left of British politics.

---

[38] In this regard, those who argued that the roots of European conflict were economic were on the right track.

[39] See Carr, *Twenty years' crisis*.

[40] Wrynn, for example, speaks of a general 'failure on the part of the socialists of Europe in the face of the European ideal': *Socialist International*, 184.

APPENDIX

The Union of Democratic Control's Four Propositions, September 1914

1. No Province shall be transferred from one Government to another without the consent by plebiscite or otherwise of the population of such Province.
2. No Treaty, Arrangement, or Undertaking shall be entered upon in the name of Great Britain without the sanction of Parliament. Adequate machinery for ensuring democratic control of foreign policy shall be created.
3. The Foreign Policy of Great Britain shall not be aimed at creating alliances for the purpose of maintaining the 'Balance of Power', but shall be directed to concerted action between the Powers, and the setting up of an International Council, whose deliberations and decisions shall be public, with such machinery for securing international agreement as shall be the guarantee of an abiding peace.
4. Great Britain shall propose, as part of the Peace Settlement, a plan for the drastic reduction, by consent, of the armaments of all the belligerent Powers, and to facilitate that policy shall attempt to secure the general nationalisation of the manufacture of armaments and the control of the export of armaments by one country to another.

Source: UDC papers, D/DC/1.

Bibliography

Unpublished primary sources

Cambridge, Churchill College
Maurice Hankey papers
Philip Noel Baker papers

Cambridge, King's College
Goldsworthy Lowes Dickinson papers
John Maynard Keynes papers

Cambridge, Trinity College
Frederick Pethwick Lawrence papers

Cambridge, University Library
Charles Hardinge papers

Edinburgh, National Library of Scotland
Richard Haldane papers

Hull, Brynmor Jones Library
Union of Democratic Control papers

Lewes, University of Sussex
Leonard Woolf papers

London, British Library
Cecil of Chelwood papers

London, British Library of Political and Economic Science, London School of Economics
Hugh Dalton papers
Independent Labour party papers
Francis Johnson papers
George Lansbury papers
League of Nations Union papers
E. D. Morel papers
Passfield papers
Graham Wallas papers

London, The National Archives, Kew
CAB 23 Cabinet minutes, 1924
CAB 24 Cabinet papers, 1924
FO 371 Foreign Office papers
FO 411 Foreign Office papers
James Ramsay MacDonald papers

Manchester, National Museum of Labour History

Labour party archive

Advisory Committee on International Questions, minutes and memoranda,
   1918–25
Arthur Henderson papers
Labour National Executive Committee, minutes, 1906–25
Labour and Socialist International papers, 1919–24
James Middleton papers
Trades Union Congress, parliamentary committee, minutes, 1914–25

Oxford, Bodleian Library
James Bryce papers
Leonard Courtney papers
Willoughby H. Dickinson papers
J. L. Hammond papers
Gilbert Murray papers
Arthur Ponsonby papers
Alfred Zimmern papers

Warwick, University of Warwick, Modern Records Centre
Amalgamated Society of Carpenters and Joiners (MSS. 78)
Amalgamated Society of Tailors and Tailoresses (MSS. 192)
International Metalworkers Federation (British Section) (MSS. 036)
International Union of Woodworkers (MSS. 78)
Iron and Steel Trades Confederation (MSS. 36)
London Society of Compositors (MSS. 28)
National Union of Bookbinders and Machine Rulers (MSS. 39)
National Union of Railwaymen (MSS. 127)
Trades Union Congress (MSS. 292)

Published primary sources

Beatrice Webb's diaries, 1924–1932, ed. M. Cole, London 1956
British general election manifestos, 1918–1966, ed. F. W. S. Craig, Chichester
   1970

The diary of Beatrice Webb, III: *1905–1924*, ed. J. MacKenzie and N. MacKenzie, London 1984

The left and the war: the British Labour party and World War One, ed. P. Stansky, London 1969

The letters of Leonard Woolf, ed. F. Spotts, London 1989

The letters of Sidney and Beatrice Webb, III: *1912–1947*, ed. N. MacKenzie, Cambridge 1978

Lloyd George, D., *War memoirs*, London 1933–6

Lord Riddell's war diary, i, London 1933

Minutes of the Rainbow Circle, 1894–1914, ed. M. Freeden, London 1989

Parliamentary debates (House of Commons)

The political diaries of C. P. Scott, 1911–1928, ed. T. Wilson, London 1970

The political diary of Hugh Dalton, 1918–40, ed. B. Pimlott, London 1986

Ramsay MacDonald's political writings, ed. B. Barker, London 1972

Report of the annual conference of the Labour party, London 1906–25

Report of the ILP, London 1914–20

Report of the proceedings of the annual TUC, London 1906–24

Thomas Jones: Whitehall diary, ed. K. Middlemas, i, London 1969

Newspapers and periodicals
Concord
Contemporary Review
Daily Citizen
Daily Herald
Foreign Affairs
Forward
Headway (journal of the LNU)
Labour Leader
Manchester Guardian
The Nation
New Europe
New Leader
New Statesman
Socialist Review
The Times
The UDC
War and Peace

Contemporary books, pamphlets and articles

Allen, C., *Is Germany right and Britain wrong?*, London c.1915

Angell, N., *The great illusion: a study of the relation of military power to national advantage*, London 1913

——— *The economic functions of the League*, London 1920

Arnold-Forster, W., *France, ourselves and the future* (UDC pamphlet xlva, 1922)

Brailsford, H. N., *Origins of the Great War* (UDC pamphlet iv, 1914)

—— *Belgium and the 'scrap of paper'* (ILP Labour and War pamphlet x, 1915)

—— *The war of steel and gold: a study of the armed peace*, 3rd rev. edn, London 1915

—— *A League of Nations*, 2nd edn, London 1917

—— 'The organization of peace', in Buxton, *Towards a lasting settlement*, 151–73

Bryce, Viscount, *Proposals for the prevention of future wars*, London 1917

Buchanan, G., *My mission to Russia and other assignments*, ii, London 1923

Buxton, C. R. (ed.), *Towards a lasting settlement* London 1917

Henderson, A., *The League of Nations and Labour*, London 1918

—— 'The outlook for Labour', *Contemporary Review* cxiii (1918), 121–30

—— *Labour and foreign affairs*, London 1923

Hobson, J. A., *A League of Nations* (UDC pamphlet xv, 1915)

—— *Imperialism: a study*, 3rd rev. edn, London 1938

Keynes, J. M., *The economic consequences of the peace*, London 1920

—— *A revision of the treaty: the collected works of John Maynard Keynes*, iii, London 1971

Labour party, *Memorandum on war aims*, London 1918

—— *Unemployment, the peace and the indemnity*, London 1921

—— *Labour and the nation*, London 1928

MacDonald, J. R., *The zollverein and British industry*, London 1903

—— *Labour and the empire*, London 1907

—— *National defence: a study of militarism*, London 1917

Masterman, C., 'The case for a Liberal party', *The Nation* (May 1920), 244–6

Morel, E. D., *War and diplomacy* (UDC pamphlet xi, 1915)

—— *The Union of Democratic Control* (UDC leaflet xiii, 1915)

—— *Free Russia and the Union of Democratic Control* (UDC pamphlet xxxvii, 1 May 1917)

Murray, G., *The foreign policy of Edward Grey*, Oxford 1915

—— *The League and its guarantees*, London 1920

Noel Baker, P. J., *The Geneva Protocol for the pacific settlement of international disputes*, London 1925

Ponsonby, A., *Democracy and the control of foreign affairs*, London 1912

—— *Parliament and foreign policy* (UDC pamphlet v, 1915)

—— *The Union of Democratic Control: what it is and what it is not* (UDC pamphlet xiv, 1915)

Salter, J. A., *Allied shipping control: and experiment in international administration*, Oxford 1921

Swanwick, H. M., *Builders of the peace, being ten years' history of the Union of Democratic Control*, London 1924

Trevelyan, C., *The Union of Democratic Control*, London 1919

Walton Newbold, J.T., *The war trust exposed*, Manchester 1913

Woolf, L., *International government*, London 1916
—— *The framework of a lasting peace*, London 1917
—— *International economic policy*, London 1920

Secondary works

Adereth, M., *The French Communist party: a critical history from comintern to the 'colours of France' (1920–84)*, Manchester 1984

Allen, V. L., 'The reorganisation of the Trades Union Congress, 1918–27', *British Journal of Sociology* xi (1960), 24–41

Anderson, P. and T. Nairn, 'Origins of the present crisis', *New Left Review* xxiii (1964), 26–54.

Angell, N., *After all*, London 1951

Barker, R., 'Socialism and progressivism in the political thought of Ramsay MacDonald', in Morris, *Edwardian radicalism*, 114–30

Bealey, F. (ed.), *The social and political thought of the British Labour party*, London 1970

Beer, S. H., *Modern British politics: a study of parties and pressure groups in the collective age*, 3rd edn, London 1982

Belloni, F. P. and D. C. Beller (eds), *Faction politics: political parties and factionalism in comparative perspective*, Santa Barbara 1978

Berger, S., *The British Labour party and the German Social Democrats, 1900–1931*, Oxford 1994

Biagini, E. F. (ed.), *Citizenship and community: Liberals, radicals and collective identities in the British Isles, 1865–1931*, Cambridge 1996

—— and A. F. Reid, 'Currents of radicalism, 1850–1914', in Biagini and Reid, *Currents of radicalism*, 1–20

—— and A. F. Reid (eds), *Currents of radicalism: popular radicalism, organised labour and party politics in Britain, 1850–1914*, Cambridge 1991

Birn, D. S., *The League of Nations Union, 1918–1945*, Oxford 1981

Blaazer, D., *The popular front and the progressive tradition*, Cambridge 1992

Black, L., '"What kind of people are you?" Labour, the people and the "new political history"', in Callaghan, Fielding and Ludlum, *Interpreting the Labour party*, 23–38

Boemeke, M. F., G. Feldman and E. Glaser (eds), *The Treaty of Versailles: a reassessment after 75 years*, Cambridge 1998

Bourne, J. M., *Britain and the Great War, 1914–1918*, London 1989

Boyce, R. W. D., *British capitalism at the crossroads, 1919–32: a study in politics, economics and international relations*, Cambridge 1987

Brand, C. F., *British Labour's rise to power*, Stanford 1941

—— *The British Labour party*, Stanford 1974

Braunthal, J., *History of the International*, II: *1914–1943*, London 1967

Briggs, A. and J. Saville, *Essays in labour history, 1886–1923*, London 1971

Brivati, B. and R. Heffernan, *The Labour party: a centenary history*, Basingstoke 2000

Brockway, A. F., *Inside the left: thirty years of platform, press, prison and parliament*, London 1942

—— *Socialism over sixty years: the life of Jowett of Bradford*, London 1946

Burgess, K., *The challenge of Labour: shaping British society, 1850–1930*, London 1980

Burk, K., *War and the state*, London 1982

—— *Troublemaker: the life and history of A. J. P. Taylor*, New Haven–London 2000

Cain, P. J. 'Hobson's developing theory of imperialism', *Economic History Review* xxxiv (1981), 313–16

—— *British imperialism: innovation and expansion, 1688–1914*, London 1993

—— and A. G. Hopkins, 'Variations on a famous theme: Hobson international trade and imperialism, 1902–38', in Freeden, *Hobson*, 31–53

Callaghan, J., S. Fielding and S. Ludlum, *Interpreting the Labour party: approaches to labour politics and history*, Manchester 2003

Cannadine, D., *Class in Britain*, London 1998

Carlton, D., *MacDonald versus Henderson: the foreign policy of the second Labour government*, London 1970

Carr, E. H., *Conditions of peace*, London 1942

—— *The twenty years' crisis, 1919–39*, 2nd edn, Basingstoke 1946

Carsten, F. L., *Revolution in central Europe, 1918–19*, London 1972

—— *War against war: British and German radical movements in the First World War*, London 1982

Ceadel, M., *Pacifism in Britain, 1915–45*, Oxford 1980

—— *Thinking about peace and war*, Oxford 1987

Cecil, R., *All the way*, London 1949

Clarke, P., 'The progressive movement in England', *TRHS* xxiv (1974), 159–82

—— *Liberals and social democrats*, Cambridge 1978

Clegg, H. A., *A history of British trades unions since 1889*, ii, Oxford 1985

—— A. Fox and A. F. Thompson, *A history of British trades unions since 1889*, i, Oxford 1964

Cline, C., *Recruits to Labour*, New York 1963

—— 'E. D. Morel and the campaign against the Foreign Office', *JMH* xxxix (1967), 126–37

—— *E. D. Morel, 1873–1924: the strategies of protest*, Belfast 1980

Clinton, A., 'Trade councils during the First World War', *IRSH* xv (1970), 202–34

Clynes, J. R., *Memoirs, 1869–1924*, London 1937

Cole, G. D. H., *A history of the Labour party from 1914*, London 1948

—— *A history of socialist thought, IV: Communism and social democracy, 1914–1931*, London 1958

Collette, C., 'The Labour party and the Labour and socialist International', *Labour History Review* lviii (1993), 29–34

—— *The international faith: Labour's attitude to European socialism, 1918–39*, Aldershot 1998

Conwell-Evans, T. P., *Foreign policy from a backbench, 1904–18: a study based on the papers of Lord Noel-Buxton*, London 1932

Cowden, M. H., *Russian Bolshevism and British Labour, 1917–1921*, New York 1984

Cowling, M., *The impact of Labour*, London 1971

Craig, G. A. and F. Gilbert (eds), *The diplomats, 1919–1939*, New York 1963

Dalton, H., *Towards the peace of nations: a study in international politics*, London 1928

—— *Call back yesterday*, London 1953

Cripps, Charles, Lord Parmoor, *A retrospect*, London 1936

Cunningham, H., 'The language of patriotism, 1750–1914', *History Workshop Journal* xii (1981), 8–33

Dockrill, M. L. and J. Douglas Goold, *Peace without promise: Britain and the peace conferences, 1919–23*, London 1981

Douglas, R., 'The National Democratic Party and the British Workers League', *HJ* xv (1972), 533–52

Downs, A., *An economic theory of democracy*, New York 1957

Dowse, R. G., 'Left-wing opposition during the first and second Labour governments', *Parliamentary Affairs* xiv (1960–1), 80–93

—— 'The entry of the Liberals into the Labour party, 1910–1920', *Yorkshire Bulletin of Economic and Social Research* iii (1961), 78–88

—— 'The Independent Labour party and foreign politics', *IRSH* vii (1962) 33–46

Durbin, E., *New Jerusalems: the Labour party and the economics of democratic socialism*, London 1985

Duverger, M., *Political parties: their organization and activity in the modern state*, London 1964

Egerton, G. W., *Great Britain and the creation of the League of Nations: strategy, politics and international organisation, 1914–19*, London 1978

Eldersveld, S. J., *Political parties: a behavioural analysis*, Chicago 1964

Epstein, L. D., *Political parties in western democracies*, London 1967

Feldman, G. D., 'A comment', in Boemeke, Feldman and Glaser, *Treaty of Versailles*, 441–7

Ferguson, N., 'The balance of payments question: Versailles and after', in Boemeke, Feldman and Glaser, *Treaty of Versailles*, 401–40

Fischer, C., *The Ruhr crisis, 1923–1924*, Oxford 2003

Fletcher, R., 'British radicalism and German revisionism: the case of Eduard Bernstein', *IHR* iv (1982), 339–70

Flournoy, F. R., 'British liberal theories of international relations', *JHI* vii (1946), 195–217

Foote, G., *The Labour party's political thought: a history*, 3rd edn, London 1997

Freeden, M. (ed.), *Reappraising J. A. Hobson*, London 1990

Glaser, E., 'The making of the economic peace', in Boemeke, Feldman and Glaser, *Treaty of Versailles*, 371–400

Goldstein, E., *Winning the peace: British diplomatic strategy, peace planning and the Paris Peace Conference, 1916–20*, Oxford 1991

Gordon, M., *Conflict and consensus in Labour's foreign policy, 1914–65*, Stanford 1969

Grayson, R. S., 'The Liberal party and international affairs, c. 1919–1988', *Contemporary British History* xiii (1999), 186–97

Gupta, P. S., *Imperialism and the British labour movement, 1914–1964*, London 1975

Haesler, S., *The tragedy of Labour*, Oxford 1980

Hamilton, M. A., *Arthur Henderson*, London 1938

Hamish Fraser, W., *A history of British trade unionism, 1700–1998*, Basingstoke 1999

Hammond, J. L., *C. P. Scott of the Manchester Guardian*, London 1934

Hanak, H., 'The Union of Democratic Control during the First World War', *BIHR* xxxvi (1963), 168–80

Harmel, R. and K. Janda, 'An integrated theory of party goals and party change', *Journal of Theoretical Politics* vi (1994), 259–87.

Harrison, R., 'The War Emergency National Workers' Committee, 1914–1920', in Briggs and Saville, *Essays in labour history*, 211–59

Haupt, G., *Socialism and the Great War*, Oxford 1972

Henig, R., *Versailles and after, 1919–1933*, London 1984

—— *The origins of the First World War*, London 1989

Hinde, W., *Richard Cobden: a Victorian outsider*, New Haven 1987

Hinton, J., *The first shop stewards movement*, London 1973

Hobsbawm, J., 'The labour aristocracy in nineteenth century Britain', in his *Labouring men: studies in the history of labour*, London 1964, 272–315

Hodge, J., *Workman's cottage to Windsor Castle*, London 1931

Horne, J. N., *Labour at war: France and Britain, 1914–18*, Oxford 1991

Howard, C., 'MacDonald, Henderson and the outbreak of war, 1914', *HJ* xx (1977), 871–91

Howe, A., 'Towards the "hungry forties": free trade in Britain, c. 1880–1906', in Biagini, *Citizenship and community*, 193–218

Howe, S., *Anticolonialism in British politics: the left and the end of empire, 1918–1964*, Oxford 1993

Howell, D., *British workers and the Independent Labour party, 1888–1906*, Manchester 1983

—— *MacDonald's party: Labour identities and crisis, 1922–1931*, Oxford 2002

Howell, S., *Anticolonialism in British politics: the left and the end of empire, 1918–1964*, Oxford 1992

Hunt, R. N., *German social democracy, 1918–1933*, Chicago 1964

Jeffery, K., *The British army and the crisis of empire, 1918–1922*, Manchester 1984

Joll, J., *The origins of the First World War*, 2nd edn, London 1992

Jones, R., *Arthur Ponsonby*, London 1989

Jones, T., *Remaking the Labour party from Gaitskell to Blair*, London 1996

Judt, T., *Marxism and the French left: studies in labour and politics in France, 1830–1981*, Oxford 1986

Kavannagh, D. (ed.), *Politics of the Labour party*, London 1982

Kendall, W., *The revolutionary movement in Britain, 1900–1921*, London 1969

Kennedy, P., *The rise of the Anglo-German antagonism, 1860–1914*, London 1980

Keohane, D., 'Labour's international policy: a story of conflict and contention', in B. Brivati and R. Heffernan (eds), *The Labour party: a centenary history*, Basingstoke 2000, 363–82

Kirby, D., 'International socialism and the question of peace: the Stockholm conference of 1917', *HJ* xxv (1982), 709–16

Klingemann, H., R. I. Hoffbert and I. Budge, *Parties, policies and democracy*, San Francisco 1994

Kruger, D. H., 'Hobson, Lenin and Schumpter on imperialism', *JHI* xvi (1955), 252–9

Laybourn, K., *Phillip Snowden: a biography*, Aldershot 1988

—— *The rise of Labour*, London 1998

—— and J. Reynolds, *Liberalism and the rise of Labour, 1890–1918*, London 1984

Lee, A. J., 'Conservatism, traditionalism and the British working class, 1880–1918', in Martin and Rubinstein, *Ideology and the Labour movement*, 84–102

Lentin, A., *The Versailles peace settlement: peacemaking with Germany*, London 1991

Leventhal, F. M., 'H. N. Brailsford and the *New Leader*', *Journal of Contemporary History* i (1974), 91–113

—— 'H. N. Brailsford and the search for a new international order', in Morris, *Edwardian radicalism*, 202–17

—— 'Towards revision and reconciliation: H. N. Brailsford and Germany, 1914–1949', in Briggs and Saville, *Essays in labour history*, iii. 163–87

—— *The last dissenter: H. N. Brailsford and his world*, Oxford 1985

—— *Arthur Henderson*, Manchester 1989

Lyman, R. W., *The first Labour government, 1924*, London 1957

—— 'The British Labour party: the conflict between socialist ideas and practical politics between the wars', *JBS* v (1965), 140–52

McBriar, A. M. (ed.), *Fabian socialism and English politics, 1884–1918*, Cambridge 1962

McKenzie, R., *British political parties*, 2nd edn, London 1963

McKibbin, R., 'James Ramsay MacDonald and the problem of the independence of the Labour party, 1910–1914', *JMH* xlii (1970), 216–35

—— *The evolution of the Labour party, 1910–1924*, Oxford 1974

—— 'Arthur Henderson as Labour leader', *IRSH* xxiii (1978), 79–101

—— The ideologies of class: social relations in Britain, 1889–1950, Oxford 1990

—— 'Why was there no Marxism in Britain?', in his Ideologies of class, 1–41

McNeilly, E., 'Labour and Internationalism, 1906–14', Twentieth Century British History xx (2009), forthcoming

Maddox, W. P., Foreign relations in British Labour politics: a study in the formation of party attitudes on foreign affairs, and the application of political pressure designed to influence government policy, 1900–1924, Cambridge, MA 1934

Mantoux, E., The Carthaginian peace, London 1946

Marks, S., 'Reparations reconsidered: a reminder', Central European History ii (1969), 56–65

—— The illusion of peace: international relations in Europe, 1918–1933, London 1976

—— 'Smoke and mirrors: in smoke-filled rooms and the Galerie des Glaces', in Boemeke, Feldman and Glaser, Treaty of Versailles, 337–70

Marquand, D., Ramsay MacDonald, London 1977

Martin, D. E., 'Ideology and composition', in K. D. Brown (ed.), The first Labour party, 1906–1914, London 1985, 17–37

—— and D. Rubinstein (eds), Ideology and the Labour movement: essays presented to John Saville, London 1979

Martin, R., TUC: the growth of a pressure group, 1868–1976, Oxford 1980

Marwick, A., Clifford Allen: the open conspirator, Edinburgh 1964

Matthew, H. C. G., R. I. McKibbin and J. A. Kay, 'The franchise factor in the rise of the Labour party', EHR xci (1976), 723–52

Mayer, A. J., The political origins of the new diplomacy, New Haven 1959

—— Politics and diplomacy of peacemaking: containment and counter-revolution at Versailles, 1918–1919, London 1968

Medlicott, W. N., British foreign policy since Versailles, London 1940

Meynell, H., 'The Stockholm Conference', IRSH v (1960), 1–25

Michels, R., Political parties: a sociological study of the oligarchical tendencies of modern democracy, London 1915

Middlemas, K., The Clydesiders: a left-wing struggle for parliamentary power, London 1965

—— Politics in industrial society, London 1979

Miller, D. H., The Geneva Protocol, New York 1925

Miller, K. E., Socialism and foreign policy: theory and practice in Britain to 1932, The Hague 1967

Miller, S. and H. Potthof, A history of German social democracy from 1848 to the present, Leamington Spa 1986

Miller, W. L., Electoral dynamics in Britain since 1918, London 1977

Milliband, R., Parliamentary socialism: a study in the politics of Labour, 2nd edn, London 1972

Minkin, L., The Labour party conference: a study in the politics of intra-party democracy, London 1978

—— The contentious alliance: trade unions and the Labour party, Edinburgh 1992

Moggridge, D., *British monetary policy*, Cambridge 1972

Morgan, A., *J. Ramsay MacDonald*, Manchester 1987

Morgan, K O., *Consensus and disunity: the Lloyd George government, 1918–1922*, Oxford 1979

—— *Labour people*, Oxford 1987

Morris, A. J. A., *Radicalism against war*, Harlow 1972

—— *C. P. Trevelyan, 1870–1958: portrait of a radical*, Belfast 1977

—— (ed.), *Edwardian radicalism, 1910–14: some aspects of British radicalism*, London 1974

Mule, R., 'Explaining the party-policy link: established approaches and theoretical developments', *Party Politics* iii (1997), 493–512

Naylor, J. F., *Labour's international policy: the Labour party in the 1930s*, London 1969

Newton, D. J., *British Labour: European socialism and the struggle for peace, 1889–1914*, Oxford 1985

Nicolson, H., *Peacemaking, 1919*, Leeds 1946

Northedge, F. S., *The troubled giant: Britain among the great powers, 1916–39*, London 1966

Nugent, N. and D. Lowe, *The left in France*, London 1982

Orde, A., *British policy and European reconstruction after World War One*, Cambridge 1990

Panebianco, A., *Political parties: organization and power*, Cambridge 1988

Peele, G. and C. Cook (eds), *The politics of reappraisal, 1918–39*, London 1975

Pelling, H., *America and the British left*, London 1956

—— *A history of British trade unionism*, London 1963

—— *Popular politics and society in late Victorian Britain: essays*, London 1968

—— *A short history of the Labour party*, 9th edn, Basingstoke 1991

Phillips, G., *The rise of the Labour party*, London 1992

Pierson, S., *Marxism and the origins of British socialism*, London 1973

Pimlott, B., *Hugh Dalton*, London 1985

—— *Trade unions in British politics: the first 250 years*, 2nd edn, London 1991

Pollard, S., *The gold standard and employment policy between the wars*, London 1970

Porter, B., *Critics of empire*, London 1968

—— *The lion's share: a short history of British imperialism, 1850–1983*, Harlow 1975

—— *Britain, Europe and the world, 1850–1986: delusions of grandeur*, 2nd edn, London 1987

—— 'Hobson and internationalism', in Freeden, *Hobson*, 167–81

Price, R., *An imperial war and the British working class*, London 1972

Pugh, M., *The making of modern British politics, 1867–1939*, Oxford 1982

Read, D., *Cobden and Bright: a Victorian political partnership*, London 1967

Reekes, A., *The rise of Labour, 1899–1951*, Basingstoke 1991

Reid, A. J., 'Old unionism reconsidered: the radicalism of Robert Knight, 1870–1900', in Biagini and Reid, *Currents of radicalism*, 214–43

Robbins, K., 'Lord Bryce and the First World War', *HJ* xx (1967), 255–77

—— *Sir Edward Grey: a biography of Lord Grey of Fallodon*, London 1971

—— *The abolition of war: the peace movement in Britain, 1914–1919*, Cardiff 1976

—— *Politicians, diplomacy and war in modern British history*, London–Rio Grande 1994

Rose, R., 'Complexities of party leadership', *Parliamentary Affairs* xvi (1963), 257–78

—— 'Parties, factions and tendencies in Britain', *Political Studies* xii (1964), 33–46

Rothwell, V., *British war aims and peace diplomacy, 1914–1918*, Oxford 1971

Ryder, A. J., *The German revolution of 1918: a study of German socialism in war and revolt*, Cambridge 1967

Saville, J., 'The ideology of Labourism', in R. Benewick, R. N. Berki and B. C. Parekh, *Knowledge and belief in politics*, London 1973, 213–26

Schneer, J., *George Lansbury*, Manchester 1990

Schuker, S. A., *The end of French predominance in Europe: the financial crisis of 1924 and the adoption of the Dawes Plan*, Chapel Hill 1976

Schwabe, K., 'Germany's peace aims and the domestic and international constraints', in Boemeke, Feldman and Glaser, *Treaty of Versailles*, 37–67

Searle, G. R., *The Liberal party: triumph and disintegration, 1886–1929*, Basingstoke 1992

Sharp, A., 'A comment', in Boemeke, Feldman and Glaser, *Treaty of Versailles*, 131–44.

Shaw, E., *The Labour party since 1945: old Labour; new Labour*, Oxford 1996

Shepherd, J., 'Labour and parliament: the Lib-Labs as the first working-class MPs, 1885–1906', in Biagini and Reid, *Currents of radicalism*, 187–213

Skidelsky, R., *John Maynard Keynes: hopes betrayed, 1883–1920*, London 1983

—— *John Maynard Keynes: the economist as saviour, 1920–1937*, London 1992

Spear, S., 'Pacifist radicalism in the post-war British Labour party: the case of E. D. Morel, 1919–24', *IRSH* xxiii (1978), 193–223

Stansky, P. (ed.), *The left and the war: the British Labour party and World War One*, New York 1969

Stedman-Jones, G., *Languages of class: studies in English working class history, 1832–1982*, Cambridge 1983

Stevenson, D., 'French war aims and peace planning', in Boemeke, Feldman and Glaser, *Treaty of Versailles*, 87–109

Stokes, E., 'Late nineteenth century colonial expansion and the attack on the theory of economic imperialism: a case of mistaken identity', *HJ* xxii (1969), 285–301

Strom, K., 'A behavioural theory of competitive political parties', *American Journal of Political Science* xxxiv (1990), 565–98

Stubbs, O., 'Lord Milner and patriotic labour, 1914–1918', *EHR* lxxxvii (1972), 717–54

Swanwick, H. M., *I have been young*, London 1935

Swartz, M., *The Union of Democratic Control in British politics during the First World War*, Oxford 1971

—— 'A study in futility: the British radicals at the outbreak of the First World War', in Morris, *Edwardian radicalism*, 246–61

Tanner, D. M., 'The parliamentary electoral system, the "fourth" reform act and the rise of Labour in England and Wales', *BIHR* lvi (1983), 205–19

—— *Political change and the Labour party, 1900–1918*, Cambridge 1990

—— 'Ideological debate in Edwardian Labour politics: radicalism, revisionism and socialism', in Biagini and Reid, *Currents of radicalism*, 271–93

—— 'The development of British socialism, 1900–1918', *Parliamentary History* xvi (1997), 48–66

—— 'Socialist parties and policies', in M. Pugh (ed.), *A companion to modern European history, 1871–1945*, Oxford 1997, 133–54

—— P. Thane and N. Tiratsoo (eds), *Labour's first century*, Cambridge 2000

Taylor, A. J. P., *The troublemakers: dissent over foreign policy, 1792–1939*, London 1957

—— *The origins of the Second World War*, Harmondsworth 1961

—— *English history, 1914–1945*, Harmondsworth 1970

Taylor, M., 'Patriotism, history and the left in twentieth century Britain', *HJ* xxiii (1990), 972–9

Temperley, H. and L. M. Penson (eds), *Foundations of British foreign policy from Pitt (1792) to Salisbury (1902)*, Cambridge 1938

Thane, P., 'Labour and local politics: radicalism, democracy and social reform, 1880–1914', in Biagini and Reid, *Currents of radicalism*, 244–70

Thomas, J. M., *My story*, London 1937

Thompson, L., *The enthusiasts: a biography of John and Katherine Bruce Glasier*, London 1971

Thompson, N., *Political economy and the Labour party: the economics of democratic socialism, 1884–1995*, London 1996

Thompson, W., *The long death of British labourism*, London 1993

Thorpe, A., 'J. H. Thomas and the rise of Labour in Derby, 1880–1945', *Midland History* xv (1990), 111–28

—— *A history of the Labour party*, Basingstoke 1997

Trachtenberg, M., *Reparation in world politics: France and European economic diplomacy, 1916–1923*, New York 1980

Trentmann, F., 'The strange death of free trade: the erosion of "liberal consensus" in Great Britain, c. 1903–1932', in Biagini, *Citizenship and community*, 219–50

—— 'Wealth versus welfare: the British left between free trade and national political economy before the First World War', *Historical Research* lxx (1997), 70–98

Tucker, R. W., *The attitude of the British Labour party towards European and collective security problems, 1920–39*, Geneva 1950

Turner, J., *British politics and the Great War: coalition and conflict, 1915–1918*, New Haven–London 1992

Van der Slice, A., *International labour, diplomacy and peace, 1914–1919*, London 1941

Vickers, R., *The Labour party and the world: the evolution of Labour's foreign policy, 1900–1951*, Manchester 2004

Waites, B., *A class society at war*, Leamington Spa 1987

Wald, K. D., 'Advance by retreat? The formation of British Labour's electoral strategy', *JBS* xxvii (1988), 283–314.

Walters, F. P., *A history of the League of Nations*, London 1952

Ward, P., *Red flag and Union Jack: Englishness, patriotism and the British left, 1881–1924*, Woodbridge 1998

Webb, S., 'The first Labour government', *Political Quarterly* xxxii (1961), 6–37

Weinroth, H. S., 'The British radicals and the balance of power', *HJ* xxiii (1970), 653–82

—— 'Norman Angell and *The great illusion*: an episode in pre-1914 pacifism', *HJ* xvii (1974), 551–74

White, S., *Britain and the Bolshevik Revolution: a study in the politics of diplomacy, 1920–1924*, New York 1980

Wilson, T., *The myriad faces of war: Britain and the Great War, 1914–18*, Cambridge 1986

Winch, D., *Economics and policy*, London 1969

Winkler, H., 'The emergence of a Labor party foreign policy in Great Britain, 1918–22', *JMH* xxvii (1956), 247–58.

—— *The League of Nations movement in England*, Metuchen, NJ 1967

—— *Paths not taken: British Labour and international policy in the 1920s*, Chapel Hill–London 1994

Winter, J. M., 'Arthur Henderson, the Russian Revolution and the reconstruction of the Labour party', *HJ* xv (1972), 753–73

—— *Socialism and the challenge of war: ideas and politics in Britain, 1912–18*, London 1974

—— (ed.), *The working class in modern Britain history: essays in honour of Henry Pelling*, Cambridge 1983

Woolf, L., *Beginning again, 1911–1918*, London 1964

—— *Downhill all the way, 1919–1939*, London 1967

Worley, M., *Labour inside the gate: a history of the British Labour party between the wars*, London 2005

Wrigley, C., *David Lloyd George and the British Labour movement: peace and war*, Hassocks 1976

—— *Arthur Henderson*, Cardiff 1990

—— *Lloyd George*, Oxford 1992

—— Widening horizons? British labour and the second international, 1893–1905', *Labour History Review* lviii (1993), 8–13

Wrynn, J. F. P., *The socialist International and the politics of European reconstruction*, Amsterdam 1976

Yearwood, P., '"On safe and right lines": the Lloyd George government and the origins of the League of Nations', *HJ* xxxii (1989), 131–55

Young, J. W., 'Idealism and realism in the history of Labour's foreign policy', *Bulletin of the Society for the Study of Labour History* i (1985), 14–19

Zariski, R., 'Party factions and comparative politics: some preliminary observations', *Midwest Journal of Political Science* iv (1960), 27–51

Zimmern, A., *The League of Nations and the rule of law*, London 1936

Unpublished theses

Bridgen, P., 'Ideology and politics in the development of a Labour party foreign policy, 1900–1924', PhD diss. London 2001

Howard, C., 'Henderson, MacDonald and the leadership of the Labour party, 1914–1922', PhD diss. Cambridge 1978

Index